Design for Learning in Virtual Worlds

Design for Learning in Virtual Worlds, focused specifically on how to design virtual worlds for educational purposes, explores:

- The history and evolution of virtual worlds;
- The theories behind the use of virtual worlds for learning;
- The design of curricula in virtual worlds;
- Design guidelines for elements experienced in virtual worlds that support learning;
- Design guidelines for learning quests and activities in virtual worlds.

The authors also examine the theories and associated design principles used to create embedded assessments in virtual worlds. Finally, a framework and methodology is provided to assist professionals in evaluating "off-the-shelf" virtual worlds for use in educational and training settings. *Design for Learning in Virtual Worlds* will be invaluable both as a professional resource and as a textbook for courses within Educational Technology, Learning Sciences, and Library Media programs that focus on gaming or online learning environments.

Brian C. Nelson is Associate Professor of Educational Technology at Arizona State University. An instructional designer and learning theorist, he has published and presented extensively on the viability of educational virtual worlds for situated inquiry learning and assessment. Dr Nelson's recent writing addresses issues related to the design and evaluation of educational games, with a focus on theory-based design principles. He is currently a Co-Principal Investigator on the SAVE Science Virtual World project, and was the Project Designer on the River City project. He was a Co-Principal Investigator on two MacArthur Foundation Digital Learning grants and was also a Co-Principal Investigator on the SURGE project, creating video games to teach high school physics.

Benjamin E. Erlandson is Assistant Professor of Instructional Science and Technology with an emphasis in Digital Media in the School of Information, Technology, and Communication Design (ITCD) at California State University, Monterey Bay. In addition to teaching several courses in interactive media design/development and instructional design, Dr Erlandson runs the Virtual Environments for Situated Inquiry of Complexity (VESIC) Lab, conducting various research studies investigating the usefulness of meso-immersive 2D and 3D virtual environments—much like those used for many popular computer games—for learning about complex systems.

Interdisciplinary Approaches to Educational Technology
Series Editor: J. Michael Spector

Current and forthcoming series titles:

Design for Learning in Virtual Worlds

BRIAN C. NELSON
AND
BENJAMIN E. ERLANDSON

Routledge
Taylor & Francis Group

NEW YORK AND LONDON

First published 2012
by Routledge
711 Third Avenue, New York, NY 10017

Simultaneously published in the UK
by Routledge
2 Park Square, Milton Park, Abingdon, Oxon OX14 4RN

Routledge is an imprint of the Taylor & Francis Group, an informa business

Library of Congress Cataloging-in-Publication Data
Nelson, Brian C.
  Design for learning in virtual worlds / Brian C. Nelson, Benjamin E. Erlandson.
  p. cm.—(Interdisciplinary approaches to educational technology ; 2)
  S Includes bibliographical references and index.
  Virtual reality in education. I. Erlandson, Benjamin E. II. Title.
  LB1044.87.N445 2012
  371.397—dc23
  2011037902

ISBN: 978–0–415–88639–0 (hbk)
ISBN: 978–0–415–88640–6 (pbk)
ISBN: 978–0–203–83637–8 (ebk)

Typeset in Sabon
by Swales & Willis Ltd, Exeter, Devon

Printed and bound in the United States of America by
Walsworth Publishing Company, Marceline, MO.

Dedication

Brian: This book is dedicated to those who shaped my understanding of virtual worlds for education: Chris Dede (virtual worlds guru and my doctoral advisor at Harvard), Diane Jass Ketelhut (a virtual worlds for science learning researcher and my best friend), Jim Gee (educational games researcher and designer), and an incredible group of PhD students at ASU who teach me more every day about virtual worlds design (Kent Slack, Younsu Kim, Cecile Foshee, and Andre Denham). This book is also dedicated to my family: to my wife Akiko Wakao, who got me interested in virtual worlds when we were graduate students together, and to my son Kohei who always comes up with the best ideas for curriculum that will actually be fun.

Ben: This book is written for all past, present, and future brave souls that don twenty hats and build virtual worlds for learning. I would like to dedicate this book to my father Stephen Erlandson, who taught me how to see the world with hiking boots and a fishing rod – and still teaches me to this day. It is also dedicated to my young nephew Bennett, who helps me experience the world through brand new perspectives. He also thinks I live in a computer, which isn't entirely false.

Contents

Illustrations

Figures

Tables

Preface

This is a volume in the Routledge series entitled "Interdisciplinary Approaches to Educational Technology." This book follows a four-part, problem-centered framework similar to that used in other books in the series, customized to our exploration of virtual worlds for learning.

Part One of this volume provides an introduction and overview of the field of virtual worlds for education. Chapter topics include an articulated definition of virtual worlds, a brief history of virtual worlds for education with an overview of several educational virtual worlds, and a discussion of the mechanics of virtual worlds including the virtual world space, movement and interaction with elements in virtual worlds, and graphical user interfaces.

Part Two provides an elaboration of the theoretical perspectives that inform the assertion that virtual worlds can be powerful spaces for learning. Chapter topics include theories of learning that are often used to justify the educational use of virtual worlds, including situated learning, constructivism, cognition, and behaviorism; an exploration of the contexts in which virtual worlds for learning are typically used, along with a discussion of the learner populations who take part in virtual world-based learning experiences, and an overview of assessment and measurement in virtual worlds.

Part Three provides a more detailed elaboration of practical approaches to designing virtual worlds for learning. Chapter topics include an overview of a framework for critiquing existing virtual worlds as learning platforms, followed by a detailed discussion of the processes used for designing a virtual world-based learning curriculum, the activities within the worlds that make up such a curriculum, and the assessments that help to demonstrate whether and to what extent learning has taken place as a result of completing virtual world-based curricula.

Part Four shifts focus from design of virtual worlds to development and implementation issues. This section includes an overview of the development process of virtual worlds, providing a practical look at moving from design to development. Implementation and evaluation issues are also covered, including practical tips for evaluating the success of a virtual world implementation in various learning contexts.

Each of the chapters is structured to provide introductory remarks followed by a discussion of the major points covered. Each chapter also includes one or more self-check quizzes and suggested learning activities related to the chapter topic, along with references to literature cited in the chapter, web links to other material, and other resources.

Acknowledgments

Brian: I must first thank Ben for being an excellent co-author, colleague, and friend. I also want to thank J. Michael Spector, the series editor, for his example, expert modeling, and encouragement; and my editor at Taylor Francis/Routledge, Alex Masulis, for his patience with this newbie author and for allowing a long time extension.

Ben: First and foremost, I wish to thank Brian for taking me on as his first doctoral student and surviving all the way through my dissertation! Your continued support, collegiality, and friendship are cherished. I wish to thank James Klein for showing me the ways of instructional design and Wilhelmina Savenye for enlightening me on the subject of evaluation. Finally, Joanna Gorin ignited and sustained my interest in measurement and assessment.

part one
Introduction and Overview

one
Definition and History of Virtual Worlds for Education

Introduction

In the popular press, virtual worlds are almost always talked about in breath-less tones of wonder and newness. They are described as the latest, emerging technology that has captured the hearts, minds, and funds of players young and old. The way you hear virtual worlds discussed, you would think that they appeared on the world stage just moments ago ... a sudden miraculous arrival in their present high-definition, full-color, ultra-realistic glory. If vir-tual worlds were sold in cereal boxes, the labels would all shout "New!" "Improved!" or "Now even better!"

In reality, though, those boxes should read something like "New look, same great taste!" Virtual worlds have been around in some form or another for decades. If you include mechanical virtual worlds, we can trace their ori-gins back even further. In this chapter, we will follow the winding trail of the evolution of virtual worlds over time. We will pay particular attention to the history of virtual worlds used for education. And we will look at some cur-rent and recent examples of virtual worlds designed especially for education. Before that, though, we need to define what we mean when we say "virtual world." We need a working definition to provide a foundation for the rest of the book!

What's a Virtual World?

What's a virtual world? On first thought, this seems a pretty easy question to answer. *A virtual world is a computer-based 3D world that you can explore by yourself or with other people.* In a virtual world, you either explore as yourself (first-person) or are represented by a computer-based character called an avatar (third-person). This definition is a good starting point, but like most definitions, the more you think about the topic, the more complex the definition becomes.

Let's start expanding our definition by describing what virtual worlds are not, at least as we are going to talk about them in this book. In this book, virtual *worlds* are distinct from virtual *reality*. So what is virtual reality? Virtual reality consists of fully immersive 3D simulations. By fully immersive, we mean that the experience of the user in a virtual reality environment is a close functional simulation of reality, or a simulation of reality with some added "superpowers." To achieve this, virtual reality-based simulations rely on a collection of software and related hardware. Virtual reality users wear head-mounted displays through which they view a simulated world or environment (Figure 1.1). These displays often include motion tracking. With motion tracking, as you turn your head from side to side or up and down, the simulated world tracks your head's movement. So when you turn your head left or right, you see what is on either side of you in the virtual world displayed through the head-mounted display. Some head-mounted displays include headphones that similarly include motion tracking connected to audio. You hear the sounds of the virtual reality environment all around you, and the sounds move appropriately has you turn your head. For example, if you hear a dog barking off to your left and turn your head in the direction of

FIGURE 1.1 Virtual reality hardware

the barking, you will both see the dog come into view in your head-mounted display, and hear the barking move from your left side to directly in front of you in virtual space.

Virtual reality simulations also frequently make use of data gloves. Users wear a glove (usually just one), and sensors in the glove track the movement of their hand through real space. This movement is then mapped onto the 3D space of the virtual world, and a cartoon-like image of the user's hand appears in virtual space. With the glove, users can pick up, carry, and otherwise interact with objects inside the virtual reality world. For example, they can pick up and throw a virtual ball. Data gloves often include some form of force-feedback that allows users to "feel" the virtual objects that they interact with via the glove. A few very elaborate virtual reality setups even include what are essentially giant hamster balls that allow the users to walk or run in all directions, with elaborate motion tracking software mapping their movements into the head-mounted display.

Virtual reality is, in a word, *cool*! But it is not the topic of this book. We are focused instead on something just as cool: virtual worlds. What's the difference? In this book, we define virtual worlds as computer-based environments that can be explored without the use of special hardware (other than a mouse or some other control device). Virtual worlds are explored by moving avatars through them or through first-person perspective. Virtual worlds can be single-player or multi-player. They can be graphical 2D or 3D worlds or text-based worlds. Virtual worlds can be simulations, but they don't have to be. Virtual worlds can be games, but they don't have to be.

Let's unpack each of the components of this long definition.

Computer-based Environment

Right off the bat, we need to clarify. Virtual worlds don't *have* to be computer-based. Depending on how you want to define them, you could say that virtual worlds have been around as long as humans. Human beings have always been very adept at creating virtual worlds in their minds based on stories they hear and books they read. Think of the last really good book you read. While reading it, you undoubtedly created your own very detailed virtual world based on the characters, setting, and storyline of the book. While deeply engrossed in reading, you probably stopped consciously noticing the words on the page at all. You achieved what game designers call a "flow state" in which the medium through which you encountered the virtual world of the story disappeared (Csikszentmihalyi, 1990). You were fully engrossed in the world of the book: experiencing it firsthand. You, in short, became a designer, builder, and participant in a virtual world.

But for the purposes of this book, we are talking about interactive electronic worlds versus non-electronic virtual worlds, such as board games, dice-based games, etc. Further, we are going to focus on the design of computer-based virtual worlds. Virtual worlds have migrated to a multitude of platforms including game consoles (i.e., Xbox 360, PlayStation 3, Wii, etc.), portable game systems (Nintendo DS, Nintendo 3DS, PlayStation Portable, etc.), and—most prolifically—smartphones (iPhone, Android, Windows Phone, etc.). But most virtual worlds designed for educational use continue to be computer-based. Within a few years, this is probably going to change, but for now we'll stick with the computer.

Exploring Virtual Worlds

In Chapters Two and Three, we will go into great detail about the mechanics of computer-based virtual worlds, looking at all aspects of how they work, how users can interact with them, and how the mechanics of virtual worlds can be used to your advantage to help people learn. For now, though, here is a brief explanation of what we mean by "exploring." Virtual worlds are usually explored in two main ways: first-person and third-person (or avatar-based). Unlike virtual reality environments, exploring virtual worlds doesn't require any special equipment beyond a computer, mobile device, phone, or gaming console.

In a first-person virtual world, you explore the world as if you are bodily embedded in it. You see the virtual world through your own eyes or, rather, through the eyes of the virtual you—your avatar. Avatars can be visible or invisible representations of the character that you play in the virtual world. In a first-person virtual world, your avatar might be a 20-feet-tall giant or a snake slithering along the ground, but you won't actually see yourself: you'll just see the world in front of your eyes. In commercial games, this form of exploration view is the standard in First-Person Shooter (FPS) games, called that for the obvious reasons that you see the virtual world from a first-person perspective, and because typically your main activity is shooting things. In an FPS game you might, and often do, see your arms represented in virtual space, frequently holding tools, guns, a chainsaw, and other objects with which to perform tasks and hunt down the bad guys. Usually, your legs are invisible in an FPS virtual world, although you are likely to hear your footsteps as you walk or run through the world.

In a third-person view of virtual-world exploration, you control a visible avatar and make it move through the world for you. Nearly all Massively Multi-player Online Role-playing Games (MMORPGs) use third-person, avatar-based controls. You spend most of the time in a third-person virtual world looking at the back of your avatar as it moves around. The only time you are likely to see your character's face is when you first select the character at the beginning of the game, when your character dies, or during "cut-scenes" (mini-movies designed to advance the storyline of the game).

Single-Player and Multi-Player Virtual Worlds

At the time we write this book, multi-player virtual worlds reign supreme both in the commercial realm and in educational virtual-world products. There is a good chance that you first became interested in the idea of using virtual worlds for teaching or training because of your exposure to and/or experiences with a multi-player game world. As we will explain in Chapter Four, there are a large number of learning benefits to be gained through well-designed multi-player virtual worlds. For example, many of the so-called "21st-century skills" we would like students to have when they enter the workplace are supported by the affordances and activities of multi-player virtual worlds: collaboration, teamwork, mentoring, competition, sharing, etc. Plus, multi-player virtual worlds are simply fun to inhabit, as a direct result of the same kinds of affordances that make them such good learning spaces.

With all the focus on multi-player virtual worlds, it is sometimes easy to forget that single-player virtual worlds offer an equally powerful set of learning benefits, including all the ones listed above. For example, like multi-player virtual worlds, single-player worlds can support collaborative skill building, mentoring and teamwork. They just do it in a different way, as we will describe in Chapter Four. Also, single-player virtual worlds have been shown to be effective platforms for science, math, literacy, and health care instruction. They are particularly good at what is called *epistemic* gaming in which players role-play real-world jobs and related skills in the safe confines of a virtual world (Shaffer, 2006). Players in epistemic games might start out doing "lowly" jobs associated with some profession, and then take on increasingly complex tasks as their skills improve. In the commercial games world, single-player games set in virtual worlds are most often designed as either FPS in which your goal is to kill everything in sight or role-playing games (RPGs), that are very similar to educational epistemic games except that you are more likely to take on the role of an elf or ranger than of a scientist or city planner.

A (Very) Brief History of Educational Virtual Worlds

Now that we have a basic definition in place, let's take a brief tour of the history of educational virtual worlds that fit our definition. As we've described, virtual worlds have been around in one form or another for decades. If we stick with our "electronic" qualifier, we still can look back to the mid-20th century to find the first virtual-world pioneers. Sensorama, a mechanical virtual world, was built in 1962 (Figure 1.2). It was designed as a kind of highly immersive personal movie viewer and featured 3D video, stereo sound, wind, and even smells (see www.mortonheilig.com/InventorVR.html).

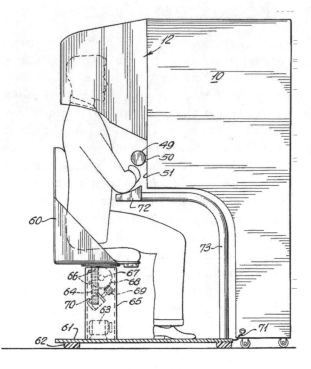

FIGURE 1.2 Sensorama

Narrowing our focus further to computer-based virtual worlds, we move a bit closer to the present day, but can still find early virtual-world examples starting in the 1970s. That is when the first computer-based text adventures appeared. These early computer games consisted of complex virtual worlds experienced entirely through the written word. Essentially these were very elaborate "choose your own adventure" books in electronic form. One of the first of these worlds, created in 1977, was called "Colossal Cave Adventure." Colossal Cave Adventure enabled players to explore a virtual cave by typing in text commands. For example, if you wanted to move north, you would type "north" or "n" on the keyboard. Each time you moved to a new location in the virtual cave, you would be presented with a new description of your surroundings, possible exits, and tasks that could be performed at that location (see www.rickadams.org/adventure).

In the late 1970s, text-based virtual worlds went multi-player with the introduction of the first Multi-User Dungeons or MUDs. The first, actually called MUD (also called MUD1 and British Legends) (see www.british-legends.com), was developed in England and played via a telnet connection (this was pre-internet after all). Like Colossal Cave Adventures, players of MUD and its descendants could explore virtual worlds using written navigational commands. MUDs also allowed groups of players to communicate with each other via text chat messages. Early text-based MUDs and MOOs

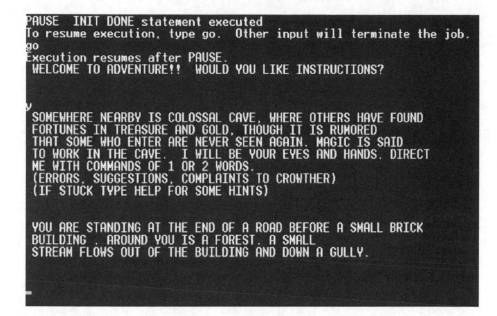

```
PAUSE   INIT DONE statement executed
To resume execution, type go.  Other input will terminate the job.
go
Execution resumes after PAUSE.
 WELCOME TO ADVENTURE!!  WOULD YOU LIKE INSTRUCTIONS?


y

 SOMEWHERE NEARBY IS COLOSSAL CAVE, WHERE OTHERS HAVE FOUND
 FORTUNES IN TREASURE AND GOLD, THOUGH IT IS RUMORED
 THAT SOME WHO ENTER ARE NEVER SEEN AGAIN. MAGIC IS SAID
 TO WORK IN THE CAVE.  I WILL BE YOUR EYES AND HANDS. DIRECT
 ME WITH COMMANDS OF 1 OR 2 WORDS.
 (ERRORS, SUGGESTIONS, COMPLAINTS TO CROWTHER)
 (IF STUCK TYPE HELP FOR SOME HINTS)


 YOU ARE STANDING AT THE END OF A ROAD BEFORE A SMALL BRICK
 BUILDING . AROUND YOU IS A FOREST. A SMALL
 STREAM FLOWS OUT OF THE BUILDING AND DOWN A GULLY.
```

FIGURE 1.3 Colossal Cave Adventure

(Multi-User Dungeons, Object Oriented) included many design characteristics and features that would be quite familiar to modern virtual-world players and designers. For example, MUDs and MOOs usually featured narrative-driven interactive stories. They typically had fantasy, sci-fi, or mystery themes. Their gameplay centered on solo or group quests, usually involving battles against enemies. Often, they included the ability to take on more than one character type, to wield weapons of various kinds, and to manage inventories of tools and objects that could help with a quest. Although players couldn't see their avatars, they could create elaborate descriptions of them, which could be read by other players.

MOOSE Crossing

One innovative MOO designed for educational use was called MOOSE Crossing. MOOSE Crossing was a text-based, multi-player educational world started by Amy Bruckman in the 1990s. Bruckman used MOOSE Crossing, with its embedded programming language called MOOSE, to teach computer programming to kids with mixed results that would foreshadow findings in many subsequent educational virtual worlds. Bruckman (2000) conducted a qualitative analysis of 50 children using MOOSE Crossing to study programming, finding that student learning of programming in the virtual world was extremely uneven: some kids learned programming in the virtual world, but many more did not. Bruckman cited low levels of participation with the programming language aspect of the MOO (more than a third of the students analyzed didn't try to do any programming while in the virtual world ... a central activity of the curriculum) as a key reason for uneven learning results.

The next step in the evolution of computer-based virtual worlds was the MUVE, or multi-user virtual environment. In brief, a MUVE is simply a MOO with graphics. MUVEs are 2D or 3D virtual worlds in which learners control avatars that represent their online personas. As with earlier text-based adventure MUDs and MOOs, players in MUVEs can explore the worlds, interact with objects, communicate with other users, and complete quests. When used for educational purposes, the content in MUVEs can vary widely, although educational MUVEs to date have centered mostly on science curricula. Most virtual worlds created for educational purposes by researchers and educational designers have been, and continue to be, MUVE-based. The earliest studies of these virtual worlds focused on their potential impact on learning and student motivation, rather than on their effectiveness (e.g., Bers, 1999; Bers & Cassell, 1998; Corbit & DeVarco, 2000). That focus is changing somewhat toward qualitative and quantitative studies exploring the impact of the worlds, and curricula embedded in them, on learning (Clark, Nelson, Sengupta, & D'Angelo, 2009; Nelson & Ketelhut, 2007).

To demonstrate the kinds of curricula and designs that have been created in educational virtual worlds, let's take a look at several educational MUVEs that have been created over time. This overview is far from comprehensive, but will give a flavor of the kinds of worlds out there. For a more comprehensive review of modern educational virtual worlds, we recommend looking through the research and review articles included in the references section at the end of the chapter.

Whyville

One of the first (and still running) very large-scale MUVE-based virtual worlds with an educational focus is Whyville (Figure 1.4). This 2D virtual world with a cartoon-like look and feel has more than 4 million registered users at the time this chapter is being written (see: http://whyville.net). Whyville was started as an environment specifically aimed at pre-teen girls, and the majority of its players are still female ... a relative rarity among virtual worlds. Players exploring the Whyville world can take part in a large number of casual games, some of which focus on science education content including biology, physics, and chemistry.

One interesting curricular unit designed for Whyville is the "Whypox Epidemic." In the Whypox curriculum, a virtual virus is unleashed on the users of Whyville. The virus spreads through the community in different

FIGURE 1.4 Whyville

ways and leads to different symptoms. Players with the virus might suddenly see their avatar's face covered with red spots. In addition, students infected with Whypox will have their text-based chat messages interrupted by sneezes. In investigating how 6th grade science classes dealt with the Whypox epidemic, researchers found that students tracked the spread of the outbreak on charts in their classroom, gathered information about disease transmission in a virtual "Center for Disease Control" in the Whyville environment, and used an "Infection Simulator" to observe how diseases spread in a population (Neulight, Kafai, Kao, Foley, & Galas, 2007). The researchers found that the participating students were actively engaged in gathering data and forming hypotheses about the virus, even outside of school (they could log in to Whyville from their home computers at night).

River City

Another recent large-scale educational virtual world was River City. Created as part of a decade-long research project (1999–2009) at Harvard University, River City was an MUVE aimed at teaching science inquiry and content to middle school students. Students explored the River City virtual world in small teams, working together to solve the mystery of widespread illness that overtook a small city. Participants entered River City as time travelers, teleporting from modern times to the late 1800s to lend modern day knowledge and skills to the suffering people of River City. At the invitation of the River City mayor, students would spread out through the city, exploring the streets,

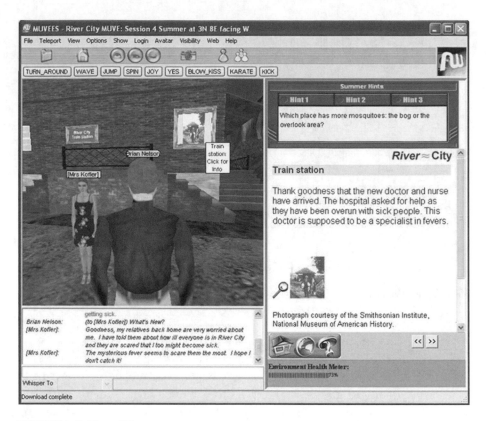

FIGURE 1.5 River City

river, neighborhoods, a hospital, public housing area, and other spots, trying to develop hypotheses about why people in town were getting sick. Designed into the embedded curriculum in River City were multiple overlapping kinds of disease afflicting the citizens including water-borne, insect-borne, and person–person transmitted illnesses—all affecting the town simultaneously. At the end of the project, student participants compared their research with other students in class, often finding that different students came up with quite different findings.

Results from a series of studies with River City showed that: It was engaging for participants, especially students who were identified by their teachers as "low achievers" in regular classroom curricula (Nelson, Ketelhut, Clarke, Bowman, & Dede, 2005); students who conducted River City science quests with the aid of a curricular "hints" system outperformed those without the hint system (Nelson, 2007); participants' belief in their ability to succeed in science (their self-efficacy) was boosted by participation in River City (Ketelhut, 2007); and boys and girls learned equally well in the virtual world (Nelson et al., 2005). Although the River City project has ended, details about it can still be found online at the time of this writing (see http://muve.gse.harvard.edu/rivercityproject). The River City virtual world was purchased by a commercial company called Activeworlds (see http://rivercity.activeworlds.com), which is still running it and is working on an updated version.

Quest Atlantis

Following in the footsteps of River City is the Quest Atlantis virtual-world project (see http://atlantis.crlt.indiana.edu). Like River City, Quest Atlantis is an educational MUVE in which students collaborate and perform quests in an effort to solve problems plaguing the virtual world and its people. One of the main curricular units in Quest Atlantis, called "Taiga," echoes the main River City curriculum: students work in teams to understand problems with the water in the Quest Atlantis world, and formulate plans to solve these problems. Hickey, Ingram-Goble, and Jameson (2009) conducted a pair of studies on the impact of the Taiga curriculum for elementary school students. The first study with four 6th grade classes found that students using Taiga outperformed students reading text covering the same material on a test covering the material. A later study saw learning gains for Taiga participants after new versions of formative feedback were designed into the virtual world. Anderson and Barnett (2007) found similarly positive outcomes (p < 0.01) on standardized learning measures in their study of a Quest Atlantis implementation with 26 elementary school students.

SAVE Science

A final example of a modern educational virtual world can be seen in the SAVE Science project (Figure 1.6). This project is focused on creating and testing new methods for assessing learning inside virtual worlds. Researchers on the SAVE Science project (two of whom developed the River City virtual world) have created a series of virtual-world modules for middle school students. Participating students complete their regular, classroom-based science curriculum, and then enter the SAVE Science virtual world to complete assessment quests related to some aspect of the content covered in class. The SAVE Science virtual world has been designed to record student interactions in the virtual world as they complete their quests. These data are then analyzed to evaluate how well students have understood the material taught in class. The umbrella curriculum in the SAVE Science virtual world is similar to that found in other educational virtual worlds such as River City and Quest Atlantis, and is centered on science inquiry skills. In SAVE Science, students have an overall goal of uncovering the likely contributors to a series

FIGURE 1.6 SAVE Science virtual world

of problems facing a virtual city and surrounding countryside (sick farm animals, weather-related crop failure, and climate-related problems with the town's water). Students enter the virtual world multiple times over the course of a school year, conducting a new inquiry quest on each visit—each related to content studied in class prior to their virtual-world quest (Nelson, Ketelhut, & Schifter, 2010).

Conclusion

Let's conclude our introduction to educational virtual worlds with a few caveats: first, the definition we provide here of virtual worlds should NOT be considered the authoritative, end-all-be-all definition. It's pretty good, though, and covers most of the virtual worlds that have been created for educational purposes to date. Technology is changing incredibly rapidly, so it is likely that elements of our definition will change just as rapidly. For example, an increasing number of augmented reality applications are being created for learning that combine virtual worlds with data or visualizations brought in from the real world. And, of course, our definition sticks to computers as the main vehicle for virtual-world delivery. As we have described, and as you certainly know, computers are one of a multitude of platforms for hosting virtual worlds. Indeed, as this book is written one of your authors is creating a version of the SAVE Science virtual world that will run on tablet computers and smartphones. Still, the design approaches, concepts, and frameworks we will cover in upcoming chapters are not exclusive to computer-based virtual worlds.

Similarly, our brief review of virtual worlds created for educational purposes is deliberately incomplete. We could easily fill a book with the history of virtual worlds, but we instead want to give you a basic foundation in some of the "biggies" that have been created over time, to demonstrate the common themes and goals of these worlds.

Armed with a virtual-world definition and with some background in virtual worlds history, you are ready to plunge into the nitty-gritty of designing virtual worlds. So, let's get to it!

TEST YOUR UNDERSTANDING

1. What is the difference between a virtual reality environment and a virtual world?
2. Do you agree with the definition offered in this chapter? Why or why not?

LEARNING ACTIVITIES

1. Pick a single "historical" virtual world to investigate. Share a short overview of your chosen virtual world with your classmates. What were its strengths and weaknesses from a learning perspective? From a technical perspective?
2. Write your own definition of an educational virtual world on a piece of paper, and put your definition away for safe-keeping. When you reach the end of this book, write a second definition, and then compare the two.
3. Imagine virtual worlds in the future. In what ways do you think they will change? In what ways will they remain the same? What would you like to be able to do in a future virtual world that you can't do in current ones?

References

Anderson, J. & Barnett, M. (2007). *The Kids Got Game: Using Quest Atlantis, a 3D virtual computer game to develop critical thinking and problem solving skills in middle school science classrooms.* Presented at Annual International Conference of the National Association for Research in Science Teaching (NARST), April 2007, New Orleans, LA.

Bers, M. U. (1999). *Zora: A graphical multi-user environment to share stories about the self.* Paper presented at the Computer Support for Collaborative Learning (CSCL '99).

Bers, M. U. & Cassell, J. (1998). Interactive storytelling systems for children: Using technology to explore language and identity. *Journal of Interactive Learning Research, 9(2),* 183–215.

Bruckman, A. (2000). *Uneven Achievement in a Constructivist Learning Environment.* Paper presented at the International Conference on Learning Sciences, Ann Arbor, MI.

Clark, D., Nelson, B., Sengupta, P., & D'Angelo, C. (2009). *Rethinking Science Learning through Digital Games and Simulations: Genres, examples, and evidence.* Invited paper, Learning Science: Computer Games, Simulations, and Education Workshop, Washington, DC.

Corbit, M. & DeVarco, B. (2000). *SciCentr and BioLearn: Two 3D implementations of CVE science museums.* Paper presented at the Third International Conference on Collaborative Virtual Environments, San Francisco.

Csikszentmihalyi, M. (1990). *Flow: The psychology of optimal experience.* New York: Harper Perennial.

Hickey, D., Ingram-Goble, A., & Jameson, E. (2009). Designing assessments and assessing designs in virtual educational environments. *Journal of Science Education and Technology, 18(2),* 187–208.

Ketelhut, D. J. (2007). The impact of student self-efficacy on scientific inquiry skills: an exploratory investigation in River City, a multi-user virtual environment. *The Journal of Science Education and Technology, 16(1),* 99–111.

Nelson, B. (2007). Exploring the use of individualized, reflective guidance in an educational multi-user virtual environment. *The Journal of Science Education and Technology, 16(1),* 83–97.

Nelson, B. & Ketelhut, D. (2007). Scientific inquiry in educational multi-user virtual environments. *Educational Psychology Review, 19(3),* 265–283.

Nelson, B., Ketelhut, D., Clarke, J., Bowman, C., & Dede, C. (2005). Design-based research strategies for developing a scientific inquiry curriculum in a multi-user virtual environment. *Educational Technology, 45(1),* 21–34.

Nelson, B., Ketelhut, D., & Schifter, C. (2010). Exploring cognitive load in immersive educational games: The SAVE Science project. *International Journal of Gaming and Computer-Mediated Simulations, 2(1),* 31–39.

Neulight, N., Kafai, Y. B., Kao, L., Foley, C., & Galas, C. (2007). Children's participation in a virtual epidemic in the science classroom: making connections to natural infectious diseases. *Journal of Science Education and Technology, 16(1),* 47–58.

Shaffer, D. (2006). *How Computers Help Children Learn.* New York: Palgrave Macmillan.

Links

The Whyville virtual world is still alive and active at: http://whyville.net. User accounts are free.

Likewise, Quest Atlantis is still running and is free, although you need permission to create an account. You can read about the latest version of the virtual world at: http://questatlantis.org.

The River City virtual world continues to be used by classes around the world, although it is no longer free. You can read about the project here: http://rivercity.activeworlds.com.

Other Resources

An interactive history of virtual worlds can be found here: www.vwtimeline.com.

two
Mechanics of Virtual Worlds

The World

Introduction

The purpose of this chapter is to differentiate between the two main parts of any virtual environment—the world and the Graphical User Interface (or GUI)—by looking under the hood and exploring the mechanics of the world. We describe what the world is (and isn't), as well as how it can work—along with plenty of examples. Before we dive headfirst into a topic as heavy-duty as virtual-world mechanics, it can help to have a clear definition of exactly what it is that we're going to be exploring. For the purposes of this chapter (and the rest of the book), we define the world as the 3D coordinate-based experiential space within which a learner can move his or her representative avatar. Similarly, we define the GUI as the interactive audiovisual information feedback system layered between the world and the user. We'll be discussing the GUI in great detail in Chapter Three, but it is good to have both definitions to better understand each.

The World

There is quite an array of virtual environments available to the public, both for entertainment and educational purposes. The world portion of each of these can manifest quite differently from one product to the next. So, despite the great definition we've supplied above, it can still be difficult to grasp exactly what the world portion of any virtual environment is. Perhaps a better way to achieve a good understanding of the world is to think about what the world IS, as well as what the world ISN'T.

What the World Is

Here is one good way to think about what makes up the world of any virtual environment: anything that could normally be perceived and/or experienced in the actual world we live in—such as that great big space outside with grass and trees and sunshine, as well as the interior and exterior space of any structure placed in that great big space—is considered part of the world in a virtual environment. If it's a 3D space that you can move around inside, no matter how big or small, then it's contained within, and is part of, the world.

This 3D space of which the world consists is actually quite interesting. The world space is based on a Cartesian coordinate space that contains three axes: the X axis, the Y axis, and the Z axis—one for each dimension (Figure 2.1). Every single location within the coordinate space of any world in any virtual environment has a unique set of coordinates assigned. Any object in the space has a three-number coordinate location. You can't move your avatar anywhere inside the boundaries of the world that doesn't have one of these coordinate sets assigned. To put it another way, if the fabric of the world exists and you can function within that world, it has coordinates assigned. Understanding the function of this coordinate system for the world is handy when you're trying to design a virtual world and place objects in specific locations within the world. These coordinates are also quite useful when displaying the location of any object within the world (or even a learner's avatar) on a graphical map of the world.

Within this coordinate space of the world, there are four main types of "stuff" that make up the substance of the world: terrain, atmosphere,

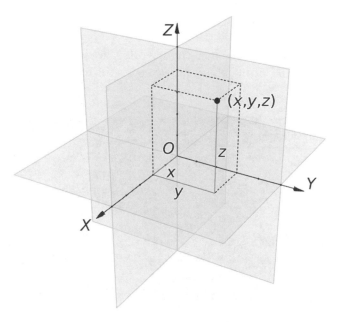

FIGURE 2.1
Cartesian XYZ
coordinate space

objects, and scripts. There are similarities between these four types of virtual-world substance with things we experience in the real world. After you finish reading this sentence, close your eyes for a moment and think about all the things you perceive as you move around through real space, either indoors or outside. Terrain is the ground we walk upon; atmosphere is the air we breathe, the clouds we see, and the water we drink; objects are the things that sit and/or move upon the ground; and scripts drive the phenomenal forces we perceive such as wind, gravity, and rain.

Terrain

In virtual worlds, the terrain serves as a platform where objects under the influence of gravity find a place to rest. The most simplistic form of terrain in a virtual world is a solid plane that serves as a smooth, flat floor upon which objects can rest or move. Much like the real world, though, often the terrain of a virtual world is quite complex, with a topography that creates a somewhat realistic resemblance of geological formations (Figure 2.2). Should you move a player-controlled character across such complex terrain using a first-person perspective, the view of the world displayed through the "eyes" of that character would change as the character travels over and across the varied elevation levels of the terrain. Similarly, objects in the world that travel from one coordinate space to another "by land"—in other words, without flying—would do so in a manner that follows the topographical contours of the terrain. In short, the terrain of a virtual world has the same properties as the terrain that exists in the real world.

Atmosphere

The atmosphere in virtual worlds doesn't actually exist, in the sense that a virtual atmosphere has no substance. A user's perception of the virtual

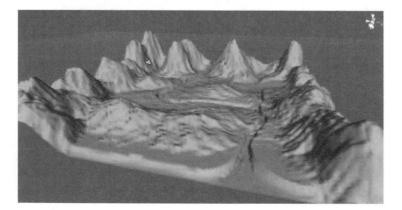

FIGURE 2.2 Geological formations in virtual terrain

atmosphere is based on the combination of auditory, visual, and kinetic elements that interact to create an experience that "feels" like a real environment. Think about your last experience outdoors on a partly cloudy day. What color was the sky? How big were the clouds? Were they dark grey, white, or all the colors of a beautiful sunset? What about the wind: which direction was it blowing and how strongly? Could you hear the ocean, or maybe some birds chirping, or perhaps the sounds of city traffic? Did it smell like a thunderstorm was about to happen? Well, almost all of these perceived phenomena can be replicated as part of the atmosphere of a virtual world—except for the smells, of course (as we described in Chapter One, the early Sensorama virtual world included smells, but no modern virtual worlds include this component). For example, take a look at Figure 2.3. The clouds in the virtual world look fairly similar to the clouds in the real world. If it were possible to embed a movie into a paper-based text, you would also be able to compare the similarities of the clouds' movement across the sky in both versions of the world.

Objects

A horse is a horse (of course, of course!) no matter which way you look at it, right? Not necessarily. Anything that sits upon (or floats above) the terrain of a virtual world is a bounded object that exists within the 3D coordinate space of the world. Buildings, trees, animals, people, machines—these are all 3D objects that occupy different amounts of space within the terrain and atmosphere of the world. Every single object within the world consists of exactly the same thing: a combination of geometric shapes (e.g., spheres, cubes, cones, etc.) that can be modeled into increasingly complex forms that closely resemble the real-world counterparts that they are intended to represent. So, while a virtual horse is in many ways a horse—it looks like a horse, it sounds like a horse, it moves like a horse—at the same time it is actually

FIGURE 2.3 Ground and sky in a virtual environment

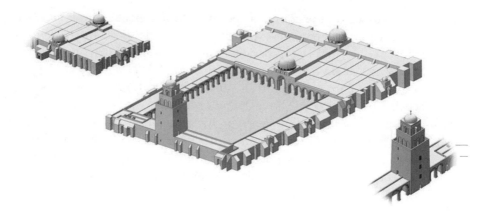

FIGURE 2.4 Complex combination of geometric forms

just a complex combination of geometric forms with similarly constructed mechanical properties (Figure 2.4).

Another important aspect of objects in a virtual world is collision. When moved, solid objects occupying space in the virtual world can collide into each other, and when this happens it is possible for the normal physical reactions to occur just as they would in the real world. Picture yourself as a virtual knight, riding your virtual horse through the virtual countryside. You're speeding along atop your galloping steed, heading toward a decrepit castle tower in the mountains in order to rescue a distressed damsel (or panicked prince) from a fire-breathing dragon. Unfortunately, you forgot to eat your virtual breakfast, and you're a little hungry because it's almost lunchtime. As you're speeding along, you are momentarily distracted by a virtual apple tree, chock full of small, similarly shaped complex geometric forms that you perceive to be delicious apples. It is at this precise moment that you should have ducked to avoid the virtual tree branch hanging a bit too low across the virtual forest path. As a result, you—along with your helmet, your shield, your sword, and your suit of armor (all of which are mere complex geometric forms)—go crashing down, feeling the effects of virtual gravity and colliding with the terrain floor of the world.

Scripts

Eventually, you collect your virtual belongings, get back on your virtual horse, arrive at the castle tower, slay the dragon, and rescue the damsel (or prince). The castle, the dragon, and the damsel are all objects, but what breathes "virtual life" into the dragon and the damsel objects, allowing them to move around within the world? Scripts are the basis of any kinetic phenomenon—such as motion from one set of coordinates to another—that occurs for an object within the world space. For example, the light rail car

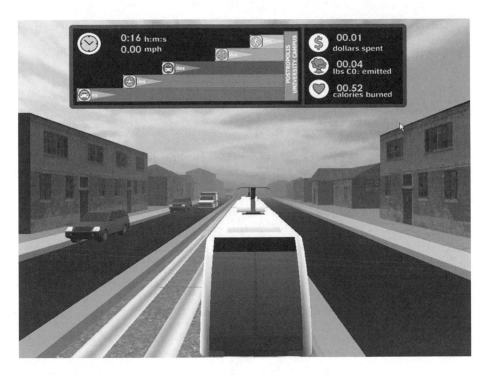

FIGURE 2.5 A light rail vehicle moves through traffic in a virtual city

pictured in Figure 2.5 is moving through virtual space along the tracks, while scripts are used to move other vehicles in close proximity so as to create the feeling of other traffic on the road.

Scripts can be applied to single or multiple objects within the world, as well as the atmosphere (remember the motion of the clouds). Scripts can also be applied as "global settings" for the entire world—such as the level of gravitational force in the environment. Think about the difference between two virtual worlds: the Earth and the Moon. In reality, the strength of gravity on the Moon is much less than that on Earth. Similar settings can be applied to virtual versions of each, thanks to the use of world-level scripts.

Terrain, atmosphere, objects, and scripts. It's a short list, but each item in the list pertains to a rather expansive concept—especially when the items interact with each other. When thinking about how these four things interact to create the entire experience of the virtual world space, it can still be quite confusing to differentiate between the 3D world and the GUI that helps a user interact with the world. This confusion is especially likely when you think about the interaction of scripts and objects. As mentioned at the beginning of the chapter, one way to clear up some of this confusion and get a better idea of what the boundaries between the world and the GUI are is to consider what the world ISN'T.

What the World Isn't

One of the reasons that virtual worlds make such great platforms for learning is the seemingly endless opportunities for interaction and engagement between the world space and additional or supplemental data and information that are pertinent to the world experienced by the learner. Thinking about this additional information and the interactions the learner has with the information can help to solidify your understanding of the boundaries of any virtual world. With this idea in mind, there are basically two categories of things that are NOT part of the world:

1. anything (sounds, objects, images, videos, animations, text) that exists outside the boundaries of the coordinate system;
2. any interactions that take place between the learner and the computer application (housing the virtual world) that occur beyond the direct interactions experienced within the coordinate system of the world.

In short, if something is not part of the world, but it is part of the experience of the computer application that houses the world, then it is most likely part of the GUI. For example, consider a painting hanging on the wall of a virtual museum. In the world space of the virtual museum, a low-resolution version of the painting image is placed on a flat rectangular object that appears to be hanging from the virtual wall. As a learner approaches this painting and clicks on it, a high-resolution version of the painting is displayed on an invisible plane that seems to exist between the virtual world space and the computer screen. By the way, this invisible plane is the space for the GUI—but we'll get to that in Chapter Three. The point here, though, is that the high-resolution version of the painting (that appears when the learner clicks on the virtual framed painting in the museum) is actually not part of the world, even though it's a picture of the same thing.

Another way to think about the defined space of the virtual world is this: if you can't experience something in the real world, then it's likely that the same experience—when it happens in a virtual-world application—is not part of the virtual world, but instead exists or occurs beyond its boundaries. Consider again the museum and the painting. If you were walking through a real museum looking at real paintings, it would be impossible for you to "click" on the actual painting and have a high-resolution image of the same painting float in front of your face for you to get a closer look.

Based on this delineation of experience, it can be tempting to draw a decisive boundary between what is and isn't in the world based strictly upon whether or not an object or experience is part of the user interface integrated into the software application that houses the virtual world. Many aspects of the world are themselves interfaces—whether virtual or real. Any museum in the real world is a constructed, curated space that is itself an interface for its contents. Paintings are hung and sculptures are displayed with purpose—to provide an engaging experience to the museum visitor. The same line of reason applies to virtual worlds. Don't fall into this trap of black-and-white differentiation between worldly and non-worldly experiences based solely on interface with information.

Additionally, the rule of thumb about "whether or not you can experience something in the real world" as evidence to define the experiential boundaries of the world space should be clarified. Just because something can't occur in the real world doesn't mean it's automatically part of the GUI. One of the things that make virtual worlds such a powerful platform for the facilitation of learning is the suspension of certain limitations typically experienced in reality—such as gravity and time. Imagine a virtual-world simulation activity where a single human can toss massive elephants with ease while completing an exercise in learning about variables affecting trajectory.

Now, hopefully you have a much less confused understanding of what is and isn't part of the world (including subjective considerations surrounding the "rules"), and as such, you might want to know where the world is. Why, you might ask, would it be important to know where the world is? Well, perhaps you'd like to put things in the world for learners to experience, or at least let other people know where to find it. So, where, exactly, is the world?

Where Is the World?

For any virtual world that can be explored by one or more users, there are two basic locations where the worlds can actually be housed: on a server (or set of servers), or on the individual user's computer. Either location type is a perfectly good space to host a virtual world, but each has specific benefits and drawbacks that can have an effect on the way a particular game or simulation is experienced.

Server-based Worlds

Many worlds are housed on one or more servers in a centralized location (or series of locations). The larger a world, the more server space is necessary to maintain the world. There are several advantages to having a world hosted on a network of servers in a central location.

First, the world can be persistent, which means that factors about the world change over time, even if a particular user is not logged in to servers to experience the world continuously. For example, if a user has a virtual farm, and she goes on vacation for three weeks, the next time she logs in to a server-based virtual world, her crops will have experienced three weeks' worth of growth. The fact that server-based worlds are in centralized locations can also be an advantage, especially from a design and development perspective. When bugs are found in the software infrastructure of the world itself, updates or patches can be applied to the world software more easily, since the world is always in one place (as opposed to distributed among thousands or millions of users). While automatic updates over the internet are becoming commonplace in software applications, this still stands as benefit for worlds hosted on centralized servers. One final benefit of server-based worlds is the fact that they are always live (which is typically required for realistic persistence). The fact that they are always live means that multiple users can work together in such worlds at any time of day that is convenient, allowing for truly global collaboration in realistic virtual spaces.

However, the "always live" aspect of server-based worlds can also be a drawback. From a development perspective, updates applied to the live world have the potential for disruption, ranging anywhere from minor glitches in the users' experience to full-blown outages of the world. If major construction work must be done upon the world for any reason, it might even be necessary to hold a planned outage for the world. While such outages are usually announced in advance as a courtesy to frequent users, such disruptions are still a cause for concern when deciding whether to house the worlds you design (or acquire) on a server. A second drawback to server-based worlds is lag. Since the world is housed on a server and not the user's local machine, the speed of the network connection between the user and the server-based world—as well as the amount of server traffic happening at a given time for multi-user worlds—serves as a limiting factor for the user's experience of the world. Slow connections and/or high traffic can lead to higher amounts of lag (or delay) between the events occurring live on the server and the interactions happening on the user's local machine.

Locally-based Worlds

Locally-based worlds are housed on the hard drive of the local machine (e.g., computer, mobile device, or game console) of the user. Local housing of the world eliminates nearly all the drawbacks mentioned for server-based worlds. There is some potential for lag based on the processing power and/or amount of memory available on a user's machine, but this is why almost any computer application involving a locally-based virtual world comes with a specific set of hardware requirements listed somewhere on the packaging (or the product website). Assuming the hardware requirements are met, the user is ensured a seamless, lag-free experience of the locally-based world in all its glory. Also, locally-based worlds can typically be more detailed—such as using higher resolution objects and applying more atmospheric effects to the world—since there is no need to push the experience of the world over a network connection.

As for drawbacks, locally-based worlds are typically not persistent, since they are not constantly functional like the server-based worlds. It is possible to achieve a semblance of persistence in these intermittently active worlds, using one or more algorithms to bring world elements "up to speed" when a user re-enters the world after an absence of any particular length. The non-centralized nature of the worlds can present a drawback to developers, since any software updates must be distributed to all end users and installed locally on each person's computer or device. As mentioned above, this process is becoming continuously more efficient as the average user's connection to the internet becomes faster.

Worldly Advances

Of course, technology advances. Our computers, mobile devices, game consoles, and as-yet-unnamed future forms of digital consumption continue to increase in power, speed, resolution, and fidelity. The networks that connect these devices ebb and flow in size, shape, and stability to keep various technological systems in constant communication, pushing and pulling information between these devices as needed. As such, the lines between which part of a world subside on the user's local machine versus any number of servers are constantly changing.

Still, though, now we know what typically is in the world, what typically isn't in the world, and options for where the world can be located. One question still remains: how does the world actually work?

How Does the World Work?

"The world works in mysterious ways," or so they say. Well, at least the real world can be mysterious. In a virtual world, functionality is much simpler and concrete, since everything that occurs within a world must be performed by a computer, which operates at the level of ones and zeros. Yes, virtual worlds can be quite complex, but from a functional perspective, they don't need to be mysterious. Here, we've broken down the functionality of worlds into three parts: how an individual world functions, how multiple worlds can function together, and what happens when multiple users interact in the same world (or worlds) over a network connection.

World Construction

As we've already mentioned, the terrain, atmosphere, and all objects of a 3D world exist within the 3D XYZ coordinate space that defines the boundaries of the world. When building a world, typically you would first set the terrain, then place objects, and then add in atmospheric elements. Sometimes these phases can happen in overlapping, iterative fashion. For example, if your world contains a significant amount of water (such as a large river running through the middle of it), you might want to set several atmospheric elements—such as water reflection, water color, water level—before placing any objects, because these aspects of the water might dictate where and how you place certain objects within the world, such as a bridge over the river, or whether or not you place any objects underwater.

Often, many objects that appear in a world are not permanent, or do not actually exist in the world before a game or simulation that takes place within that world has been launched. These objects that appear when the game is begun are objects that populate the world at runtime. This process of runtime population is accomplished using various scripts attached to the world and the objects. For example, think about the streets of a virtual metropolis filled with cars, buses, trucks, pedestrians, and cyclists. These streets would probably have quite a few taxicabs zipping around, carrying people from one place to another. As a world designer or developer, it would be quite inefficient to place an individual taxicab object into the world for each taxicab you would want to have zipping around. Additionally, you'd have to take the time to place an individual script on each car that would tell it where and how to move through the streets without crashing into another car.

A much more efficient way to populate your city world with a gaggle of taxicabs is to create world-level scripts that automatically populate the city with a certain number of taxicabs based on any number of other conditions (such as the time of day or what the current location of the user is). Based on this script, each taxicab would appear in the world and function at some level of autonomy until its job was done, and then it could be removed from the world just as easily.

Why would it be necessary to add and remove objects from the world at any point during the time one or more users explores the world? Think about yourself walking down a real city street. What do you see? Buildings, sidewalks, pavement, landscaping, vehicles, people, animals, and probably lots of other things ... as far as the eye can see. *As far as the eye can see.* There are taxicabs all over the city. As you walk through a real city, though, you can't see all of them. In fact, you can only see the ones that are within your range of vision and not blocked (or *occluded*) behind other objects, such as buildings. You know that other taxicabs are there, picking up and dropping off any number of passengers. You don't need to see them to know that, most likely, all is right with the world and the taxis you can't see are still performing this worthwhile endeavor. The same holds true for everything else going on beyond what you can actually see in the city. The same holds true for virtual worlds. Scripts can be used to populate a small portion of the world around a user—a portion of the world that is within that user's defined perceptual range.

No matter which way the user turns, she has a defined range of distance around herself that she can see. The imaginary circle that delineates this range can also serve as a useful boundary. Objects populated at or after runtime only need to appear within this bounded range around the user. This boundary moves along with the user, though, so it's often useful to make the range of populated objects slightly larger than the user's perceptual range. Anything that is assumed to happen beyond the perceptual range of the user doesn't actually need to appear in the world, since the user won't be able to see it anyway. This brings up an important point for virtual worlds. What are the options a user has for perceiving the world around her?

World Perception

A person can explore a virtual world much like he would in the real world, a mobile body navigating the terrain and perceiving its environment through a pair of eyes contained within a head that has the option of looking in a different direction from that in which the body is moving. In other words, the body can be moving forward as the head looks to the right or left, or the body can strafe to one side or the other as the head maintains a forward gaze. In a virtual world, this perceptual mechanism is achieved through the use of a virtual camera that serves as the eyes of the user. So, if a user is exploring the world in first-person perspective mode, then her ambulatory body is, essentially, a walking camera moving through the environment.

If you've ever engaged with any software applications that integrate meso-immersive 3D worlds (such as computer games) before, you'll know that first-person perspective isn't the only option for perceiving the world. Third-person perspective is common too. The main difference between first-person and third-person is that in third-person mode, the user sees his character moving through the environment, and he is essentially floating above the character at some predetermined distance.

It is not uncommon for a user to continuously swap between perspectives as she navigates the world. In many virtual-world applications, there are points in time where the system will automatically swap from one perspective to the next. For example, the perspective could automatically swap from first-person to third-person when a user reaches a certain benchmark location in the world, and the software begins an automated sequence involving the user's character engaging in some pre-scripted action, such as crossing a bridge over a moat and entering a castle at the end of a quest, or the system could also automatically swap from third-person to first-person when the user enters and begins driving a jeep after walking through a virtual jungle. With all this discussion of crossing bridges and driving jeeps through the jungle, you might be wondering exactly what happens as a user navigates through a particular virtual world. Luckily, that's coming up next!

World Navigation

As a user navigates a world, there is a constant stream of information collected by the back-end system about the location of her avatar, based on the three-axis XYZ coordinate system we've already described. These location coordinates can be continuously analyzed to provide appropriate surroundings for the user as she moves through the world—remember her perceptual range and the addition and removal of objects from the world.

In order to move through the world, the user typically has several options for controlling her avatar (or in first-person mode, the camera). Often the options for control involve some combination of directional control using the keyboard (such as the four arrow keys), as well as a combination of mouse movements and button clicks to control the perceptual gaze of the camera (in first-person mode, of course). Many times additional combinations of keys can be used to change certain aspects of the directional motion, such as holding down a particular key to run instead of walk while using the directional arrow keys. As a designer or developer of educational virtual worlds, you can provide several different levels and/or types of control to the individual user, depending on the context and learning goals of the virtual world.

One such decision involves aspects unique to navigation in virtual worlds: teleporting and flying. As of now, we haven't yet successfully developed a working teleportation device for the real world, so we're limited to such activities occurring in a virtual space. However, teleportation can be a handy way to move around a virtual world. A user can instantaneously transport herself from one coordinate location to another, no matter how far apart "geographically" these two locations might be—even if the two locations are in two different worlds! Think of it as navigating through different scenes of a movie on a DVD, or skipping around to different chapters of a book. Maybe there are three different locations in a world that a user consistently visits, say, a police station, a diner, and a crime scene. Instead of having to take the time to mobilize overland from each of these locations to another, a user can instantly transport her character between the locations using teleportation. As a designer, you can decide whether or not this function should be available to the users of your application.

Finally, there's personal flight. Over time, mankind has come up with some pretty nifty contraptions to move humans through the air at increasing speeds, ranging from hot air balloons to supersonic jets and rocket ships. However, to date, no human has successfully flown through the air and maintained an aloft trajectory without the use of supplemental technology.

Luckily, in a virtual world, users can fly around without any assistance whatsoever. Designers and developers make the rules in these worlds.

If you want to let your users fly around unassisted, knock yourself out! All that this entails is moving the character or camera (in first-person) to a particular coordinate space that is at an altitude above the elevation of the terrain in the surrounding area—no special equipment necessary. Once the user has reached this altitude, she can fly wherever she wants, as long as her intended flight path doesn't take her beyond the boundary space of the world. This raises an interesting question about worlds: what happens when the user gets to the edge of a virtual world?

Living on the Edge

Everything comes to an end, even virtual world spaces. Currently, it is impossible to create an infinite contiguous world space. However, some of the more sophisticated game engines are able to create the illusion of an infinitely contiguous world space by dynamically generating world terrain as needed, therefore creating a seemingly seamless infinite world for the user. Either way, at any given time, there is an upper bound and a lower bound to every 3D coordinate space that defines a given world. If a user's location reaches these coordinate boundaries, then he has officially found the edge of the world. Despite the plethora of myths describing the myriad monsters that live just beyond the edge of the world, it is impossible for a user to get there from here. Depending on the type of terrain that exists in the world, these world edges can have horizons that are anything from perfectly flat to deathly steep. And in the case of the sophisticated game engines that build dynamic terrain on the fly, well, this is where the building happens.

In most cases (other than dynamic terrain generation), the edge of the world presents a problem. If the user were able to keep moving beyond the edge, she would fall off into empty space, falling perpetually downward into a bottomless darkness. As designers, how do we avoid this possibility of perpetual nosedives for our users? One way to protect the users is pretty simple—don't let them get too close to the actual edge of the world.

If you don't want the user to get too close to the edge, a world-level script can be applied that prevents the user from further forward motion when the user's location reaches a certain predetermined boundary range that you have defined for the world. Let's say the world is 10,000 meters across. This means that the coordinate space of the world extends from −5,000 to +5,000 meters in the X and Y coordinate spaces. As a designer, you can describe a motion boundary that corrals the users of the world within a space that is slightly smaller than the world boundaries, so that a user can never actually

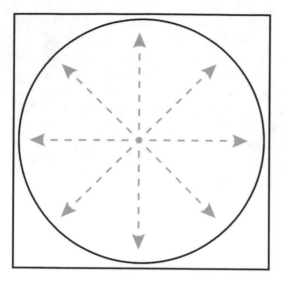

FIGURE 2.6 Overhead view of world boundary and motion boundary in a world

reach the world boundary itself. Figure 2.6 shows an overhead view of a generic world space. The outer square represents the world boundary, and the inner circle represents the motion boundary.

It seems like there is still a little problem with the relationship between the world boundary and the motion boundary. Can you spot the problem? Based on the layout in Figure 2.6, there are some spots in that world where even though the user can't fall off the edge, they still might be able to see past the edge of the world. When trying to design an engaging meso-immersive experience for the users of any world, you really don't want this situation to be possible. How can you avoid allowing users to see past the edge of your world?

Remember the perceptual buffer? Let's say that within your world, the maximum allowed size of a user's perceptual buffer is 200 meters (you can also think of this perceptual buffer as a range of vision). In this case, you would want the difference between the world boundaries and the defined motion boundary to always be greater than 200 meters—even 201 meters will suffice. Another way to think of it is that the radius of the perceptual buffer should never be longer than the distance between the world boundary and the motion boundary—that way the user can never see over the edge (even if new terrain will be built before he gets there!).

So we've prevented the user from falling off the edge. We've prevented her from seeing over the edge into the vast black virtual nothingness that lies beyond. One thing is still missing from our perceptual masterpiece. You guessed it: the horizon. Imagine yourself sitting on the top of a craggy peak in the Himalayas, enjoying a cup of tea after a satisfying climb. As you sip your Darjeeling delight, you gaze at your surroundings, turning to see all 360 degrees of the horizon. Depending on the current weather conditions and the quality of your own eyesight, you can probably see pretty far in every direction. At some distance away is the edge of your own sight capability, and this serves as your visual horizon; however far you can see, the edge of that range of vision defines your perceptual horizon. As a designer of any virtual world, you must account for the substance of this perceptual horizon.

Even if a user is prevented from traveling close enough to the edge of the world to fall off or see beyond the edge of the terrain, he can still see past the edge of the terrain from the ground level up to the sky (just like we can in the real world). An illusion of this visual horizon can be created in virtual worlds using a skybox or skydome. The skydome is a half-sphere that serves as a perceptual bubble surrounding the world from the ground level up to the "top" of the sky. What? There's no top of the sky in the real world ... that's crazy talk!

You're right, but imagine yourself on the craggy peak once again. You look directly to the west, eyes level with the horizon. You turn your gaze up until you are staring straight up into the sky. Keeping your gaze straight up, you turn your body 180 degrees so that you are now facing east. Bring your gaze back down to an eye-level view of the eastern horizon. The perceptual journey you've just made with your eyes covered 180 degrees of a sphere. This happens to be exactly half of a sphere, which, conveniently, is the same shape as the skydome surrounding your virtual world. Exactly halfway through that journey across the sky, when you were looking straight up, is a 90-degree angle from one horizon to the top of the sphere. If you own a mixing bowl, place it upside down on a flat surface. Everything inside the bowl is your virtual word, and the bowl is the skydome.

Around the bottom of this half-sphere, you can arrange a series of generic scenery images (such as endless horizon views of an ocean, a forest, or a meadow) that will provide a sort of visual fence for the user as he gazes toward the horizon of your world in any direction. These images are blended together horizontally to create a seamless 360-degree horizon along the horizontal edges of the world. Usually the top edges of these images are completely full of a singularly-colored sky (the same for all images) so that these images can be easily blended with the sky color settings of the world. This provides a seamless transition between the image itself and the rest of the colored skydome above the top edge of the images in the visual fence (as the user raises her gaze up into the sky to look at the virtual clouds). Imagine a series of cards glued to the inside bottom edge of the mixing bowl.

So, with that last horizontal detail, we've accounted for all angles of protecting the perceptual illusion of seemingly infinite horizons and skies for those users that like to live dangerously, on the fringes of the world. There are times, though, when we do want to allow users to move past the edge of the world, hopefully without even noticing.

Multiple Worlds

Many applications that implement virtual worlds as the theater of interaction with content can be quite expansive, with the contextual space of the virtual world requiring much more territory than is feasible for the mechanics of a single world. Think about an educational adventure game that involves traveling to the far reaches of the world to various archeological dig sites to put together clues about the interactions between various ancient civilizations throughout the history of human existence. Should the entire topography of the planet—detailed at the level necessary to sell the desired realism of the game—be contained within a single virtual world? No. Multiple worlds can be used in a variety of combinations to create the entire contextual space of any application that implements these worlds. Some examples of implementing multiple worlds include: different levels within a game, nested worlds, and juxtaposed worlds.

Game Levels

Many commercial virtual worlds are conceptually structured into a series of levels for gameplay, often with the difficulty of gameplay increasing with successive levels. In the case of meso-immersive games, each of these levels typically consists of one or more worlds—if there is more than one world in a level, these worlds are either nested or juxtaposed, and we'll get to these arrangements momentarily. Think about this series of levels like a series of rooms in a labyrinth, with each room set up in a way so as to make it more difficult to get from the entrance to the exit of the room; perhaps each room has more monsters (or smarter monsters) than the previous room. In any case, singular worlds arranged in this level-based format are typically experienced in a linear fashion, with substantial perceptual breaks between levels—such as the game screen fading to black.

Nested Worlds

Worlds can be nested within each other. When this happens, the worlds aren't actually housed inside one another (like those egg-shaped Russian dolls you might've seen). Instead, these nested worlds are just conceptually linked together in a hierarchical fashion (Figure 2.7).

The figure represents a conceptual map of the arrangement of worlds as they should be experienced by a user as she explores the outermost (external) world on the conceptual map. Each of the internal worlds within the hierarchy of the conceptual map represents a space that should be perceived by the user as fitting "inside" the territorial space of the external world. For example, consider the external world to be an island in the ocean. The internal worlds within the hierarchy of that external world would be structures that

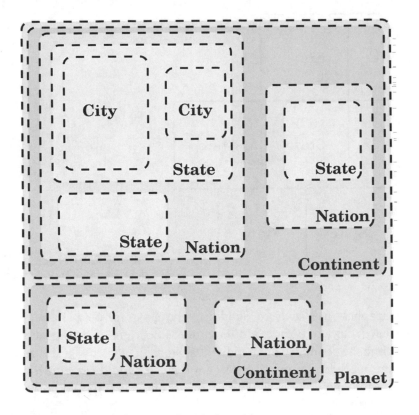

FIGURE 2.7 Conceptual diagram of nested worlds

exist on that island. One internal world could be a huge cave inside a mountain on the island. Another could be a mansion on the island (perhaps the lair of an evil villain intent on world domination or destruction). These worlds, existing as separate entities housed on the user's local machine—or a server, or even multiple servers—are linked together using application-level scripts that recognize and uphold the conceptual hierarchy of the game design.

There can be multiple levels to the hierarchy. Think of the mansion on the island. There are multiple floors to the mansion, including a cavernous basement that holds all the evil-doing technology of the villain. Each floor of the mansion has many different rooms, each of which could, technically, be a world nested within the floor world, which is nested within the mansion world, which is nested within the island world, which is ... well, you get the idea.

Juxtaposed Worlds

Worlds can also be linked to each other in a non-hierarchical fashion—or in other words, juxtaposed. Each world is "touching" another world on at least one side (Figure 2.8).

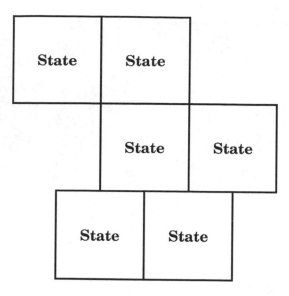

FIGURE 2.8 Conceptual diagram of juxtaposed worlds

Cartographers use grids to divide up the geography of the real world (planet Earth) using latitude and longitude. Each one of these grid squares could define the boundary of an individual world in a virtual globe. As a user goes from one side of a continent to another, he would travel through any number of juxtaposed worlds. These worlds can be juxtaposed horizontally, vertically, or both.

There are many other practical applications of world juxtaposition in applications that implement virtual worlds. One example would be the different floors of the villain's mansion (vertical juxtaposition) or the different rooms within each floor of the villain's mansion (horizontal juxtaposition). What about a huge chunk of virtual outer space? That would probably require both horizontal and vertical juxtaposition of the worlds representing each 3D sector of the overall space.

So we can have worlds touch each other and get along like one big happy family. That's great news. What happens, though, when a user wants to cross from one world to the next? For example, what if a user wants to fly (not teleport) from one planet to another in the chunk of space represented by the 3D collection of worlds, and the planets are on opposite corners of the chunk? Well, she's going to need to fly her spaceship through several different worlds to get there.

From One World to Another

As a designer, you'll need to ensure that any transitions between worlds are seamless—if necessary. In much the same way that the cuts between scenes of a movie are best when unnoticed, the same holds true for transitions between worlds in a single level of a game or simulation. Picture this: a user—experiencing the world in first-person perspective—navigates through the island world that contains the villain's mansion. As the user arrives at the mansion, he passes through the front door. This front door serves as a portal between two nested worlds (the island world and the mansion world). As the user passes through the front door, he shouldn't notice anything out of the ordinary, right? What happens when you get home from work (or anywhere) and walk through the front door of your living space? Is there a noticeable gap in your experience? Unless you have some cool new transcendental powers that the rest of the world hasn't yet discovered, then your answer to the previous question should be a resounding "NO!" You pass through the door, and nothing special happens. You keep moving forward without a hitch in your perception. The same thing should happen when you transition from an external world to an internal world in a nested world hierarchy—and the same holds true for when you pass between two juxtaposed worlds.

If you're still struggling with the concept of seamless transitions, think of the following path. The user enters the mansion (external world to internal world). He moves through several rooms (juxtaposed worlds) on the first floor of the mansion. At some point he discovers a secret stairwell (nested worlds) in the study that leads down to the basement (juxtaposed worlds) where the evil villain stores his secret massive weapons. In the back of the basement is a secret elevator (nested worlds) that serves as an escape route for the villain, leading to an escape pod housed in the island cave (juxtaposed worlds).

The journey for the user should feel absolutely seamless as he moves through each of these worlds. Even though he's been through several different worlds to get from the front door of the mansion to the escape pod in the cave below, the entire experience should feel like it took place in one big world. What happens, though, when multiple users are interacting with each other in the same world (or hierarchy of worlds)? This usually only happens in networked spaces, and luckily that's the topic we're covering in the next section of the chapter.

Networked Worlds

There are three main things to keep in mind when designing or acquiring virtual-world applications for use by multiple users simultaneously over a network: world instances, representative avatars, and sound issues.

World Instances

Most of the time, when two or more users are simultaneously interacting with the same virtual world, they're actually not in exactly the same world. Well, they are, but they aren't. Remember the taxicab objects we mentioned before? Multiple copies (or "instances") of the same taxicab could be added to the city world at any point during the simulation. The same concept holds true for multi-user worlds housed on a network. User A and User B might be interacting in the same island world, but each user has a different instance of the world served up to his or her local machine.

Good news! This allows you, the designer, to have certain aspects of each user's experience maintain a balance of separation and similarity within the same world at the same time. Don't worry if this confuses you at the moment—we'll describe this maintenance of balance more fully in a later section of the chapter. However, continuing within this conceptual vein of separation and similarity, what happens when User A and User B happen to cross paths within the island world?

Representative Avatars

In multi-user worlds, all human-directed characters in the world are continuously represented by avatars. This means that even when a user is exploring the world in first-person perspective, there is still an avatar embodying the user's moves through the environment. This attachment of representative avatars is done so that when users interact with each other, even if both are in first-person mode, each user will see a recognizable character as a representation of the other user—as opposed to an invisible camera. This reduces the confusion that would ensue should two invisible people try to have a conversation (or maybe a playful fistfight duel) with each other.

On a more serious note, imagine there are two people in a virtual-world program for training emergency medical technicians, and one person is the trainee, and one person is the fake victim. The trainee must interact with the fake victim's representative avatar to apply the appropriate first aid for the current situation. This would be quite difficult to do if the victim's character did not have a representative avatar.

Representative avatars can also actually be useful in worlds occupied by a single user. What happens in the real world when you walk past a store window, a rain puddle, or, say, a mirror? That's right, you see a reflection of yourself. If that is a level of detail that needs to be designed into your world, then the user of your world will need to have a representative avatar attached to his character as she comes within perceptual range of these reflective surfaces. Luckily, in a single-user world, you won't typically need to worry about users having conversations with themselves—but what about conversations among users in these multi-user worlds?

Sound Issues

If you've ever played any of the popular commercially available online games that implement meso-immersive virtual worlds, you likely already know about one or more ancillary programs that are also available to facilitate gamers' conversations about and within the gameplay. Typically, these software applications are referred to as "voice chat" programs, and one example of such an application is Mumble (http://mumble.sourceforge. net)—which also happens to be open source! These programs enable people to speak to one another over VOIP (Voice Over Internet Protocol) connections as they interact with each other (or other objects and characters) in the world.

An additional design issue related to conversational in-world audio is directional sound. Directionality of sound is an option for in-world conversations, meaning that as two players converse with each other using voice chat software, the listening user will hear the speaker's voice as if it were coming from the direction of the speaker's location relative to the listener. Take a look at the spatial relationship between three users at a random location in the island world (Figure 2.9).

User B is attempting to convince Users A and C to meet her by the bank of the river. She speaks intermittently to each user. When User A responds, his voice sounds as though he's ahead and to the left of User B. When User C responds, her voice sounds as though she's behind and to the right of User B. By the way, in case you're curious, the three users eventually do unite to defeat the evil villain, thwarting his master plan for world domination.

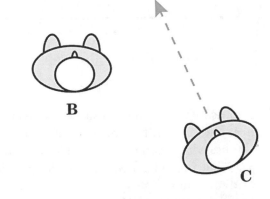

FIGURE 2.9 Overhead diagram of three users (A, B, C) in island world

Conclusion

That just about sums up the discussion of the mechanics of the world. We've got to move on to the other half of the meso-immersive experience: the GUI. To review, in this chapter we've defined the world and the GUI in the context of 3D meso-immersive virtual applications. We've described the what, the where, and the how for the world. Hopefully, you've absorbed a substantial portion of this information and learned a thing or two. However, to facilitate further absorption and synthesis, below we've provided a host of additional examples, as well as some self-paced activities and exercises that you can do to continue your exploration of these topics.

TEST YOUR UNDERSTANDING

1. In your own words, describe the boundaries of a virtual world.
2. How do scripts and objects work together in virtual worlds?
3. Describe the difference between nested and juxtaposed worlds.

LEARNING ACTIVITIES

1. Use graph paper to map out three different sets of X, Y, Z coordinates for an object, and then try to replicate those positions with a small object (such as a tennis ball).
2. Draw a conceptual map of the place you live, work, or go to school as a series of nested and juxtaposed worlds—all the way from the nation (or planet or solar system!) down to different rooms on the same floor of a building.

Links

http://mumble.sourceforge.net—from the website: "Mumble is an open source, low-latency, high quality voice chat software primarily intended for use while gaming. ... Mumble is a voice chat application for groups. While it can be used for any kind of activity, it is primarily intended for gaming."

Other Resources

Game Engines are one primary tool for the construction of virtual worlds. If you're the type that likes to tinker, then you're in luck! There are plenty of good free game engines available for your experimentation. If you're more of a window shopper, then these links can give you access to a good buffet of what's available in the game engine world.

www.devmaster.net/engines—from the website: "This database is committed to providing you with the most accurate and up-to-date information for current engines around the web. Each engine contains a brief description as well as a list of supported features and general info (platform, API, etc.)."

www.moddb.com/engines—from the "about" page: "Mod DB is the largest website dedicated to supporting independent development of games (user generated game content), including mods, addons and DLC. The aim of Mod DB is to unite developers, players and their ideas, empowering them to shape the games we play."

three
Mechanics of Virtual Worlds

The GUI

Introduction

Just like Chapter Two, the purpose of this chapter is to differentiate between the two main parts of any virtual environment—the world and the Graphical User Interface (or GUI). Since we investigated the world in Chapter Two, in this chapter we'll be looking under the hood and exploring the mechanics of the GUI. We describe what the GUI is (and isn't), as well as how it can work—along with plenty of examples.

The World and the GUI Defined

In case you skipped directly to this chapter, let's start with definitions. For the purposes of this chapter (and the rest of the book), we define the world as the 3D coordinate-based experiential space within which a learner can move his or her representative avatar. Similarly, we define the GUI as the interactive audiovisual information feedback system layered between the world and the user.

The GUI

In Chapter Two, throughout the process of describing what the world is and isn't, we frequently alluded to the existence of the GUI as a way to draw the boundary around certain aspects of the world. So, now we'll do the same thing with the GUI—tell you what it is, what it isn't, and some basics about how it works.

What the GUI Is

Remember, GUI stands for *Graphical User Interface*. Essentially, any information content (in form, function, or both) that you normally wouldn't have access to as you explore the real world would most likely be part of the GUI in a meso-immersive virtual-world application. In such an application, the GUI is an ancillary platform for user interaction with the world. Typically, this information lies somewhere between the user and the world space. If you were to hold up a piece of plexiglass between your face and the world around you, this would be a space for a GUI.

Consider a real-world scenario where a GUI might come in handy: finding food. For the most part, we humans are no longer hunter-gatherers, but we still do have to find food to feed ourselves, even if it comes from a factory in a plastic bag. But let's be more optimistic and think about a trip to the local farmers' market (Figure 3.1). The typical routine is to go around to each of the market booths—which are usually segregated based on whether the produce is organically or conventionally grown—and see what the farmers have to offer, making purchases when you deem the produce suitable to your culinary needs. You may enter some booths to inspect the produce and talk to the farmer, and likely you'll pass by several booths without even a glance.

FIGURE 3.1 A local farmers' market

Once your bags are full and your pockets are empty, you load your produce into the paniers on your bike and pedal your way back home.

Think more specifically about your interactions in one particular booth—perhaps a local farmer specializing in stone fruits (such as plums and peaches). You approach the booth, and the first thing you notice is a sign on the front of the booth indicating where the farm is located and that all the produce is certified organic (including a logo from the certifying organization). Perhaps you question the standards for certification implemented by the particular organization? Were this a virtual experience, you might be able to pull up a translucent window that would appear on your screen between you and the booth. This window would contain information about the standards implemented by this particular organic certification organization. Perhaps you could then pull information from other certification organizations to compare standards.

Why is this important? It could be that the organic certification method chosen by this farmer is not up to your own standards for the food you wish to consume. Having this information available to you before you converse with the farmer can prepare you to ask the right questions and find out why this particular organization was chosen over others with better standards for certification. Pertaining to virtual worlds, though, the point is that the information you were able to view and compare between the various organic organizations was presented in a way that is not yet possible in the real world, so such information (and the function of comparison) would certainly be part of the GUI in a virtual-world application.

The GUI provides mechanisms for the user to supplement the actions he or she can perform directly in the world environment. The content of the GUI is any audiovisual information or feedback provided for the user that is not directly emitted from the world environment. Let's dive into each of these aspects—the function and the form—with a greater level of detail.

GUI Function

As we've already stated, the function of the GUI is the facilitation of a user's supplemental interactions with the world. This facilitation occurs primarily through the visualization of relevant information, based on a push/pull relationship between the user and the system—the user and the system are pushing and pulling information back and forth through one or more channels of interaction.

Different meso-immersive experiences provide different levels of interactivity with the GUI displays. Some can be oriented toward rather passive consumption, much like the ticker display that runs constantly along the bottom of the screen on most cable television news channels. They are passive because the user can't do anything with the information other than consume it. Most of the information in a GUI for a virtual world designed for learning should be actively consumed by the user as she works toward the learning goals of the world, otherwise the information shouldn't be taking up valuable screen space. The user can view the information presented in the GUI, make decisions about what's happening in the world, and then take action to change in-world behaviors. One last function of the GUI for the user is active production of information. Tools can be made available in the GUI for the user to produce information based on her in-world interactions. For example, a user playing the role of a scientist investigating one or more ecological issues in a virtual watershed could use a digital log book to keep notes about her observations.

GUI Form

As the technological platforms supporting the user's experience in a virtual world continue to improve, GUIs are becoming more dynamic and advanced—including the visual or interactive form taken by the GUI at any given moment during the experience. Still, though, GUIs can typically be grouped into two styles: those separated from the world, and those integrated into the world.

As you might expect, separated GUIs maintain a certain level of visual or formic separation from the world in a meso-immersive virtual application (Figure 3.2). As shown in the figure, these separated GUIs usually have no spatial overlap with the world. The user must focus his attention on either the world or the GUI, but attempting to view both at once might result in crossed eyes and headaches.

Integrated GUIs, however, can be well intertwined with the world space. Typically, though, these GUIs exist as a translucent layer between the user and the world, much like the aforementioned sheet of plexiglass. This type of GUI is more often used in the more technologically advanced platforms implemented by most commercially available games. Heads up displays, or HUDs (Figure 3.3) are a real-world analogy to this type of GUI.

Is one type of GUI better than the other? The answer to this question depends on your needs as a designer (or acquirer) of the virtual world that will serve as the best solution for you, and on the learning goals of the virtual world. From a strictly cognitive perspective, integrated GUIs will likely induce much less mental effort from the user than separated GUIs (we will explore cognitive aspects of virtual worlds in Chapter Four). When designing or acquiring virtual-world applications for learning, it is good to think of the GUI as the platform for learning, since much of the structured information consumed by the learner during her experience of the application comes from the GUI.

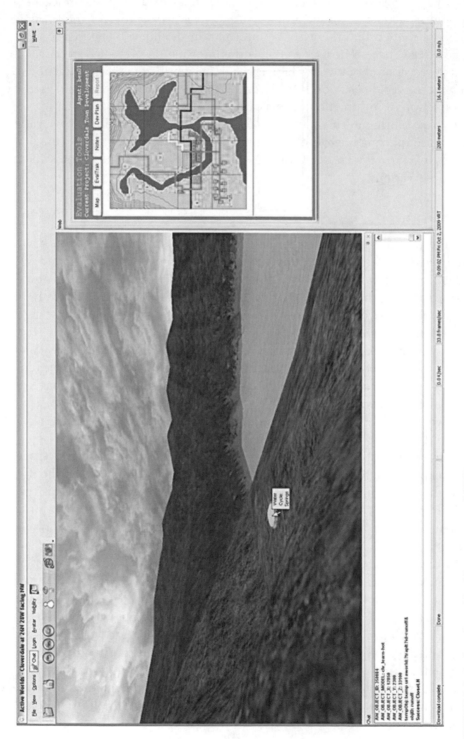

FIGURE 3.2 A virtual world with a separated GUI

FIGURE 3.3 A HUD in a large airplane

What the GUI Isn't

So we know what the world is and isn't. And we know what the GUI is. But what *isn't* the GUI? If it's in the world, it isn't in the GUI. If it's in the GUI, it isn't in the world. Or, anything happening within the boundaries of the world that would normally be perceived in the actual world we live in is not part of the GUI for that world. Seems simple enough, right?

Well, maybe it's still a little difficult to grasp this concept. Maybe an example would help: consider an air raid siren (Figure 3.4). If you're not sure what an air raid siren is, these were used to warn citizens during wartime when opposing forces were preparing an air raid on the city. This would allow citizens of the city to take appropriate measures to avoid injury or death from the resulting destruction of buildings in the city. The air raid sirens are interesting because they have such a distinctive sound—much like the noise a walrus might make if it were given a root canal.

Such a distinctive sound would come in handy as a recognizable notification mechanism in a GUI, no matter what the theme of the virtual-world application may be. The same exact sound could occur in the world, especially a virtual world that replicates the experience of being a citizen of a vulnerable European city during World War II. The form of the sound is

FIGURE 3.4 An air raid
siren on the roof of a
building

consistent across the GUI and the world, but the function is distinct from one form to the next.

The same phenomenon can occur with visual elements as well. Look again at the cockpit of an airplane (Figure 3.3). The instruments that are typically available in most airplane cockpits are physical entities that exist in the real world as tangible objects.

The same cockpit instrumentation can be presented in graphical format as a GUI layered between the pilot (user) and her view of the world—as is the case in most commercially available flight simulator applications. In this case, the plane itself doesn't actually exist in the virtual world—the plane is embodied as a camera, and the GUI creates a visual form that functions both as the illusion of a real plane body and the feedback mechanism for the pilot. It's also possible that a similar cockpit could be modeled as a virtual world in and of itself. Part of a pilot's training could involve learning the spatial layout of a cockpit in such a virtual world before she ever sits down in a real version of the same plane.

Hopefully all this talk of form and function has given you a much better understanding of what the GUI is and isn't. You may still be curious to know more specifics about function, and luckily that's where we're headed next.

How Does the GUI Work?

The GUI, as we've mentioned, serves as a sort of external interface for in-world interactions—either supplementing or extending the range of interactions available to the user in the world. In any case, the functionality of the GUI is directly or indirectly tied to the functionality of the world. The software application that drives the GUI can be separate or integrated from the world—in terms of how the application (or system of applications) interacts with the data being produced by the world.

The level of integration (or separation) of the GUI application(s) from the world data likely dictates the development process for the GUI. Using modern virtual-world development tools, the GUI application can be developed separately from the world—and in multiple pieces or stages (conducted by multiple programmers) if necessary. No matter the integration or separation of the GUI in terms of end-user (learner) experience with the virtual-world application, every attempt should be made to design the GUI so that development can occur separately and synchronously with the development of the world. Additionally, the GUI should be designed in such a way that the entire GUI can be changed or replaced without disrupting the functionality of the world (and vice versa).

From Chapter Two to this point, we've discussed the ins and outs of both the world and the GUI (what they are, what they aren't, how they work). In the process of describing all these attributes for both the world and the GUI, many instances of overlap have been touched upon. The next section of this chapter explores the relationships resulting from this overlap. Hopefully exploring the overlaps will give you an even better understanding of how both work, and the possibilities these worlds really offer for learning.

Between the GUI and the World

As the technologies for delivering meso-immersive virtual experiences to learners become increasingly sophisticated, the world and the GUI are converging. Eventually, the world will become the GUI (or, technically, the functionality currently provided by the GUI will become completely integrated into the objects of the world, and the GUI itself will actually disappear).

Until this complete integration happens, the GUI and the world must continuously communicate in order to serve up a seamless interactive experience for any learner traversing the world. These communications between world and GUI fall into three general categories: interactions, navigation, and feedback. Communications between the world and the GUI (and the user) that happen in each of these categories can best be described using an information push–pull framework. Simply put, information push occurs when the system sends information to the "client" (or learner) as needed, and information pull occurs when the client/learner requests information from the system. For better understanding of how the push–pull relationships manifest in each of these three categories, consider a fictitious example: a virtual-world application built for learning about appropriate methods for identifying flora—or, more specifically, different species of trees. Let's call this application TreeFinder. The goal of the TreeFinder application is for learners to explore several open-ended virtual natural environments and learn the appropriate methods for identifying trees as they would in the real natural environments.

As an example, we will discuss one particular method of tree species identification involving a series of decisions about the leaves of a given tree—including leaf patterns, twig spines, leaf margins, leaf arrangements, and leaf lobes. One possible series of decisions made while using this method to identify a particular tree is presented here in this decision tree (Figure 3.5). Such an approach to tree identification would be appropriately scaffolded for the individual learner as he or she explores the virtual worlds of the TreeFinder application.

Interactions

Interactions consist mostly of pull operations. The learner wants to interact with the world, and does so (mostly) through the GUI. These interactions are combinations of requests for information made by the learner. To better understand how these interactions occur, let's look at how a learner might interact with the GUI for TreeFinder.

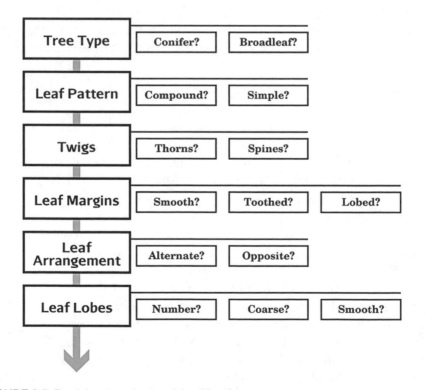

FIGURE 3.5 Decision tree for tree identification

Susanna is a middle school student who likes trees. She doesn't realize it yet, but she likes them so much that she's an aspiring dendrologist. She's exploring one of the virtual worlds of the TreeFinder application, and she's positioned her avatar right in front of a virtual tree: a beautiful, 100-feet-tall specimen of *Acer saccharum*, more commonly known as the sugar maple. She's ready to begin the identification process using the TreeFinder GUI, and we've provided a simplified diagram of how this interaction happens (Figure 3.6).

As you can see, the process of tree identification, as facilitated by the GUI, is fairly straightforward. However, in order to interact with the tree in the first place, Susanna must arrive at the tree's location within the world space of the TreeFinder application. So, how does Susanna get to the tree in the first place? And where (or, rather, how) does she go once she's identified the glorious *Acer saccharum*? Susanna moves from one place to another through navigation processes which we describe in the next section.

Navigation

Susanna has many options for moving from one place to another within the world of TreeFinder. She can navigate her representative avatar from one

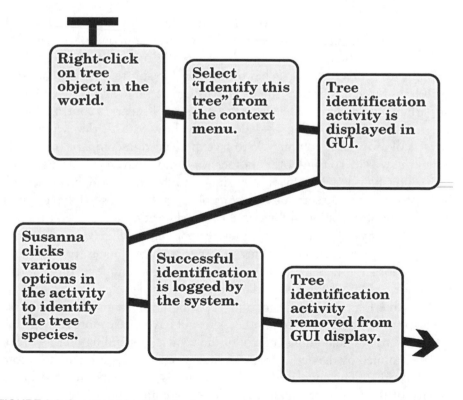

FIGURE 3.6 Susanna identifies an *Acer saccharum*

location to another in the TreeFinder world either by manipulating her avatar directly in the world, or by providing location movement commands (in some fashion) through one or more tools in the GUI. In-world navigations are information pull operations, and GUI-based navigations are typically pull operations that may be based on information pushed by the system to the user. Each of these two options for navigation can manifest in many ways, depending on how the TreeFinder application has been designed and developed.

Let's assume that the designers of TreeFinder have implemented a movement mechanism that allows for direct navigation of the world space using the arrow keys on the keyboard. Susanna can move her avatar through the world of TreeFinder much like she could transport her own body through the real world. If she wants to walk her avatar forward, she presses and holds the "up" arrow key. Thanks to the designers, she also has the option of looking around as she moves through the world using a combination of the arrow keys and mouse movements—the arrows controlling body movement and direction; the mouse controlling gaze direction (up/down or left/right).

The designers have also decided to provide Susanna with additional mobility options in the world, thanks to modes of transportation that become available to her for a variety of reasons, such as achieving other goals in the world or simply finding these vehicles after some amount of wandering. In this case, Susanna has a bicycle she can use to move from one place to another at higher speeds than walking, and she eventually comes across a jeep that is available to access further reaches of the world in shorter amounts of time.

Perhaps Susanna controls the bicycle using the same arrow key controls, or perhaps the designers have included additional separate controls for this alternative mode of transport—depending on how realistic they wish for the physics of movement on a bicycle to be experienced in comparison to walking in the world. To think of it another way—how hard is it for Susanna to control the bicycle's movement? Is it similar to the real world, inasmuch that if she stops paying attention to the control of the bicycle, she'll have trouble maintaining its stability and increase her likelihood of a crash? Either way, the level of physical realism of the bicycle experience will have consequences for Susanna's perception of her surroundings as she navigates from one location to another—she may or may not notice certain unique features of trees that she would if walking instead of riding the bicycle.

The same logic holds true for the jeep. Should Susanna choose to drive the jeep from one location to another, she will have many more responsibilities inherent in maintaining control of the vehicle, depending on the level of realism imbued by the designers (with higher realism resulting in more complex controls). This increased need for controls due to the increased complexity of the jeep functionality can necessitate additional interactive control between Susanna and the world, and additional feedback provided in the GUI. As such, the GUI is often used as a supplementary mechanism for allowing the user to fully navigate the world.

In the real world, we often use our own supplemental devices for navigation. GPS devices are increasingly pervasive, or perhaps you're one of those folks who still knows how to read a topographical map and triangulate your location manually. In any case, we're used to the idea of implementing instrumentation to help ourselves find our way through the world. The GUI associated with the world of any virtual application is a place to house much of the instrumentation that can be used to navigate that world. Often these instruments are presented as a part of the HUD that is continuously visible to the user (Figure 3.3).

One common navigation instrument available in such a HUD is the compass. In many virtual worlds, cardinal directions are irrelevant—at a fundamental structural level, anyway. However, based on the narrative of many games and simulation activities that implement these worlds, direction of travel can become an important factor. Consider Susanna's adventure through the TreeFinder application. Over the course of her experience, she's learned that certain types of flora are more likely to grow on the northern slopes of mountains, and she's on a mission to find three different species. Two of these species happen to be fond of north-facing slopes. As Susanna explores the world of TreeFinder, she will need to know which direction she's facing. If it's a rather overcast day, she might not have the sun as a reference. Having a compass tool available as part of the GUI for the TreeFinder application should make it much easier for Susanna to determine the northern slope of the mountain range she has recently located in the world following a quick drive in the jeep.

The mentioning of Susanna's jeep driving highlights another aspect of the GUI: it can change its content and layout of instrumentation depending on the current mode of interaction. When Susanna is actually inside the jeep, driving from one location to another, the GUI for the TreeFinder application would change to accommodate the instrumentation necessary for controlling the movement of the jeep. Any controls or feedback mechanisms specific to this mode—such as the speedometer and the fuel gage—would appear in the display as needed. So, the GUI changes based on the mode of user interaction. The compass might stay separated from the "dashboard" of the jeep (say, up in the top right-hand corner of the screen), or it might be integrated into the dashboard whenever Susanna is actually using the jeep. Such decisions are, of course, up to the designers of the TreeFinder application.

What if Susanna needs to cover more ground even faster than is possible in the physical limitations of a motor vehicle traveling over rugged terrain? Or what if she follows her compass and drives her jeep to the edge of a large lake and needs to get to the mountain range she can see in the distance on the other shore, but there is no boat in sight? Perhaps there is a map of the entire world of TreeFinder that she can call up into the GUI (an information pull request). This map is interactive. Susanna can click on certain icons appearing on the map and teleport directly to the represented location. This functionality would serve her well, considering that jeeps can't function under water, and she can see from the map that the lake is rather large and would therefore take quite a bit of time to circumnavigate.

In fact, teleportation is a key element of meso-immersive virtual-world applications, a functionality that can give these applications a unique affordance for learning about real-world problems in a manner that is much more efficient, at least from the perspective of traversing through space in shorter periods of time. Because teleportation is currently impossible in the real world, creating appropriate interface forms for this function can be both challenging and liberating. Because there is no real-world instrument or application for comparison, the teleportation function and/or instrumentation can take any form that designers may choose—in the GUI, the world, or both. We've mentioned GUI teleport functionality: the interactive map of the TreeFinder world. Teleportation "hot-spots" can also be implemented into the world itself using recognizable icons, much like a phone booth—or a shimmering diamond that hovers a few feet off the ground.

These hot-spots are, without a doubt, objects in the world. However, the sole purpose they serve is to function as a transportation interface for the world. So, as an element that exists solely as a part of the interface for the application, should these hot-spots be considered part of the GUI as well? The same argument can be made for Susanna's travels with the jeep. Technically, the jeep is an object in the world, but when Susanna drives the jeep, the dashboard of the jeep is strictly part of the GUI. In fact, it's most likely that Susanna isn't actually inside the jeep as she drives—most likely it's just a camera moving through the world, with the dashboard GUI layered on top, giving Susanna the first-person perspective illusion that her avatar is actually driving the jeep.

Well, we've gone and muddled things up once again. Where does the GUI stop and the virtual world begin? The boundary isn't always clear. But we know that they need to work together to provide the best experience possible for the user (learner). We've hinted at this cooperation while discussing Susanna's control of the jeep, and the transformation of the GUI for different modes of travel. The key factor of this cooperation and transformation is feedback.

Feedback

Feedback consists entirely of information pushed by the virtual world to the learner. This push can be the direct result of an information pull request instigated by the user/learner, or it can be the result of a decision made by the system underlying the virtual world based on any number of variables pertaining to the current status of the world and/or the user. In any case, the action–reaction relationship of feedback can manifest in both the GUI and the world, resulting in four possible combinations:

1. in-world action, in-world reaction;
2. in-world action, GUI reaction;
3. GUI action, in-world reaction;
4. GUI action, GUI reaction.

Within each of these four categories is a plethora of possible manifestations of the action–reaction interplay of user and feedback. Consider four interaction sequences from Susanna's navigation through the world of the Tree Finder application as brief examples of the myriad possibilities in each of the categories. First, as Susanna navigates her avatar to walk through the world in search of a specific species of tree, she cuts through a meadow of tall grass. Suddenly, there is a flurry of grass and wings all around her as she has just flushed a covey of quail out of hiding. This in-world feedback (quail objects flying away from Susanna's avatar) occurred because of an in-world action (Susanna's avatar moved within a certain proximity of the location of the group of quail objects). Second, after Susanna nearly falls over in surprise from the flushed quail, she regains her composure and seeks to find her bearings. She knows she needs to head north to find that mountain range. She takes a look at the compass in her GUI and realizes that, in all the recent confusion, she is now facing east. She turns her avatar 90 degrees to the left to face north and continue the journey. As she makes this turn (in-world action) the compass needle moves simultaneously (GUI reaction) to reflect the direction that she is currently facing.

Third, Susanna realizes it will take her quite some time to walk from her current location in the world to the mountains where her tree hunt might prove fruitful, so she decides to teleport. She locates the mountain range on the map, finds the teleport icon closest to the mountain, and clicks the icon. As she clicks the icon on the map (GUI action), her avatar is instantly relocated to the coordinate location represented by this icon (in-world reaction). It turns out that the location where Susanna landed is still relatively far away from the mountain, but she is closer to one end of the north face than the other. She knows that the species she's looking for is more likely to be found at higher elevations and fairly close to a water source. If the far end of the mountain is more likely to meet these species-friendly conditions, then it will be worth her time to travel that further distance (as opposed to the near end of the north face of the mountain). Susanna will need more information to make a decision. She looks at the world map in the GUI, and clicks buttons (GUI action) to make additional elements of the map—topographical elevations and water systems—visible (GUI reaction).

This entire sequence of events—starting with Susanna's unexpected quail experience and ending with her interaction with supplemental elements for the map—could feasibly happen within 30 seconds of real time. And it's likely that most 30-second segments of any person's experience in any meso-immersive virtual application are going to contain more than just four relatively simplistic action–reaction sequences—a lot more, actually. And with all these action–reaction sequences occurring so quickly, that means that there will be a whole lot of data flying around between the world and the GUI. How does the system keep track of all this information and properly handle this big information push–pull dance that happens constantly while a user is experiencing the world? There is a rather complex communication network and a collection of tables in one or more databases that support the push–pull of information flow. The specifics of how these networks function to deliver and store data are quite interesting, but also rather complicated—and beyond the scope of this book. However, it's important to know that such a dance is happening, especially concerning the topic of in-world measurement, which we'll cover in upcoming chapters.

Conclusion

In this chapter, we've described the what (and the what *not*) and the how of the GUI. We covered the interaction, navigation, and feedback processes that can happen between the world and the GUI. Hopefully, you've absorbed a substantial portion of this information and learned a thing or two. However, to facilitate further absorption and synthesis, below we've provided a host of additional examples, as well as some self-paced activities and exercises that you can do to continue your exploration of these topics.

TEST YOUR UNDERSTANDING

In your own words, describe the form and function of a GUI.

LEARNING ACTIVITIES

1. Think about an activity you do on a regular basis, such as grocery shopping or swimming laps for exercise. How would an integrated HUD-style GUI facilitate completion of this activity? What would it look like? How would it work?
2. With this imagined GUI, describe how the GUI interacts with the world in terms of interaction, navigation, and feedback for the activity you've chosen.

Other Resources

Even though GUIs are an integral part of 3D virtual worlds, most if not all of the content in any GUI is 2D multimedia—text, graphics, audio, and video. There are tons of good resources for good design and development of multimedia for learning, but we think that these books are two of the best resources.

Clark, R. C. & Lyons, C. C. (2004). *Graphics for learning: Proven guidelines for planning, designing, and evaluating visuals in training materials*. San Francisco: Pfeiffer.

Mayer, R. E. (2005). *The Cambridge Handbook of Multimedia Learning*. Cambridge, UK: Cambridge University Press.

part two

Theoretical Basis for Learning and Assessment in Virtual Worlds

four
Theoretical Basis for Learning in Virtual Worlds

Introduction

We've taken a tour of the history of virtual worlds and been on a detailed exploration of their mechanics. In this chapter, we're going to examine the reasons why so many people believe that virtual worlds can offer uniquely powerful platforms for learning. Why, exactly, are more and more virtual worlds being designed and deployed to help children and adults learn about science, math, health, business, fire-fighting, etc.? Let's find out.

In the earliest attempts to create educational virtual worlds, much of the motivation for making the worlds seemed linked to a basic "wow" factor: virtual worlds were exciting and new. People were just starting to figure out what they could do; trying out different things, and using them for learning seemed a natural avenue for this kind of exploration. In this approach, early educational virtual-world designers followed a familiar pattern that has been repeated multiple times through modern history. If we look back through the past hundred years (or further back, really), we see that each time a new technology was developed, it quickly was taken up as a magical new tool for learning. Radio, films, television, multimedia software, and the internet—each enjoyed a rush of enthusiasm as a possible panacea for improving education. And each ultimately failed to make much of an impact on learning, except perhaps the internet. As Todd Oppenheimer wrote in his book *The Flickering Mind* (2003), early proponents of successive technological platforms were universally wrong in their optimistic pronouncements of learning potential of their chosen tool. For example, Thomas Edison, Oppenheimer recounts, claimed that films would replace not just books, but schools themselves within a few years of their introduction.

This string of failures of past technologies offers a cautionary tale for virtual-worlds designers. Enthusiasm for a tool is not enough. Belief in the inherent power of a tool for learning won't produce that power. A "build it and it will work" attitude will most likely result in failure. Instead, virtual-world proponents and designers must develop a keen understanding of the "why" and "how" of virtual worlds for learning. And to do that, it is critical to have a strong understanding of the theoretical basis for designing educational experiences embedded in virtual worlds. There is a lot known about how people learn. By studying that knowledge and applying it to the creation of virtual worlds, we can make the best use of them as tools, and succeed in improving learning.

In this chapter, we'll go on a quick tour of several theories of learning that match well with the affordances and features offered by virtual worlds. We will look at some of the studies showing how these theories have been applied more or less successfully to the design of educational virtual worlds.

Theoretical Basis for Learning in Virtual Worlds

To provide a hook on which to hang our discussion of learning theories and how they are actualized in the making of educational virtual worlds, we are going to make use of a virtual world called River City. As we introduced in Chapter One, River City is a virtual world created at Harvard University by Professor Chris Dede and his students. River City was one of the first "modern" virtual worlds to be built and studied in a systematic way, but it wasn't the only one. As we described earlier, some others include Quest Atlantis, SAVE Science, and Whyville. Each of these makes use of a virtual world to help kids learn, among other things, about science content and inquiry skills by conducting scientific investigations. Because River City has been around for so long, and because both of the authors of this book worked on the River City virtual world, we will use it as an example to show how multiple learning theories can be applied to the design of virtual worlds for education.

Dede realized in the late 1990s that the commercial virtual worlds available at the time might work well to give kids the experience of being a "real scientist." Virtual worlds could offer students the chance to conduct an investigation that would have them using the same kinds of procedures real-world scientists use to explore problems: gather data, formulate questions, gather more data to explore those questions, formulate hypotheses, and then test those hypotheses (Dede, Ketelhut, & Ruess, 2002). Learning these steps in the classroom was most often accomplished through readings (in the more boring cases) or inquiry projects (in more interesting cases). The River City research team wondered if virtual worlds could do a better job by setting the learning of science inquiry in a relatively realistic setting in which students are asked to solve a mystery. As we covered previously, it worked pretty well. River City implementations consistently showed that a virtual world-based science inquiry curriculum could be engaging for students, offer the chance for students to conduct realistic inquiry, and lead to better results on assessments of science learning, particularly for students who traditionally do not do well in science class (Nelson & Ketelhut, 2008).

River City's design incorporated elements of several theories of learning including situated learning, constructivism, socio-constructivism, cognitive processing, and behaviorism. Let's take a look at each of these in turn, and examine how they might be applied to the design of virtual worlds.

Situated Learning

Situated learning simply means learning that takes place within a context that looks and acts like the situation in which the thing being learned will actually be used in the real world (Brown, Collins, & Duguid, 1989). Leaving aside virtual worlds for a moment, think about a lesson focused on learning to cook a hamburger at a fast food restaurant (we'll call it MacNasties). If you are a new employee, the best way to learn how to make a burger is probably to watch somebody make a bunch of them at a MacNasties restaurant, and then to make some yourself at a real grill in a real MacNasties, with somebody watching and giving advice and feedback. That's situated learning.

Situated learning theorists argue that all learning is situated in specific contexts, and that the contexts in which people learn can help or hinder their learning. If there is a good match between the thing being learned and the context in which it is learned, that match will help promote learning. If the match is not good, it will be harder to transfer the thing being learned in one setting and/or through activities unmatched to the target setting into the context in which it might actually be used. Learning in a typical school is situated in a context: the classroom. For some things, this context makes a lot of sense. For example, if a lesson's goal is to demonstrate how to sit in a classroom while somebody at the front of the room talks, the classroom is a perfect setting. We're all probably experts at this. If you were to walk into a classroom tomorrow, no matter how long you've been away, you'd know what to do immediately.

For other learning goals, the classic classroom context, setting, and activities don't make as much sense. Think about how you learned to drive a car. Depending on your age, you probably learned either in classes at your high school or through a commercial driving school. You might have read a book about the mechanics of operating a car, and about the rules of the road. You probably watched films showing these same things. The books and films might have helped a bit. But the real learning took place in one or two settings: a driving simulator and in a real car. It was only when your driving lessons were "situated" in the context in which you would actually use the skills and knowledge you needed to drive that you really learned how to drive.

So what does this have to do with virtual worlds? Probably the number one reason why educational researchers and designers are excited about virtual worlds as platforms for learning is that they are terrific at supporting situated learning.

To demonstrate why this is the case, think about what happens when you play a virtual-world-based computer game. We'll use the game Oblivion: Elder Scrolls IV as our example. In case you've never heard of Oblivion, take a look at the game's website (see www.elderscrolls.com/oblivion). Oblivion is a single-player RPG. It takes place in a very large virtual world. In Oblivion, like most commercial virtual-world-based games, your character embarks on a long narrative-driven quest. Your goal is to complete the large overarching quest, along with a collection of sub-quests. While doing so, you can also spend a huge amount of time just wandering around, exploring the virtual world. You can talk to people, pick up objects, fight, steal, perform magic spells, read documents, and generally inhabit a well-realized virtual life.

Everything you do and see in Oblivion seems pretty realistic. The graphics are a bit cartoonish, relatively outmoded by today's standards (and the cutting edge standards of today will be outmoded within a year). But you still feel as if you are inside a real world, doing real things, and talking to real people. When you learn how to do something in the virtual world (say, shoot an arrow), it feels as if you are really learning to do that thing: and doing it in a way that makes sense within the context of that world.

In other words, the things you do and learn are situated in the context of the virtual world. If you need to talk to an NPC (non-player character), you aren't likely to stop playing and go read the manual to figure out how to interact with them. Instead, you'll probably just walk up to them and start "talking" in the virtual world itself. Going back to our arrow example, you might be given the option to have a lesson on how to shoot the first time you pick up a bow and arrow. If so, the lesson will be given by a computer-based character in the virtual world, and will involve shooting the arrow at something in the world itself under the watchful eye of your in-world teacher. You are unlikely to be given a digital book and told to go read about the mechanics of arrow shooting.

How might somebody apply ideas of situated learning to the design of an educational virtual world? River City offers a good example. River City was designed from the start to provide students with the chance to conduct a scientific investigation in a setting that looked and acted like a simplified version of the real world. Upon entering the virtual city, students can investigate why town residents are getting sick by interacting with computer-based city residents, exploring possible contamination sites such as muddy streets or an insect-filled bog, and reading through records such as the admissions log at the local hospital. The world itself also provides realistic "atmospheric" elements that offer information such as the sounds of people coughing and mosquitoes buzzing, and changing weather patterns over time (Ketelhut, Dede, Clarke, & Nelson, 2007).

Like many educational virtual worlds, River City doesn't look particularly realistic (check back in Chapter One for a reminder of its look). In fact by modern gaming standards the graphics are quite poor. But the tasks that the players in River City need to perform are based on real-world science inquiry tasks, and the world is realistic enough that students who take part in the River City curriculum have reported "feeling like a real scientist"—a major change over what they reported feeling like when sitting through in-class lectures on similar topics (Clarke, Dede, Ketelhut, & Nelson, 2006).

Constructivism

Constructivist theory is another favorite of educational virtual-world designers. Some researchers will argue that constructivism is less a theory than an approach or point-of-view toward learning (Alessi & Trollip, 2001). We won't argue the point here because for our purposes it doesn't matter that much. Basically, though, constructivism in education focuses on the idea that learning isn't about getting a student to memorize a bunch of instructional material. Instead, with constructivism, learning is an act of building, or constructing, understanding of some content or processes from the inside out (Jonassen, Peck, & Wilson, 1999). Proponents of constructivism believe that it is a philosophy distinct from so-called objectivist philosophy (both behaviorism and cognitivism can be categorized as objectivist). Objectivist theories, according to constructivist designers, are based on the idea that knowledge and truth exist independently of students. In accordance with this view, the aim of learning is to absorb that external knowledge, either through passive transmission or active "intake" (Jonassen, 1991, 1994; Perkins, 1991).

Constructivism, on the other hand, states that knowledge and truth do not possess universal, external existence. Rather, each person constructs his or her own knowledge, an individual version of truth (Bednar, Cunningham, Duffy, & Perry, 1992). (Jonassen et al., 1999: 3) state that:

> individuals make sense of their world and everything they come in contact with by constructing their own representations or models of their experiences. ... Teaching is not a process of imparting knowledge, because the learner cannot know what the teacher knows and what the teacher knows cannot be transferred to the learner.

This knowledge construction is achieved through the formation and testing of hypotheses based upon previous personal experience and interaction with external "objects." Since each person has a slightly different set of background experiences and interpretative viewpoints, each will have a unique knowledge construction. Constructivist researchers are quick to note that this does not imply that all versions of personal truth are equal. Rather, the merit of an individual's knowledge about any given topic is its viability. Viability in this case is defined as how well one's ideas "work"; how well they mesh with some larger group's beliefs about those ideas (Jonassen, 1991). The objective of the learner then is to build increasingly sophisticated, viable individual models of understanding about the world.

As with any theory of learning, there are widely divergent ideas about what constructivism actually means. Dalgarno (2001) describes three interpretations of constructivism: endogenous, exogenous, and dialectic. He defines endogenous constructivism as emphasizing self-directed learner exploration, without any direct instruction or overt external guidance. In contrast, exogenous constructivists recognize the value of direct instruction, but still emphasize student control over learning and opportunities for construction of knowledge. Finally, dialectic constructivism focuses on the role of social interaction among learners as they construct knowledge. In addition, this brand of constructivism emphasizes the need for a kind of collaborative scaffolding.

Ultimately, a student learning something designed with a constructivist theory base will likely end up meeting the same learning goals as might be defined in a curriculum based in some other theoretical framework, but the path to that goal is thought of differently from a constructivist perspective than from other theory-based views. For example, a truly constructivist approach to curriculum design would not involve groups of kids sitting in a classroom listening to a lecture. Instead, a constructivist designer might set up learning projects through which students "discover" firsthand the things they are supposed to learn. Constructivist design is student centered and active. On a practical level, constructivist thinking finds its way into curriculum design in the form of project-based learning, discovery learning, and other student-led kinds of approaches.

It is easy to understand the appeal of constructivist design approaches to people interested in creating virtual worlds for learning. Virtual worlds are active, user-centered environments almost by definition. Commercial virtual-world-based games typically involve players exploring the cities, forests, spaceships, or other locations as they work to understand the virtual world, its rules, its mechanics, and their place within it. Instead of being led through a storyline, players in a virtual world designed with a constructivist curriculum might be given an initial bit of guidance from another player or from an in-game computer-based character and then be set loose to try things out for themselves. This approach also follows closely the theoretical idea of "guided constructivism."

The River City virtual world, in addition to being designed as a situated learning science curriculum, incorporated elements of guided constructivism.

Students entering River City were told by the mayor of the town (a computer-based character) that they were to explore the town and gather information on the illnesses with their teammates. To conduct their investigation, students had open access to go anywhere in the world, look at or interact with any object or person in the world, and build their own understanding of what was going on. They could decide for themselves when they thought they had gathered enough information about the illnesses in town to formulate a hypothesis. Once they did so, they could test out their hypothesis as many times as they liked (until time ran out in class) before crafting a letter to the mayor of the town explaining and defending their ideas (Nelson, Ketelhut, Clarke, Bowman, & Dede, 2005).

Socio-constructivism

Closely related to both constructivism and situated learning, and also a favorite of virtual world designers, is socio-constructivism. Socio-constructivism takes all the user-centered knowledge-building ideas of constructivism and adds a collaborative component. The basic idea is that nobody learns anything by him- or herself. Instead, each person learns by trying things out, getting feedback from the world and from other people, and then modifying their approach based on the feedback and trying again. Learning from a socio-constructivist perspective is a kind of social activity, taking place in a community of people who are also learning a given thing, or who already know that thing and can act as mentors, coaches, or guides to novices (Lave & Wenger, 1991).

Learning in a socio-constructivist curriculum often involves trying out new roles. For example, if you want to learn how to be a teacher, you can take on the role of teacher and try it out. You don't do this by yourself (at least not for long). Instead, you might test your teaching skills and build your knowledge about teaching with other people who are trying to do the same thing, under the mentoring eyes of people who are already experts at teaching and can give feedback on how you are doing.

Returning to the River City virtual-world example, it was designed both as a situated learning environment and simultaneously as a guided socio-constructivist one. Students in River City worked in small teams to complete their scientific investigation. Each member of the team was expected to play the role of "apprentice scientist." In that role, and with their team members, they were expected to try out inquiry skills as they would be practiced by a real scientist. To figure out how to do this, players gathered information from characters in the virtual world, both computer-based experts and real people, who acted as expert mentors and coaches. And students were also provided with a lot of peer feedback from other members of their investigation team, and from other students in their class who were completing the same virtual-world-based curriculum.

Behaviorism

Educational researchers and designers, when they talk of behaviorism at all, sniff that curricula based on behaviorist theory lead to "passive learners" and "rote memorization." Neither charge is true: behaviorist-based curricula are no more likely than any other theory-based curricula to lead to such dire consequences. Theories of learning rise and fall in popularity. It is the nature of academic life to be critical of previously heralded approaches to teaching and learning. Indeed, one of the best ways to advance as a researcher is to tear down formerly sacred views and replace them with new, or seemingly new, ones. Such is the case with behaviorism as a basis for the creation of curricula and learning environments in which to teach that curricula.

We believe that behaviorism offers a powerful theory for designing activities in virtual worlds for learning. Indeed, if designers are to create successful learning experiences in virtual worlds, they would do well to incorporate aspects of behaviorism in their design. To demonstrate why, let's start with a definition of behaviorism as it applies to designing virtual worlds. For our purposes, we're mostly interested in the "operant conditioning" aspect of behaviorism. This idea, put forward most famously by B. F. Skinner, centers on the use of designed activities to modify a person's behavior in the service of learning. Operant conditioning makes use of reinforcement and/or punishment in response to a person's voluntary behavior to "condition" that person to behave in a specified manner. A person performs some action in response to a stimulus, and is then either punished or rewarded (reinforced) for their behavior. These rewards and punishments, given repeatedly, are supposed to alter the person's behavior: in other words, they learn the specified behavior (Skinner, 1958). This is a wild oversimplification of just one view of behaviorism, but it will do for our discussion of behaviorism as an approach in virtual-world activity design.

How might operant conditioning play out in an educational virtual world? Behaviorism, or at least operant conditioning, is useful in getting a learner to achieve a very specific, carefully defined and scoped goal. But educational virtual worlds are frequently designed in service of ill-defined, large-scale learning goals such as "learn to act like a real scientist" or "understand and model complex systems." It seems unlikely that behaviorist ideas could be called upon to support such goals. But they can be, and are regularly used to do just that. In designing virtual-world-based curricula using behaviorist ideas, it is important to deconstruct large and/or ill-defined learning goals into smaller and smaller units. Ultimately, you end up with a large number of very small interactions for a user to work through, usually in sequence, and you can provide feedback (reinforcement) after each interaction until the user gets each one right.

Think about that last point now from a designer's perspective: it is what is done all the time in creating commercial virtual worlds. The designer starts with some very large game goal, say, "the player will become ruler of the virtual world, starting as a poor prisoner of the current ruler." Then, the designer begins to define the primary path to achieving that large-scale goal, typically working backwards from the goal to the initial player condition upon entering the world. For example, the designer may come up with a 10-step program to advance the player from prisoner to ruler. The designer would next deconstruct each of the 10 steps into a series of substeps, and probably further subdivide each of those steps into an even smaller series of sub-substeps. Eventually, the design would consist of a very elaborate organizational structure for the virtual-world-based game, featuring lots of very specific activities in service of many small goals, all under the umbrella of the original main goal for the game.

Commercial virtual-world designers, in other words, are behaviorists. And you, as a designer of educational virtual worlds, can make use of these aspects of behaviorism as a tool for creating virtual-world-based curricula and activities that are clearly defined, carefully constructed, and that operate in service of your own large-scale learning goals.

Returning one last time to our River City example, it too features activities that are relatively behavioristic. For example, there are water testing stations placed close to bodies of water in the River City virtual world (the river, water wells, and a bog). These stations let students take samples of the water at various locations to check for levels of harmful bacteria. Figuring out that it might be a good idea to take multiple samples from more than one location is up to each student (a constructivist and situated approach). But the actual process of sampling, counting bacteria, and recording results is a procedural task that is essentially behavioral. Students repeatedly perform a series of prescribed sequential steps to sample the water. If they perform each step correctly, they are "reinforced" for their successful display of a desired behavior by being able to proceed to the next step in the process. If they complete all the steps correctly, their behavior is positively reinforced by the receipt of a set of numbers showing information relevant to their quest.

Cognitive Processing

Finally, elements of cognitive processing theory can be used to support learning when they are incorporated into virtual worlds. Mayer's (2005) Cognitive Theory of Multimedia Learning (CTML) serves as the starting point for investigating the cognitive aspects of learning from media—especially more traditional 2D interactive media—using the concept of cognitive load as a foundation. CTML is built upon three assumptions: (1) humans' information processing occurs in a dual channel framework (visual and verbal)—based on Paivio's (1986) dual-coding theory; (2) humans' cognitive architecture has a limited capacity for the amount of information it can process for either of the two channels at any given time; and (3) humans actively process incoming information. Cognitive load (Chandler & Sweller, 1991; Sweller, 1994) is, essentially, mental effort sorted into three general types: intrinsic, extraneous, and germane.

Briefly, a learner's intrinsic load is good, attributed to the actual content difficulty of the learning material being processed. Depending on the nature of the curricular content, virtual-world designers might or might not be able to directly manipulate intrinsic load—unless the curricular content is directly affected by aspects of the world itself. A learner's extraneous load is bad, attributed to the nature of information presentation—poor information presentation increases a learner's extraneous load for a variety of reasons, such as split attention. Finally, a learner's germane load is good, attributed to the self-induced information processing in which a learner engages as he or she works through the curricular content presented. Generally, a reduction in extraneous cognitive load "frees up" space within a learner's cognitive capacity for more germane load (assuming the learner is motivated to do so).

Additionally, Mayer (2005) suggests five distinct processes for information processing in CTML:

1. selecting relevant words for processing in verbal working memory;
2. selecting relevant images for processing in visual working memory;
3. organizing selected words into a verbal mental model;
4. organizing selected images into a visual mental model;
5. integrating verbal and visual models and connecting them to prior knowledge.

Basically, this boils down to three processes—selecting, organizing, and integrating information—which Mayer uses as a foundation (along with the three assumptions) to create a series of principles for multimedia learning.

These principles offer a great set of guidelines for the development of the more traditional 2D multimedia learning environments you might be familiar with—applications that are, essentially, digital "page-turners." However, there are many gaps between these principles and 3D virtual worlds. We have previously written about suggested practices for developing educational virtual worlds using CTML as a starting point (Nelson & Erlandson, 2008). As noted in our article, certain principles of CTML are a better fit for virtual worlds than others, and CTML is primarily oriented toward content delivery with low-level interactivity in a "flat" environment, typically featuring relatively few learner choices of which content to view next, minimal stimulus/response activities, and rote interaction with practice and assessment items such as text input and item selection.

Obviously, cutting-edge 3D virtual worlds are a whole new ball of wax. The two primary differences that set virtual worlds apart in terms of cognitive processing-based design are the addition of a third dimension of interaction and support for increased physical realism across these three dimensions in real time. Despite its shortfalls in regard to these differences, CTML still has its place in virtual worlds. Any user interface element that presents information to the learner typically does so using—you guessed it—2D multimedia.

Conclusion

We've covered a lot of theoretical ground in a very short amount of text. "Real" learning theorists would probably complain at our simplified descriptions of the theories we have covered. But we don't care. We are practical people who want to design virtual worlds for learning that incorporate a kind of "best of" parade of ideas from a spectrum of learning theory frameworks. We're not purists, and we hope you won't be either. Be a messy pragmatist! Feel free to mix and match theoretical concepts as you see fit in service of your learning and design goals. Some theory-based ideas won't work for your learning goals, your audience, your setting, or your budget. Take what works, and dump the rest. Bring together constructivism, situated learning, behaviorism, cognitive processing, and any other useful theory in service of your virtual world's goals. Ultimately, your job as a designer is to design a virtual world that will benefit your target learners. Design in a way that you think will work for those learners, and call upon whatever mash-up of theories you wish.

TEST YOUR UNDERSTANDING

How do you define each of the following as it relates to virtual-world design? With each definition, provide an example activity showing how the theory could be applied in the design of a virtual world whose goal is to teach a player to bake chocolate chip cookies:

1. Situated learning
2. Constructivism
3. Socio-constructivism
4. Behaviorism
5. Cognitive processing

LEARNING ACTIVITIES

1. Pick a commercial or educational virtual world and analyze the theory or theories of learning that exist behind the gameplay.
2. Choose a learning goal for curriculum in a virtual world: decide on one or more theories to use as the basis for the curriculum and world design. Write a short proposal for the world and curriculum, weaving your chosen theories into the justification for the design.

References

Alessi, S. M. & Trollip, S. R. (2001). *Multimedia for Learning: Methods and development* (3rd ed.). Boston, MA: Allyn and Bacon.

Bednar, A. E., Cunningham, D. J., Duffy, T. M., & Perry, D. J. (1992). Theory into practice: How do we think? In T. M. Duffy & D. H. Jonassen (Eds), *Constructivism and the Technology of Instruction: A conversation* (pp. 17–34). Hillsdale, NJ: Lawrence Erlbaum Associates, Inc.

Brown, J. S., Collins, A., & Duguid, P. (1989). Situated cognition and the culture of learning. *Educational Researcher, 18(1)*, 32–41.

Chandler, P. & Sweller, J. (1991). Cognitive load theory and the format of instruction. *Cognition and Instruction, 8(4)*, 293–332.

Clarke, J., Dede, C., Ketelhut, D., & Nelson, B. (2006). A design-based research strategy to promote scalability for educational innovations. *Educational Technology, 46(3)*, 27–36.

Dalgarno, B. (2001). Interpretations of constructivism and consequences for Computer Assisted Learning. *British Journal of Educational Technology, 32(2)*, 183–194.

Dede, C., Ketelhut, D., & Ruess, K. (2002). Motivation, usability, and learning outcomes in a prototype museum-based multiuser virtual environment. In P. Bell, R. Stevens, & T. Satwicz (Eds), *Keeping Learning Complex: Proceedings of the Fifth ICLS* (pp. 530–531). Mahwah, NJ: Erlbaum.

Jonassen, D. H. (1991). Objectivism versus constructivism: Do we need a new philosophical paradigm? *Educational Technology Research & Development, 39(3)*, 5–14.

Jonassen, D. H. (1994). Thinking technology: Toward a constructivist design model. *Educational Technology, 34(4)*, 34–37.

Jonassen, D. H., Peck, K. L., & Wilson, B. G. (1999). *Learning with Technology: A constructivist perspective.* Upper Saddle River, NJ: Prentice Hall.

Ketelhut, D. J., Dede, C., Clarke, J., & Nelson, B. (2007). Studying situated learning in a multi-user virtual environment. In E. Baker, J. Dickieson, W. Wulfeck, & H. O'Neil (Eds), *Assessment of Problem Solving Using Simulations* (pp. 37–58). Hillsdale, NJ: Lawrence Erlbaum Associates.

Lave, J. & Wenger, E. (1991). *Situated Learning: Legitimate peripheral participation.* Cambridge, UK: Cambridge University Press.

Mayer, R. (2005). Cognitive theory of multimedia learning. In R. E. Mayer (Ed.), *The Cambridge Handbook of Multimedia Learning* (pp. 31–48). New York: Cambridge University Press.

Nelson, B. & Erlandson, B. (2008). Managing cognitive load in educational multi-user virtual environments: reflection on design practice. *Educational Technology Research and Development, 56(5–6)*, 619–641.

Nelson, B. & Ketelhut, D. J. (2008). Exploring embedded guidance and self-efficacy in educational multi-user virtual environments. *International Journal of Computer-Supported Collaborative Learning, 3(4)*, 413–427.

Nelson, B., Ketelhut, D. J., Clarke, J., Bowman, C., & Dede, C. (2005). Design-based research strategies for developing a scientific inquiry curriculum in a multi-user virtual environment. *Educational Technology, 45(1)*, 21–27.

Oppenheimer, T. (2003). *The Flickering Mind: Saving education from the false promises of technology*. New York: Random House.

Paivio, A. (1986). *Mental representations*. New York: Oxford University Press.

Perkins, D. N. (1991). Technology meets constructivism: do they make a marriage? *Educational Technology, 31(5)*, 18–23.

Skinner, B. F. (1958). Teaching machines. *Science, 128(3330)*, 969–977.

Sweller, J. (1994). Cognitive Load Theory, learning difficulty, and instructional design. *Learning and Instruction, 4*, 295–312.

Links

For a quick summary of a large number of theories, and how those theories have been realized in technology-based learning—see http://education.ufl.edu/school/EdTech/theories.htm

River City Project Information—http://muve.gse.harvard.edu/rivercityproject

Other Resources

Learning Theories (Capella University)—www.learning-theories.com

The Handbook of Research on Educational Communications and Technology (3rd ed.) provides an overview of theories used more generally in instructional design—www.aect.org

five
Defining the Context of Virtual Worlds

Introduction

Whether you're designing and developing a new virtual world or acquiring and integrating an existing virtual world for your needs, before doing so you need to make several informed decisions about the intended context of use for your world. The main areas of concern for this decision-making process are: the subject domain of the curriculum you will design for the world; the learning context; characteristics of the target learner population; world boundaries; and participant roles. In fact, the order in which you make these decisions is important. For example, decisions you will make about world boundaries and participant roles are contingent upon decisions you've already made about the domain, the context, and the population. As such, we've ordered the sections of this chapter to mirror the chain of decisions that should be made as you design a virtual world for learning.

There are also distinct differences in the way you might make each of these decisions depending on your approach: designing a new world vs. acquiring an existing world. As part of each section in this chapter, we will describe the nuances of these two approaches as appropriate. Considering this idea of appropriateness, one issue you should keep in mind throughout your decision-making process—whether you're designing or acquiring—is this: are virtual worlds an appropriate fit for the target learning context? The last thing anyone should do is apply virtual worlds as a solution to a problem that doesn't really exist. In other words, don't use the technology if it's not an appropriate venue for the learning goals. Luckily, this concept feeds nicely into the first set of decisions you will need to make, concerning the subject domain.

Subject Domain

The overarching question you should ask yourself about the subject domain involved in your decision-making process is this: is the domain in question a good fit for the affordances provided by virtual-world technology? A good way to answer this question is to think about which subject domains are a good fit (and why), and then think about why and how other domains aren't as good a fit for the affordances of this technology.

What Makes a Good Fit?

One way to think about virtual-world technology as a good or bad fit for any given subject domain is a seemingly simple comparison to a more static medium, such as a textbook. Is a curriculum that takes place in a virtual world better than the learning experience that can be provided by visual information on a static page? The same comparison can be made between virtual-world technology and more traditional 2D multimedia: does the third dimension add to the learning experience for the subject domain in a meaningful way? Several other characteristics of a subject domain make for a good match with the affordances of virtual-world technology.

First, subject domains that are activity oriented or consist of more tangible concepts are a good fit for virtual worlds—especially those domains where audiovisual content is essential, or where location and movement, object interaction, and/or communication activities are integral to the subject matter. An obvious domain that comes to mind is physics. Many of the basic concepts of physics lend themselves to being learned in a virtual world. This is because the concepts may best be understood in three dimensions, animated throughout this space (in all three dimensions) and over time. The SURGE project is one good example of using virtual worlds to learn basic concepts of physics (Figure 5.1). In SURGE, players learn about concepts of Newtonian motion by guiding a sphere-shaped character through a series of 2D and 3D maze worlds. Space and Earth sciences, biology, chemistry, architecture, civil engineering, kinesiology, medicine, and interpersonal communication skills are also all good examples of subject domains that are a good fit for virtual worlds for these reasons.

Second, subject domains conducive to synchronous multi-user interactions occurring over a distance—specifically those which require communication activities involving highly animated audiovisual signaling between activity participants—are a good fit for virtual worlds. Can you think of any examples of this type of subject domain? A virtual world designed for synchronous sign language learning practice comes to mind.

Third, domains that necessitate the ability for the learner to transcend space and time—either individually or collaboratively—are a good fit for

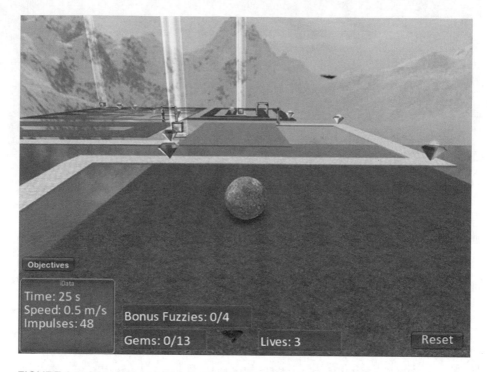

FIGURE 5.1 Screenshot of one of the SURGE physics virtual worlds

virtual worlds. Geology and archeology are two fine examples. Think about a virtual world where a learner could instantly teleport across the entire planet (or other planets) to explore and compare changes in geological formations that occur over vast spans of time. It is true that this third aspect of subject domains could also be considered a learning context. However, if the context is inherent in the subject domain—or, if the subject in question could not be learned as well (or at all) in a different context, then the context becomes an aspect of the domain.

In addition to these three characteristics of subject domains, there are a couple of additional aspects of virtual worlds that you can take into consideration when making decisions about the intended context of your project. First, virtual worlds are an excellent platform for the provision of simulations of experiences not yet feasible or possible for the learner in the real world, such as flying through space or extended underwater exploration, activities which both currently require expensive equipment and substantial training and thus are not feasible to most of the human population. Two examples of simulated experiences that are not yet possible in reality, yet happen relatively simply in virtual worlds are teleportation and time travel. Virtual worlds present the possibility for humans to interact with live dinosaurs, and even imaginary creatures that as far as we know have never actually existed.

Second, and perhaps most importantly, virtual worlds allow for the provision of a safe environment that allows for repeated mistakes without the risk of physical harm to the learner—or destruction of expensive equipment or fragile property. Think about civil engineers building bridges and the ability to do thousands of iterations of virtual stress testing before any concrete ever gets poured. Or, a learning environment for ecological systems in which budding environmental scientists can test the introduction of any number of toxins on various local ecosystems without actually creating any pollution.

Finally, can you think of other aspects of the subject domain that we might have missed? Can you think of your own specific uses of virtual worlds that take advantage of these unique affordances? One other way to figure out what makes virtual-world technology a good fit for any subject domain is to think about what makes this technology a bad fit for any subject domain.

What Makes a Bad Fit?

Deciding what makes a virtual world a bad fit for any given subject domain comes down to a rather binary outcome: either the virtual world is overkill for the learning goals, or it is insufficient. In both cases, the unique affordances of virtual-world technology are not a good fit for the subject domain in question. If the technology is overkill, it is likely that virtual worlds are simply fluff that do not add in any meaningful way to the learner's approach to the subject domain. If the technology is insufficient, then it is likely that virtual worlds simply cannot support the reality necessary for learning in the subject domain. In other words, it's impossible to learn the subject domain in a virtual space; reality is required for learning.

Many of the aspects and characteristics of subject domains and virtual-world technology we've discussed in this section could also be construed as aspects and characteristics of the learning context. Based on the relative youth of virtual worlds as a platform for learning, this makes sense. We don't yet fully grasp the range of possibilities virtual worlds present for human learning, since we as researchers, designers, and developers are still exploring the virtual frontier. In other words, we're still unclear as to which aspects of virtual worlds are strictly relevant to content (the subject domain and curriculum), and which are strictly relevant to context—or even if such strictness of delineation is appropriate. As such, when any of us make these types of context decisions, there is still quite a fuzzy overlap in our distinction between subject domain and typical contexts of learning activities. Even so, in the next section, we approach learning contexts from a more traditional perspective and see how they fit into the decision-making process for implementing virtual worlds.

Learning Context

When making decisions about designing or acquiring virtual worlds for a given learning context, we are concerned with three primary aspects of learning: formality, environment, and activity. In this case, formality is concerned with the level of accountability of learning outcomes, with formal contexts having much higher accountability than informal contexts. Our use of the term 'environment' refers to the institution in which the learning is intended to be experienced, such as educational, recreational, commercial, industrial, or governmental. Finally, our use of the term 'activity' is concerned with the type of learning activities requisite to (or happening as a result of) the particular learning context: namely consumption, interaction, and production. Now that we've established the basis for our three aspects of learning contexts, we can dive into each aspect in more detail. As we explore the details of each of these three aspects, one primary question that can serve as the common thread of exploration is: "Is use of a 3D virtual world the best approach for this aspect of the learning context for the subject domain in question?"

Formality

The formality of the learning context, while seemingly binary in nature—formal vs. informal—does indeed exist on a spectrum (i.e., certain formal contexts are "more formal" than others, and likewise for the informality of informal contexts). Yet, there can be no middle ground: formal contexts cannot be informal, and vice versa. However, it is certainly possible for informal learning to occur in formal contexts. Or, to think of it another way, "unscripted" learning often occurs in formal environments based on a given student's motivation and opportunity "in the moment." This is learning that is technically informal, even though it is occurring because of exposure to learning materials designed for a formal context. In the case of the argument made here, the primary basis for the formality of any context is the level of accountability inherent in the prescribed outcomes for learning. In other words: is there an official purpose of the learning and, if so, what is this purpose? Using this basis for formality, formal contexts are those involving high stakes and accountability, such as students learning science (among other subjects) to pass the 6th grade, or physicians learning the latest research-based patient treatment solutions to obtain re-certification for practicing medicine. The outcomes of the learning context are formalized in a way that the learner is aware of the stakes riding on his performance. The learner knows that if he does not learn the required material and successfully satisfy the formalized outcomes, he will not achieve the associated prize.

Informal contexts are those involving low stakes and accountability, such as a hobbyist who learns about aerodynamics to improve her model airplane constructions, or a nature photographer who learns about regional flora so as to better identify the beautiful purple flowers he photographed on a recent hiking trip. The informality of these learning outcomes is based on the fact that they were formed by the learners with the intention of self-improvement. The hobbyist and the photographer are not likely to become experts in either aerodynamics or regional flora. In fact, if the hobbyist learns nothing about aerodynamics or if the photographer learns nothing about the regional flora, they will most likely continue building airplanes or photographing flowers with just as much enjoyment as before—there is no external accountability for the outcomes of this learning.

Pragmatically, though, how does the level of formality of the chosen learning environment affect your decisions about designing or acquiring virtual worlds for learning? There are two main issues to consider when taking a pragmatic perspective of learning environments and virtual worlds: accountability and cost effectiveness. When the formality is high (i.e., when accountability is high)—especially when large groups of learners are involved (such as end-of-grade testing)—virtual worlds might not be a good option ... yet. Researchers have yet to establish substantial evidence for the reliability and validity of virtual worlds as measurement instrumentation for the types of assessments that typically occur in these high-stakes contexts. Second, due to the amount of sophisticated computing power needed to run highly realistic 3D environments, virtual worlds are also not always cost effective for learning—especially in informal learning contexts. One exception to this notion would be a case where the demographic of learners (like the previously mentioned hobbyists) is willing and able to pay out of pocket for expensive virtual experiences.

It would behoove you fairly early on in the decision-making process to ask yourself the big question: "Is a 3D virtual world the best approach for the level of formality we've chosen for our project?"

Environment

Typically, the types of environments for which implementation decisions for virtual worlds will be made can be categorized broadly into educational, recreational, commercial, industrial, and military institutions. Much of this categorization has to do with the level of formality we discussed in the previous section, combined with particular subject domains at various levels of professionalism. Of course, there is always the potential for crossover as well. Consider a virtual world designed for simulated training for boat control and navigation. Such a virtual world could easily be used in a formal classroom setting, at recreational facilities (including science centers, museums, etc.), in industrial contexts (shipping companies), and within several branches of the military. In any case, there are four primary issues of concern when making decisions about the implementation of virtual worlds for any of these learning environments: space, time, learner motivation, and, of course, funding.

Let's go ahead and address the issue of funding first: we've established that virtual worlds can be expensive to run and might or might not be cost effective—but cost effectiveness doesn't matter if the money doesn't exist. Somebody has to pay for the implementation, and it will either be the institution, the learner, or a combination of both. Either way, if the money isn't there, the project can't happen—so make sure to get proof of secured funding early on in the decision-making process. Yes, this issue seems so obvious that it doesn't need mention, but it's better to be safe than sorry!

Assuming the institution has the requisite funding, does it have the space to conduct the implementation? Does it have—or plan to acquire—the appropriate facilities for implementing virtual worlds, such as computer hardware and an appropriate amount of floor space to house the workstations necessary for implementation? If not, will the learner be responsible for having or acquiring their own equipment and/or facilities for implementation? For example, will the learner be expected to implement the virtual world in question at home, or in a public library, etc.? Before these questions should be answered, though, a more important issue must be addressed: Is it even possible to use appropriately powered computers in the places where implementation of this virtual world must occur? Think of some places where it's not possible: outdoors, away from a power supply for several days on end, or perhaps in a highly volatile industrial environment where sophisticated computer workstations might be at risk of destruction on a constant basis. Many more examples of such "technology-unfriendly" environments exist and you should ensure that your client doesn't have unrealistic expectations about implementation before you get too far along in the design or acquisition process.

As you clarify the issue of space and equipment, so you should clarify the issue of time. Is the target institution planning to provide appropriate amounts of time to the learner for implementation of the virtual world? Is pre-training necessary for some or all of the learners who will be using the virtual world and, if so, will enough time also be allowed for this pre-training? Are the learners expected to continue learning in the virtual world on their own time? As you can see, the time and space issues for implementation are heavily interrelated. You shouldn't make final decisions about design or acquisition until you have satisfactory evidence for both space and time.

Finally, we cannot forget learner motivation. Based on the outcomes of your inquiries into the three previous issues, an understanding of the motivation of the targeted population of learners to actually engage with the implemented virtual world can have a rather large impact on how you move forward with design or acquisition. Are learners in the target implementation site typically motivated to sit down in front of a computer (or stand around with a digital tablet in hand) and spend time with virtual worlds? More importantly—do they have a choice in the matter? In other words, is learner participation mandated by the institution? Depending on the level of require-ment versus choice, the actual motivation of the learners serves as a different factor in the decision-making process. If participation is required, then less motivated learners must be accounted for with a different perspective than if participation is by choice. Also, what are the consequences of non-participa-tion for the unmotivated learner? These consequences will likely be greatly varied, depending on the type of institution—consider the difference between a 7th grader who doesn't want to participate in a required virtual science lab versus a new recruit in the armed forces who doesn't want to participate in a virtual-world-based simulation for training about appropriate defusion of explosives in the field.

Activity

There are three primary types of activities that a learner can conduct while participating in a virtual-world implementation, each increasing in com-plexity: consumption, interaction, and production. Consumption involves learner intake and processing of information presented in the virtual world. Interaction of the learner with the content presented in the virtual world can range from rather passive (making simple choices when presented) to highly active (continuously driven exploration of an open virtual world). Learners become productive in virtual worlds when they create new artifacts (such as documents or structures) as a result of in-world actions. For each of the three types of activity, virtual worlds can be both good or bad platforms—depend-ing on one or more factors.

Depending on the type of information to be presented in the environment, virtual worlds can be good or bad for pure consumption activities. Virtual worlds are great for learning through consumption alone if the information presented can't be fully experienced in any other way than within a volumet-ric 3D coordinate system. One example of such information is any 3D plot of complex statistical data—or 3D animated infographics of the same data. It could be argued, though, that these are merely 3D objects, but if they are animated and the user is moved "through the space around the object, then it's a virtual world. Another good example is animated display of complex molecular structures (Figure 5.2).

On the other hand, virtual worlds are bad for mere consumption of infor-mation if the 3D information is unnecessary or "overkill." For example, if a printed poster hung on a wall is just as good as—if not better than—a 3D meso-immersive version of the same information, then there is no need to have the 3D version. The 3D version is overkill, an egregious waste of resources—time, space, and funding. To put it another way, if it feels like

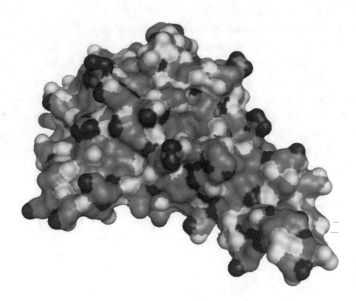

FIGURE 5.2 Complex molecular structure

eye-candy, it's probably overkill. A great example where 3D might be considered overkill is Google Streetview (Figure 5.3).

As you can see in Figure 5.3, the combination of the overhead map view and the street level photographic view is good enough to get the point across. If, as a consumer of information all you need is to know what the turn-off to someone's house looks like before you set off on your adventure, then Streetview is good enough. There's no need for a virtual-world-based driving simulation to display the same information in a photorealistic fashion—this would be a waste of resources to present the same information. Obviously, Google Maps and its Streetview functionality are highly interactive, which makes for a good segue to the next point.

FIGURE 5.3 Screenshot of Google Streetview in split-screen mode

Beyond consumption lies interaction, and virtual worlds can be good or bad for interactive activities—again depending on the type of interaction intended for the learner. If a user cannot learn the material with which he must interact without interaction in three distinct dimensions, then the use of a virtual world to realize and facilitate movement and interaction along those three dimensions is, indeed, justified. Flight simulation is a perfect example of this necessity, so a flight simulator such as FlightGear (Figure 5.4) is an example of a good use of virtual worlds for learning through interaction in three dimensions.

One could certainly learn the trifecta of flight dynamics (Figure 5.5)—pitch, yawl, and roll—using a variety of mediums, but to experience such dynamics in action (or even to see simulation of these dynamics in an animated, inter-active fashion), a virtual world would be the best solution. Throw in the four forces—lift, weight, drag, and thrust—and you've got a perfect recipe for the absolute necessity of virtual worlds for learning about flight dynamics with "heavier than air" machines.

Just as we discussed with consumption of information, virtual worlds can be overkill if the interactions for learning do not warrant expression in three dimensions, such as a more traditional 2D point-and-click or "click-through" style interface. Think about the issue another way: If the interactions do not require motion in three different dimensions of space, then a 3D virtual world is overkill. Or, consider the use of a virtual billiards table to learn about geometry (Figure 5.6).

FIGURE 5.4 Screenshot of FlightGear flight simulator

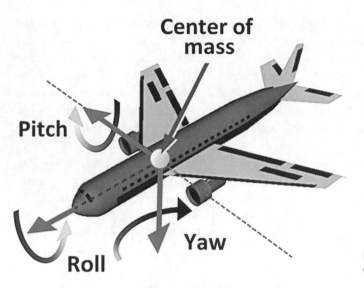

FIGURE 5.5 Flight dynamics

In Figure 5.6, a 2D animation of an overhead shot of billiard balls bouncing off each other and the bumpers of the table might suffice for basic geometry, but the same 2D approach likely wouldn't be sufficient for someone hoping to learn how to shoot these same balls with a cue. A different perspective for interaction is necessary, and a full-blown 3D virtual world (Figure 5.7) would be justified in this case. Context creeps into the picture once again!

Finally, we must consider production. Researchers are still exploring the possibilities of what can be produced by learners as they interact with content in virtual worlds, but the same "overkill" rule applies to production at this point in time. Virtual worlds are a good platform for learner production activity if the artifact to be created cannot be feasibly produced in any other digital medium—for example, if a learner is asked to demonstrate his or her ability to navigate between planets in our solar system, using an astronomi-

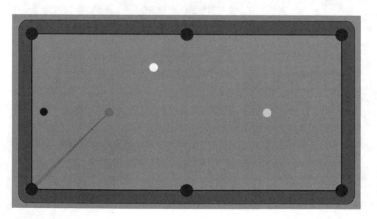

FIGURE 5.6 Simple billiards simulation

FIGURE 5.7 A 3D virtual billiards experience

cal simulator such as Celestia (Figure 5.8)—or produce accurate 3D models of the planetary orbits.

Virtual worlds are not a good fit for learner production if the artifact could just as easily—if not more efficiently and effectively—be produced in a non-3D environment. For example, if the learner needs to produce a simple text document as the primary artifact of his or her learning process, a simple word processor program—or better yet, a pencil and paper—is still probably the best set of tools for the job. Perhaps a simple principle to follow when making this decision is the idea that any artifact that doesn't have three physical dimensions shouldn't need a 3D environment to be produced. This seems pretty simple, right? However, from a pedagogical perspective, if the environment for artifact production needs to be maintained within the virtual world, even if the artifacts to be produced are not 3D—such as entering observations into a research logbook during a science exploration activity—then such simple tools should be seamlessly integrated into the virtual world experience.

To review, the three main aspects of learning context are formality, environment, and activity. While these three certainly do not offer exhaustive coverage of the nuances of every potential implementation for which you will need to make decisions about whether or not to design a virtual world for learning, they offer a solid foundation for your decision process. Depending on the specific nature of your project, the prioritization of importance of formality, environment, and activity factors will likely change, but based on

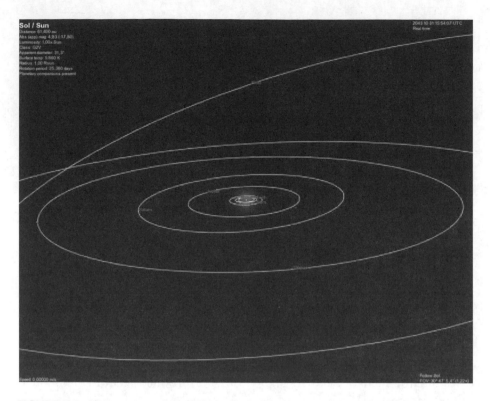

FIGURE 5.8 A view of our Sun in Celestia

the information we've provided here, hopefully you should be able to recognize the importance of each and prioritize your decisions accordingly.

Learner Population

No matter the context for learning of your intended implementation of virtual worlds, it is likely that your decision-making process will involve the participation of many types of learners—even if you've targeted a fairly specific audience. The first three factors of learner population to consider are age, gender, and ethnicity. Each of these three has similar effects on your decision-making process—concerning learner engagement with technology. Do learners in the age groups (or gender or ethnic groups) of your targeted population typically choose to engage with virtual worlds when learning? It's easy to see how engagement based on these three factors (especially in a less specific target audience) can become quite complex quite quickly. In any case, you should check available research literature to verify your intuitions about learners' tendency toward use of virtual worlds. If the research literature about your particular targeted group of learners' use of virtual-world technology is sparse to non-existent, then a good alternative strategy would be to find evidence from studies of your target group's inclination toward similar technologies.

The extant culture(s) of learners in your targeted audience can have a variety of effects on these learners' individual perspectives on age, gender, and ethnicity, especially if the group of learners is formed based on factors external to the person—such as workers with few things in common other than the fact that they work for the institution where training must occur. As such, consider all the research you do on your target audience—based on age, gender, and ethnicity—and realize that your findings from this research process will need to be viewed through a pragmatic lens that welcomes the (potential) chaotic reality of this culture effect on the participation of your targeted audience of learners in the implementation of your designed or acquired virtual world.

On a less ambiguous note, the issue of drastic cultural differences in a targeted group of learners can have a very simple effect on the number of languages you must consider offering as part of the virtual-world learning experience—especially if you are acquiring a virtual world instead of designing one. You must ensure that the acquired world has the capability of language localization if you must accommodate a multitude of languages. Obviously, if you are designing your own world, simply include localization as a feature to be developed in the virtual world.

Another major factor to consider for your targeted audience of learners is the potential for an extreme range of prior knowledge and experience—with both the subject domain and the use of virtual worlds as a platform for learning. Depending on the nature of your subject domain, it is possible that you will need to deal with a vast number of different levels of learner knowledge and ability as you plan for scaffolding within the virtual-world experience. A simplified example comparing subject knowledge and familiarity with virtual worlds in a binary fashion (low vs. high) results in four groups of learners to be accounted for (Table 5.1).

Table 5.1 2 × 2 Categorization of Learners' Prior Knowledge and Familiarity with Virtual Worlds

		Prior Knowledge	
		Low	High
Familiarity with virtual worlds	Low	Low prior knowledge and low familiarity with virtual worlds	High prior knowledge and low familiarity with virtual worlds
	High	Low prior knowledge and high familiarity with virtual worlds	High prior knowledge and high familiarity with virtual worlds

Obviously, the more factors you have (e.g., multiple requisite types of knowledge, skills, abilities, or experience), the more groups you will need to account for when considering learner scaffolding in your decision-making process for design vs. acquisition of virtual worlds. No matter how you end up dividing your learners into subgroups based on knowledge and experience, due to the nature (and potential complexity) of user interaction with virtual-world technology, you should consider dividing your targeted population into groups based on familiarity with virtual worlds. One good strategy for this approach is Cooper's method of three groups: beginners, intermediates, and experts (Cooper, Reimann, & Cronin, 2007). Not only should you account for the specific needs of each of these three groups, you should consider how the virtual-world learning experience will enable users to transition up to the more sophisticated groups (if necessary). As a side note, if you plan to do a lot of designing and developing of virtual worlds (especially if you're fairly new to the field), the Cooper book is a rather comprehensive volume focusing upon interaction design—it would be well worth keeping a copy handy on your desk.

Age, gender, ethnicity, culture, knowledge, skills, wisdom, technological savvy: these are quite a few learner factors to consider when making decisions about your targeted learners' probable interactions with your intended virtual world. Obviously, you won't come close to perfect prediction, but the take home message is this: Do ample appropriate research on your target population (e.g., a review of the literature, interviews, focus groups, etc.) before you get too far along in the design process—but likely after you've established the primary parameters for the context of learning. For specific strategies on conducting the necessary research about your targeted learners, consult any of the numerous quality texts available on the topic of needs analysis. A well-conducted needs analysis for the learning context and its associated learner population provides a proper foundation for good decisions about world boundaries and participant roles in the intended virtual world.

World Boundaries

Another major issue to consider when making your decisions about designing or acquiring a virtual world for learning is: Should the world be open or closed? Open worlds are those that have no additional barriers other than the edge of the actual world itself—an edge that can actually be defined by the limitations of the computer system within which the world exists, meaning the world can be rather large. Closed worlds, on the other hand, are those that have established boundaries of play that limit a user's range of exploration (and, therefore, experience) in the virtual world.

Why would you want to consider implementing an open world for your intentions? Open worlds offer the option for non-linear gameplay and a mode of world exploration—and potentially production—that is often referred to as "sandbox mode." If you think of a virtual world as a big open environment with boundaries at the edge of the world (the box) and an environment that doesn't have any preconceived narrative structure (the sand), then this metaphor makes pretty good sense. If a sandbox mode approach to learning is a good fit for your subject domain, learning context, and target population, then you should certainly consider an open world as a potential strategy. Open worlds, by their nature, tend to be more complex under the hood, since the range of possibilities for learner consumption, interaction, and production are much larger (and much more dynamic). If you are leaning toward design and development as opposed to acquisition of a virtual world, this increased complexity of the mechanics of open worlds should be taken into serious consideration as a potential developmental obstacle. This complexity is heightened even further if non-linear gameplay is factored into the equation. Non-linear gameplay goes above and beyond sandbox mode in open worlds, offering a variety of narrative outcomes to the learner. Such non-linearity is readily applicable to virtual worlds for learning, simply from a different set of perspectives—namely, curricular and pedagogical.

This complexity is operationalized through a concept called procedural generation, which essentially involves the creation of dynamic content "on the fly" based on any number of computed algorithms. In terms of virtual worlds, this means that much of the world content is generated after the world has initially loaded on the user's computer. For you as a decision maker, creation of open world sandbox experiences and/or non-linear learning narratives (or scenarios) for your designed or acquired virtual world means that procedural generation is a likely requirement. This means that your virtual world—especially one that you're going to design and develop—will likely require much more time to develop.

If, due to this complexity (or for any reason) you decide to go with a closed world instead, you should certainly consider implementing the "illusion of choice" for the learning scenario(s) taking place in the world. You might be wondering what, exactly, is entailed in the provision of illusion of choice in a virtual world. A closed virtual world is, to all intents and purposes, a maze. Learners must get from point A (the start of the scenario) to point B (the end of the scenario) within a certain period of time, within a finite space (Figure 5.9).

With the illusion of choice, learners must still get from point A to point B within a certain period of time, within a finite space. However, the learners do not perceive this A-to-B travel as that which occurs within a maze, due to the provision of alternative scenario options or tangential routes (or a combination of both). Alternative scenario options—multiple ways to finish the

FIGURE 5.9 A simple labyrinth-type maze

learning scenario—are essentially multiple solution paths through the same finite space (Figure 5.10).

Tangential routes are harmless side paths that don't deviate too far from the main world path (or scenario framework). These routes might take the form of a short path through the woods on the edge of a suburban development, an open-air market in the middle of a busy metropolis, or even an optional "side mission" the learner must complete before finishing the

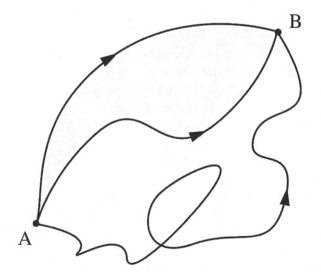

FIGURE 5.10 Multiple solution paths from A to B

main scenario. In other words, these tangential routes can be literal in world spaces or metaphorical narrative structures. In either case, these tangential routes help maintain the illusion of choice—the closed world is a maze, but it doesn't feel like a maze to the learner.

To reiterate, the main factor you should consider when making a decision about open versus closed worlds is the needs of your learners in the particular subject domain to be learned. Of course, the multiple aspects of learning context will also play into your decision, but context should be a lower priority than learners and subject when making your decision about world boundaries for your intended virtual-world implementation. Ultimately, the choice you make—open vs. closed world—has a major impact on the final decision you've got to make about participant roles in your virtual world.

Participant Roles

While participant roles is the last area of concern we cover in this chapter, it is certainly not the least important. While each area of concern we've covered has a definitive impact upon the virtual world you ultimately choose to design and develop or acquire, your decisions about participant roles have the biggest impact on the way the virtual world has to function in relation to your target audience. In other words, your decisions about participant roles directly affect the amount and types of interactivity that must be hosted within your world, which directly affects the relationship between the world and the GUI (which we described in detail in Chapters Two and Three). The more complex and (inter)active your participant roles need to be, the more complex and interactive the communication between the GUI and the world of your virtual-world application will need to be. There are three main decisions to make about participant roles, and each is oriented toward one major participant in the virtual world for learning: the learner, the instructor, and the computer. To better understand the distinct decisions you'll need to make about each of these three primary roles, let's consider a virtual SCUBA diving virtual world (Figure 5.11).

The primary decision you will need to make about the learner's role in the virtual world is whether the world and its scenarios are intended to be experienced individually or collaboratively. Do you need a single-user or multi-user world to host the types of learning activities necessary for your audience, subject domain, and context? Perhaps you need a mixture of both? (If you are not sure how to make this decision, take another look at our discussion on socio-constructivism and collaboration in Chapter Four). In the SCUBA world example, perhaps there are initial training exercises in underwater species recognition that the learner must complete individually, and these are followed by lessons in underwater communication via hand signals that must be completed collaboratively with other learners present. In this

FIGURE 5.11 A virtual SCUBA simulation

case, the best decision would be to design or acquire a virtual world that is capable of hosting multi-user activities—in order to account for the collaborative activities that come later in the sequence of training. You can always conduct individual activities in a multi-user world, but collaborative learning in a virtual world designed for individual users is not typically an option.

Another factor to consider is whether or not an instructor, trainer, or coach needs to play a participatory role in the virtual world alongside the learner. In the SCUBA example, will the instructor conduct virtual dives with the learner(s)? Will the instructor need to have additional capabilities—as an operative character in the virtual world—above and beyond the learners? In the SCUBA example, would the instructor have the ability to change characteristics of the reef or local species activity should the learning scenario unfold in a certain way? Could the instructor trigger the entry of a shark into the waters if the lesson were about quick, efficient underwater communication in such emergent situations? Essentially, for which in-world activities—consumption, interaction, and production—must the instructor have virtual abilities above and beyond those of the learner? Differentiation in virtual ability levels among users (learners vs. instructors) means that multiple participant role types for human participants within the virtual world must be created, which is a substantial factor in the design and development of virtual worlds—and therefore a factor that also weighs heavily in acquisition decisions. Plus, why stop at two roles? Are there additional participant roles that might be necessary at some point during the learning process for participants in a given virtual world—such as guest lectures, experts' opinions, etc.?

As a decision maker, do these additional human roles also require additional participant role differentiation, or could they simply be grouped in with the learner(s) or the instructor(s)—in terms of necessary virtual capabilities?

Finally, you should consider the non-human roles that might occur in your virtual world. Computer-controlled characters, or "agents" are a vital part of the realism of virtual worlds, and many of these agents can be judiciously implemented to take advantage of what virtual worlds have to offer above and beyond learning in the real world. In the SCUBA example, perhaps each species of fish could be controlled by a schooling agent, or each individual fish could actually be an autonomous agent that abides by several key rules (such as "swim in the other direction when divers get too close"). Depending on the level of instruction necessary, it's possible that some of the teaching in the world could be conducted in the form of guided practice, with the learner collaborating with a computer-controlled diver agent that behaves in a slightly more advanced way than the currently assessed ability of the learner diver. This concept highlights another issue about computer-controlled agents populating your virtual world: How much artificial intelligence will each agent have? Most computer-controlled agents have some level of artificial intelligence, even in its most basic form. A rather basic example of artificial intelligence is pathfinding: an agent can get from point A to point B using a set of rules (imbued in the agent via some programming language) to navigate between these points along a choice of different successful paths (Figure 5.12).

In any case, the more computer-controlled agents you wish to include in your virtual world, the more complex your world will become. It's likely that this increased complexity of agency will increase the processing power necessary to operate your virtual world in a seamless fashion for the learner's meso-immersive experience.

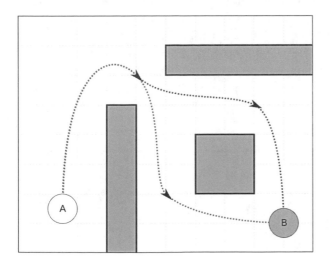

FIGURE 5.12 Two successful paths around an obstacle (using pathfinding)

Conclusion

As you can see, when it comes to defining the context of virtual worlds for learning, there are many decisions to be made, and these decisions should be made early—especially if you are designing and developing your own world—and in the right order. Hopefully the examples presented in this chapter have convinced you that world boundaries and participant roles are indeed contingent upon subject domain, learning context, and target audiences of learners. In other words, don't put the cart before the horse. Granted, you can't be certain that the context decisions you make early in the design or acquisition process will turn out to be the best decisions, but the only way to know is to try—make your decisions and implement them. Just be sure to plan for appropriate evaluation techniques so that you can collect evidence from outcomes—leading to answers about the quality of your design/acquisition decisions. To help you do this, we'll cover implementation and evaluation in later chapters.

TEST YOUR UNDERSTANDING

Choose any subject domain and describe any aspects of that domain that make virtual-world technology a good or bad fit for the domain.

LEARNING ACTIVITIES

1. Choose any existing virtual world—your own design or another—and analyze the application using the basic criteria described in this chapter. Choose a domain, context, and population and write up a brief categorized critique of the application. Consider as well how the domain, context, and population can affect each other, as well as world boundaries and participant roles.
2. Write a formal needs analysis for a given population of learners in a specific context learning about content from one or more specific subject domains.

Reference

Cooper, A., Reimann, R., & Cronin, D. (2007). *About Face 3: The essentials of interaction design*. Indianapolis, IN: Wiley.

Other Resources

Needs analysis or needs assessment is a fundamental part of defining the context of your virtual world. Three primary tools for assessing the needs of any population are the survey, the interview, and the focus group. Here we provide citations for a good place to start reading about each of these three tools.

Survey Research
Fowler, F. J. (2002). *Survey Research Methods*. Thousand Oaks, CA: Sage Publications.

Interviewing Techniques
King, N. & Horrocks, C. (2010). *Interviews in Qualitative Research*. Los Angeles, CA: Sage Publications.

Focus Groups
Krueger, R. A. & Casey, M. A. (2009). *Focus Groups: A practical guide for applied research*. Thousand Oaks, CA: Sage Publications.

six
Measurement and Assessment with Virtual Worlds

Introduction

It is often the case—unfortunately—that assessment is an afterthought (or, even worse, a non-thought) as one designs curriculum for a given subject domain. Assessment is a key component of design for learning, and assessment of learning within virtual worlds is no exception—and, of course, good assessment requires good measurement. This chapter covers several important aspects of measurement and assessment of learning within virtual worlds, beginning with an overview of the distinct differences between measurement and assessment, followed by a brief review of reliability and validity—oriented specifically toward learning in virtual worlds. This section is followed by a discussion about what can (and should) be measured in virtual worlds.

Measurement and Assessment

The primary reason we design virtual worlds for learning is (or at least should be) to facilitate learning about one or more concepts within one or more subject domains. We invest extensive thought into making a large number of decisions about various aspects of these worlds to ensure that the curricular goals can be achieved by the learner—to ensure that substantial learning occurs as intended. How can we as designers and educators be sure that learning occurs within the virtual world as intended? We can evaluate learners' progress individually or collectively—at various times before, during, and after the learning should be occurring—to see if the results for which we planned are indeed manifest. Good evaluation technique requires good assessment technique. Good assessments are essentially decisions based on valid inferences drawn from reliable data sources. Reliable data sources are created using reliable measurement instruments. (If you're a little rusty on reliability and validity, don't despair, we'll get to these old friends in the next section of the chapter.)

We've established the rough connection: evaluation needs assessment, and assessment needs measurement. We evaluate our virtual world for two main reasons: to see if learning has indeed occurred, and to judge the quality of the virtual world itself (based on any number of predetermined factors relevant to the particular implementation). Why, though, are assessment and measurement so important in virtual worlds for learning, and why should you remember to keep the processes of assessment and measurement distinct? Let's answer these questions, one at a time.

Assessment is important for virtual worlds because it allows us to determine whether or not learning has occurred, and to what extent—measurement alone cannot indicate this outcome. This is why assessment is vital for the evaluation of learning. Further, good assessment (based on valid inferences) is of utmost importance for virtual worlds due to the fact that virtual worlds are as yet unproven as a better platform for learning in a majority of subject domains over existing approaches. Evaluative evidence collected about learning in virtual worlds for any subject domain is much more convincing—either for or against the use of such worlds for learning the subject domain in question—if the methodology for collection of such evidence is sound. In this case, the sound methodology is simply well-designed (and appropriately conducted) assessment plans.

Consider an assessment plan to evaluate something rather simple: clothing. How long is the sleeve of your shirt? What is a good assessment plan to evaluate the length of your shirt sleeve? Why do you need to know the length? If you are looking to get duplicate shirts tailored to the exact specifications, your assessment plan should involve some unit of measurement—preferably the same unit used by your tailor. If your shirt sleeve is 34 inches long, you want the tailor to make all your future shirts with 34-inch sleeves as well. However, if you are standing in a store, trying on a shirt, the unit of measurement is your arm. Is the sleeve of this new shirt too long (more than one arm in length), too short (less than one arm in length), or just right (exactly one arm in length)? Now consider another example perhaps a bit more important: infants. A new mother wants to know if her infant child has a fever. Does she rely on the back of her hand as a surefire method, or does she resort to a thermometer?

What about assessment plans specifically for learning in virtual worlds? What is the best way to assess learning in virtual worlds? Does it matter whether the measurement occurs before, during, or after the learner engages with the world? What should be measured before, during, and/or after the learner engages so that you may have the best information from which to draw inferences about learning? What sorts of inferences should you be attempting to make to best support the efficacy of virtual worlds as a platform for learning in a given subject domain? These are the sorts of questions that should guide the design of assessments for evaluating learning in virtual worlds.

Still, why is measurement important? Measurement is important for virtual worlds because assessment is important for virtual worlds. The best laid assessment plans are essentially useless when shoddy measurement instruments are used to measure the constructs the assessment designers have defined. Think back to the shirt and the tailor. If the tailor uses the metric system and cuts fabric to the centimeter, then your measurement (in inches) of the length of your arm is not the best information. However, if the tailor and you are both using inches as the measure of choice, but the manufacturer of your measuring device printed the inch markings at slightly lesser widths than those of the device used by the tailor, the assessment plan has been completely foiled. The metric problem is easily resolved with a quick conversion of units. The faulty device problem, though, is much worse—as both you and the tailor will likely assume that your device's version of 34 inches is accurate, when in fact the difference is quite substantial, and you end up with a shirt sleeve over your fingertips since you've unwittingly provided the tailor with inaccurate evidence of the length of your arm. The same problem could occur with the young mother and the feverish baby. A faulty thermometer could send them on an unnecessary trip to the emergency room at the local hospital, or worse yet keep the mother at home, comforted by an inaccurately low temperature reading. In both cases, you and the mother made "good" assessment decisions using bad measurement tools.

Again, what about measurement for assessment of learning in virtual worlds? Should the measurements occur within or separate from the virtual world? Can you acquire or build precise, accurate measurement instruments that function within the virtual world? If your intent is to use an existing virtual world, the question may be moot: in-world measurement might not be possible in the virtual world you're planning to use. If so, which *types* of measurement are possible? However, if your intent is to design your own virtual world, you'll want to make sure to decide whether to measure learning within or outside your virtual world very early in the design process—such as when you are creating a list of specifications that will help you choose the best platform for development. The parameters of how and where you can measure what needs to be measured for the evaluation of learning with your virtual world have a great impact on the rest of your design plan for the virtual world.

This sentiment—decisions about measurement implementation as a guide for design and development of virtual worlds—leads us back to the importance of keeping measurement and assessment separate as distinct processes. Generally speaking, it's best to keep these two concepts separate to avoid confusion on many fronts (implementation, conversation, judgment, etc.)—and the easiest way to differentiate between the two is to remember that assessments are decisions, and measurements are instruments. This differentiation is quite relevant when evaluating learning in virtual worlds: based on today's cutting-edge technology, virtual worlds can now serve as quite sophisticated measurement instruments, but not yet as truly sophisticated assessment decision makers. Thankfully, humans still need to be involved in the assessment process with virtual worlds—and, frankly, always should be involved in the process.

A quick example of measurement and assessment with virtual worlds is the use of these worlds as performance testing in formal educational settings (such as a classroom). SAVE Science, the virtual-world project we discussed earlier in the book, is this kind of world. Students perform a series of tasks (with some level of complexity) within the confines of a virtual world. The virtual world records this performance in a variety of dimensions—the world itself is the measurement instrument. The evidence provided by the instrument is then used by the classroom teacher to make assessment decisions about the individual student's performance—including whether this performance-based evidence indicates the presence or absence of learning by the student. We'll explain this concept in more depth further along in this chapter, but first let's look at reliability and validity.

Reliability and Validity

In the measurement, statistics, and methodological studies community, both the differentiation between, and comprehensive nature of, reliability and validity are continuously debated. Many texts about these concepts have been written, both theoretical and practical in perspective. However, for the purposes of this book, we will make a relatively simple distinction between reliability and validity—and how each applies to virtual worlds for learning. Essentially, the difference between reliability and validity comes down to precision vs. accuracy. To demonstrate this distinction and apply the concepts to virtual worlds, let's consider a standard dart board (Figure 6.1) and the game of darts.

In a variety of different games involving darts, you and an opponent take turns throwing three darts at the board. The darts stick into the board, and the arrangement of the three darts forms a pattern (Figure 6.2).

The three darts in Figure 6.2 have been thrown fairly precisely in that they form a tight pattern close together on the dartboard. They are also fairly accurate throws, assuming the dart thrower was aiming for the bull's-eye. In any case, the precision of the three throws is related to reliability, and the accuracy of the three throws is related to validity. In other words, precision

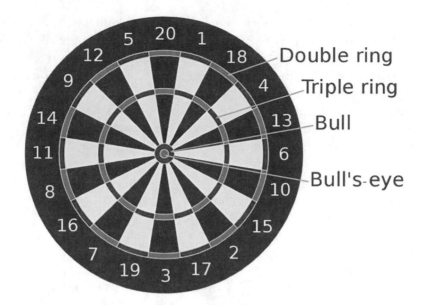

FIGURE 6.1 Diagram of a regulation dartboard

FIGURE 6.2 Darts in a dartboard

has to do with the function of the repeated throws, and accuracy is a value judgment of the location of the three throws combined. It is quite likely that a precisely thrown pattern of three darts will be completely off target—such as tightly clustered on the edge of the dartboard (outside the double ring)— and therefore highly inaccurate.

Considering measurement and assessment, reliability typically applies to the former (precision), and validity typically toward the latter (accuracy). As educators, we ideally use reliable (precise) measurement instrumentation to gather evidence that helps us to make valid (accurate) assessment decisions. It is possible that we use a highly reliable measurement instrument in a non-valid manner, resulting in an inaccurate set of decisions despite implementation of a precise instrument. A very common case of non-valid assessment is the use of a test X that is intended to measure construct X, and we think we're trying to measure construct X when we really need to be measuring construct Y (and, of course, should be using test Y). We plow forward using test X, and then we use the precisely collected evidence of levels of construct X in learners we've tested to make decisions about levels of construct Y with those learners.

When designing evaluation plans for learning, we should make choices about constructs that must be reliably measured so that we can make valid assessment decisions to inform the evaluation process. If any link in this chain—construct choice, measurement, and assessment practice—is weak, it's likely that the evaluation process will be mistaken or even break down completely.

Choosing Constructs to Be Measured in Virtual Worlds

First things first. In case you haven't already heard, it's impossible to measure learning. Yes, we can assess "learning," but to do so we must gather evidence about *measurable* constructs relevant to aspects of learning that are of interest to the context of evaluation. Looking specifically at assessment in virtual worlds, once you've defined the measurable constructs that you wish to measure for your assessment of learning, you must then decide which of these constructs can be measured in virtual worlds—and which constructs *should* be measured in virtual worlds. Of course, this begs two pressing questions:

1. What can be measured in virtual worlds?
2. What should be measured in virtual worlds?

What Can Be Measured?

Much as we split the description of virtual worlds into two chapters in this book—the GUI vs. the world—an understanding of what can be measured with virtual worlds is best achieved with the same strategy. Certain constructs are better measured as in-world performances of specific tasks by the individual learner (or a group of learners). Likewise, certain other constructs are best measured using instruments embedded into the GUI.

The World: Measuring Performance

Which constructs associated with learning are best measured in the world itself? Those constructs that require demonstration in three dimensions over time. In other words, compelling evidence for assessing construct X for a given learner cannot be fully measured in less than three dimensions. Plus, the continuous measurement of these performance data in three dimensions *over time* provides even more compelling evidence of learning, due to its ability to measure *change (or growth) in all three dimensions*. This type of evidence can't easily be captured using the pencils and bubble sheets of standardized testing (much less the 2D digital versions of these same tests).

Still confused? One way to better understand which constructs are a good fit for assessment in virtual worlds is to consider what it is that will actually be conducting the measurements and gathering data as evidence for your assessment decisions about the constructs. *Computers* will be conducting these measurements, so let's approach the measurement of in-world performance data from the perspective of a computer. How might a computer "see" a learner's in-world performance?

One way to parse out the way that a computer understands the evidence produced by a learner during in-world performances is to categorize the evidence as data—in a way that is recognizable to a computer. We've done this categorization already (Nelson, Erlandson, & Denham, 2011), and we call our categories channels—global evidence channels, to be exact. There are three primary channels of evidence to be sourced from a learner's performance in a virtual world: location and movement; object interaction; and communication activities. Table 6.1 provides examples of specific forms that evidence may take within each of these channels.

With some planning, a virtual world residing in a computer system can distinguish rather discretely between these three different types of evidence as it conducts measurements of the performance occurring in the world. Think

Table 6.1 Global Evidence Channels: Primary Evidence Sources

Primary Evidence Sources

Location/Movement (LM)	Object Interaction (OI)	Communication Activity (CA)
Location Tracking	Interaction Types	Simple Communication
• XYZ coordinates • Location visited • Time spent in X location	• Click/select object • Pick up (grab) object • Release (drop) object	• Sign • Signal • Speak (if integrated into world)
Movement Tracking • Direction • Speed • Acceleration/Deceleration		

though, about how complex even a simple task would be when performed in the real world, if all the actions were recorded to a database. Take, for example, buying a pack of chewing gum. A gum-buyer moves between various locations within a store to locate the chewing gum. A recording of location coordinates (X, Y, Z) and a timestamp are recorded to the database every second that the gum-buyer is in the store. This serves as evidence for movement throughout the store area, and these coordinate recordings can be compared to determine direction, speed, and acceleration.

Our gum-buyer interacts with various objects including the pack of chewing gum to be purchased. She might interact with several different "gum pack objects" (picking each one up and then releasing it as she sets it back down) in the world before choosing the pack of gum that she wishes to purchase. Each of these object interactions could be recorded in the same database, with information such as a timestamp, the name of the object, and the type of action that occurred. This evidence of object interaction can be investigated for patterns of interaction that are relevant to the activity.

Our gum-buyer communicates with the cashier at the store, asking him which aisle contains the chewing gum section. This voice communication event is logged in the database with a timestamp and event description, perhaps including a recording of the actual spoken words. Evidence for this event could be compared with location/movement data to determine when our gum-buyer asked the cashier for help—before or after exploring a large portion of the store floor herself?

As you might have noticed, quite a substantial bit of evidence can be collected across these channels just for something as simple as one person walking into a room to buy a pack of gum. And nobody was even being tested! Moving into a virtual world, these same complex actions occurring via these channels can easily be recorded for use as evidence of learning. Can you think of specific examples of how in-world events might serve as evidence for learning in your own world?

It should become obvious quite quickly that for a typical learner's performance in a virtual world these three channels of evidence rarely occur independently from one another. Further, consider the goal of truly authentic assessment and the complexity of evidence collected in performances that go beyond the simple act of buying a pack of chewing gum. Luckily, these evidence channels can be combined into dyads (pairs) and—if we're really going to push the envelope of authentic assessment in virtual worlds—all three channels simultaneously. Let's start with the dyadic combinations of channels (Table 6.2).

There are three potential sources of complex evidence when location/movement and object interaction are combined: movement to or from objects, movement of objects, and movement with objects. For example, does the

Table 6.2 Global Evidence Channels: Dyadic Channel Combinations

Dyadic Channel Combinations		
LM and OI	LM and CA	OI and CA
Movement to/from Objects	Movement to accomplish Communication	Communicating through Object Interaction(s)
Movement of Objects		
Movement with Objects	Communicating about Movement	Communicating about Object Interaction(s)

learner (task performer) approach or depart one or more objects in the virtual world? Movement of objects can include projectiles shot or thrown by the performer, objects set in motion by the performer (such as a spinning top), or automatons not initiated by the performer. Movement of the performer with objects include carrying the object—during which the object is in motion and only touching the performer's embodied avatar—as well as pushing, rolling, or dragging the object—during which the object is in motion and touching both the performer's avatar and the environment (either simultaneously or intermittently, depending on the parameters of the motion).

When the channels of location/movement and communication activity are combined, two types of complex evidence about learning can be collected: movement to *accomplish* communication and communication *about* movement. Movement to accomplish communication can include simple demonstration tasks such as: all or part of the learner's character moves (without objects) to help communicate an idea or process to another human- or computer-controlled character in the virtual world. For example, if the character waves her virtual hand to attract the attention of others standing nearby, this is a movement to accomplish communication. Conversely, if the learner communicates through location or movement in a self-referential fashion, the performed task is a communication act *about* the movement. Consider the actor's bow, or the gymnast's revolving pose at the end of her routine, and you've got two examples of self-referential communication about movement. The communication does not need to be self-referential, however. Think of the use of hand signals to communicate about others' movement—for example, the police officer directing traffic with her hands.

Similarly, when the channels of communication activity and object interaction are combined, two types of complex evidence about learning can be collected: communication *through* object interactions and communicating *about* object interaction. The first type of evidence is based on the creation of signs or signals by the learner—or the "marking" of in-world objects (or spaces) with stationary interactions to leave messages for other human- or computer-controlled characters. "Stationary interactions?" you say. Yes. Remember that this is communication and interaction without movement (we'll get to the triads soon enough). Essentially, the learner interacts with an object in a way that creates a sign or symbol through the way in which the object (or space) has been altered—with the caveat that the signifier cannot require motion to be understood. For example, think if someone rearranged all the furniture in your home or office while you were absent. Upon your return, none of the objects in the room would necessarily be in motion, but you would notice that each of them had been interacted with at some point. As another example, think of the piles of stones that are often used for way-finding on trail systems in various parts of the world (Figure 6.3). Stacks of rocks—not in motion—used for communication. Interestingly enough, these purposed stacks of rocks are called cairns.

The second type of evidence—communicating *about* object interactions—is likely to occur rarely in a virtual world, since most in-world communication requires motion of some sort. However, if a learner modifies previously created objects with further interactions—in a way that serves as commentary about the original interaction—then such evidence can actually occur. Quite possibly the best example of object interaction to modify previous object interaction—as commentary on a signifier—is political graffiti on a dividing wall, such as the graffiti by Banksy on the Israeli West Bank barrier (Figure 6.4). This graffiti does not move, but it is evidence of object interaction, created on top of (and in response to) another object which was placed to define space—object interaction within a space.

With graffiti, we wrap up the dyads and move on to triadic channel combinations (Table 6.3). As you might have already suspected, much of the complex evidence for learning collected in virtual worlds will come from

FIGURE 6.3 A cairn in Oyggjarvegur

FIGURE 6.4 Graffiti in the West Bank

performances that contain triadic combinations—just as a majority of the performances that occur in the real world are triadic in nature: movement, interaction, and communication.

Further, it should come as no surprise that the three distinct triadic combinations of complex evidence all hinge upon communication: communication *about* object movements, communication *while* moving objects, and communicating *through* object movement. Communication about object movements occurs when the learner performs communication actions specifically about the motion of objects, whether these objects are in motion caused by the learner, another character (human- or computer-controlled), or through other physical forces. Think about two children in a park, one holding a balloon. The child loses his grip on the string, and the balloon begins to float

Table 6.3 Global Evidence Channels: Triadic Channel Combinations

Triadic Channel Combinations
LM and OI and CA
Communicating about Object Movements
Communicating while Moving Objects
Communication through Object Movements

away unnoticed. The second child sees the balloon's escape, and she pokes the first child to get his attention, then gestures skyward toward the rising balloon. Both children watch the balloon continue its flight, and the boy waves goodbye to the balloon.

Communication while moving objects in a virtual world occurs when a learner performs communication actions during the process of actively moving one or more objects. As the learner (or group of learners) applies continued force to maintain the object's motion, the learner communicates with other characters, either in reference to the moving object or the context of motion. Further, the object's movement would not necessarily continue without sustained effort managed through this communication process. If you have ever helped a friend move his or her belongings from one house to another, you probably know how much communication is necessary to successfully carry a long couch or coffee table down a flight of stairs—especially if the stairs have a turn.

Finally, communication through object movement might be considered the essence of non-verbal communication between human-controlled characters in a virtual world. Typically, this type of complex evidence can be created through visual demonstrations involving the motion of one or more objects, or through the creation of signs or symbols that involve the motion of one or more objects. A perfect example of complex demonstration as communication through object movement is fencing—or, rather, virtual fencing (Figure 6.5). If an expert models fencing moves—such as the "lunge" in Figure 6.5— to the novice within a virtual training ground, the expert is communicating to the novice by modeling the motion of the object—in this case, the foil.

A good example of signs or signals that require the motion of objects is the semaphore signaling system, which involves two identical red and yellow

FIGURE 6.5 Diagram of a "lunge" maneuver in fencing

FIGURE 6.6 A US Navy Signalman uses semaphore to communicate with an approaching ship

flags, one in each hand of the signaler (Figure 6.6). Depending on the position of each flag, a different letter is represented. It is, essentially, a visual Morse code, used to convey messages over large distances within the line of sight.

One last thought: the communication action performed by a learner is not necessarily intentional. Communication through object movement can certainly be done in a mistaken fashion, when the intent of the learner is to avoid communication—such as attempting to sneak closer to a rare species of songbird in hopes of getting a better view, but accidentally kicking a stone, alerting the bird and causing it to fly away. This can serve as a perfect example of how one aspect of learning—learning from mistakes—can be measured in a virtual world. Let's say our accidental stone kicker—we'll call him Jack—was attempting to complete a specific "field studies" practice quest as part of an ornithological learning simulation set in a virtual forest. In his first run through the practice quest, Jack kicks the stone and scares the bird, which renders his task impossible to complete in the allotted time, resulting in his failure of the quest. Part of the feedback delivered to Jack at the conclusion of his quest attempt (back at the virtual ornithological research center headquarters) would include guidance based on an assessment of the evidence automatically recorded during his stone-kicking incident. Upon retrying the same practice quest for observation of the rare songbird, we hope he might be more careful to avoid the same clumsy mistake again.

In some ways, the types of measurement made possible through in-world instrumentation and Global Evidence Channels might seem limiting—

especially if you focus on each channel individually as opposed to the dyadic and triadic combinations—but it can also allow for direct digital measurement of performance in a way that has before been impossible. If used in concert with measurement instrumentation administered through the GUI, this performance evidence has the potential to revolutionize the practice of assessment.

The GUI: Embedded Instrumentation

Many learner traits or constructs can be measured with instrumentation administered through the GUI, ranging from affective constructs such as engagement and self-efficacy to knowledge constructs such as declarative and procedural knowledge—as well as metacognitive traits such as self-regulation. In short, if a trait or construct can be measured using traditional paper- or web-based survey applications, it can be measured using instrumentation delivered through the GUI of a virtual world. Items are presented to the learner through the interface, and responses are recorded into a database to track the learner's progress over time. The benefit that GUI-based instrumentation has over traditional survey instrumentation for assessment is that the GUI-based instrumentation can be presented to the learner in a way that is integrated into the narrative of the virtual world scenario, without breaking the learner away from the learning experience in the world—thus preventing the potential reduction of learner engagement.

For example, in the Cloverdale Virtual Watershed (Erlandson, 2010), a learner is repeatedly tested for his or her ability to recognize the emergent properties of the water cycle (Figure 6.7). The test is conducted four times throughout the learning scenario, based on the learner's individual exploration of the various (16) elements of the water cycle. Each learner explores the elements based on the order in which they interview different residents of Cloverdale, and after each fourth element view, the test is delivered in the form of an "urgent lab transmission" from the learner's research assistant.

The tests are dynamically populated to include text labels that align with the four elements of the water cycle most recently viewed by the learner— such as Atmospheric Storage, Transpiration, Surface Runoff, and Springs. Each rendition of the test consists of the same three items, presented in a narrative format that maintains the "feel" of the learning scenario:

> *Research Assistant*: "Hi, {UserName}! I've just received a transmission from your observational responder, and I need a status report on your evaluation. I've got a few questions for you about the four most recent elements you've logged in the system:
>
> 1. Could you please describe any emergent properties of the water cycle you've noticed based on {these four recently observed elements}?

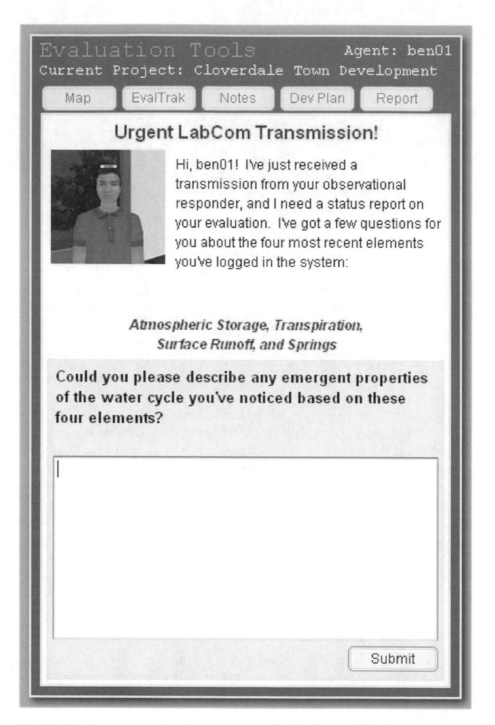

FIGURE 6.7 Measurement instrumentation embedded in the GUI of the Cloverdale Virtual Watershed

2. Can you help me understand how {these four recently observed elements} fit within the context of the water cycle?
3. Could you please describe any interesting forms or patterns of interactions you may have noticed in the water cycle, involving {these four recently observed elements}?

The learner is able to answer these questions (via open-ended response) without leaving the context of the virtual-world scenario, and the integration into the narration—getting the research assistant up to speed—helps to keep the test from feeling like an actual test. Additionally, the timestamps for the responses provided by the learner to each of these test questions can be associated with timestamps from in-world performance evidence. With the ability to match up these two types of evidence for each learner, correlations between responses and performance can lead to better understanding of the affective and knowledge-based values of different patterns of in-world performances.

We've established what can be measured in both the virtual world and the GUI, and even hinted at the potential power of these two measurement techniques to work in concert to revolutionize the assessment of learning. Still, though, there is a major difference between what can be measured, and what *should* be measured in virtual worlds. As with almost everything in life, just because you can doesn't mean you should. This adage rings especially true concerning appropriate applications of technology.

What Should Be Measured?

How does one decide what should be measured using virtual worlds versus more traditional methods of measurement and assessment? The decision process is deceptively simple. For each construct you've identified and defined for inclusion in your measurement protocol, you must answer the following question: Does the context of construct measurement within the protocol—at the measurement, assessment, and/or evaluation levels—necessitate in-world performance or embedded instrumentation? Answer yes, and score a point for virtual worlds. Answer no, and score a point for traditional measurement protocols. For each of the constructs garnering a yes answer to the first question, you must then decide whether it can be measured in virtual worlds—either in-world or through the GUI. If the answer to this second question is also yes, then the construct keeps its scored point. If the answer to this second question is no, then the construct loses its point.

Once you have established which of your defined constructs can and should be measured in virtual worlds, you can tally the scores. If the tally for using virtual worlds is greater than the tally against virtual worlds amongst your constructs, then you've got a strong case for the implementation of virtual worlds within your measurement protocol. Of course, quantity is not the only deciding factor. Certain constructs you have identified within your measurement protocol will likely hold priority over others. In this case, constructs with higher priority might hold more weight—perhaps being worth two or three tally points instead of just one. As such, if the majority of your constructs—judged either by sheer quantity or qualitatively weighted priority—should be measured in a virtual world, then you should heavily consider building or acquiring a virtual world to appropriately measure the constructs defined for your protocol. Otherwise, it's probably a waste of resources to apply a virtual-world measurement solution to a learning assessment problem that doesn't actually require virtual worlds. This is a fundamental concept you should keep at the forefront as you design assessment procedures which integrate virtual worlds as measurement instrumentation—the topic of focus in Chapter Nine.

Conclusion

Based on the hierarchy of evaluation, assessment, and measurement, we've established the importance of both assessment and measurement in the evaluation of learning—and the importance of maintaining the discretion between the two processes. In our brief review of reliability and validity, we emphasized the relationship between reliability, validity, precision and accuracy (remember the darts), and how these concepts fit within measurement and assessment concerning virtual worlds. Finally, we discussed at length the process of choosing appropriate constructs to be measured using virtual worlds, both in the world and in the GUI.

TEST YOUR UNDERSTANDING

1. Describe the main differences between measurement and assessment.
2. Describe the main differences between reliability and validity.

LEARNING ACTIVITIES

Consider the following challenges to help you review the content of the chapter.

1. Which subject domains would be a good fit for measurement and assessment using virtual worlds, and why?
2. Which domains might be a poor fit, and why?

3. Similarly, which learner populations would be a good fit for measurement and assessment using virtual worlds, and why?
4. Which populations might be a poor fit, and why?
5. Choose a particular subject domain, and think of several learning goals and objectives associated with this subject domain. Consider the potential of these learning objectives to be defined as constructs for assessment—and whether or not these constructs can be effectively demonstrated and measured inside a virtual world.
6. For each construct you've identified and defined for inclusion in your measurement protocol, you must answer the following question: Does the context of construct measurement within the protocol—at the measurement, assessment, and/or evaluation level—necessitate in-world performance or embedded instrumentation?

References

Erlandson, B. (2010). *Fostering Ecological Literacy: Recognizing and appreciating emergence in a complex virtual inquiry environment.* Arizona State University. ProQuest Dissertations and Theses.

Nelson, B., Erlandson, B., & Denham, A. (2011). Global channels of evidence for learning and assessment in complex game environments. *British Journal of Educational Technology, 42(1),* 88–100.

Other Resources

If you want to learn more about measurement and assessment, here are four books that can serve as an excellent foundation:

DeVellis, R. F. (2003). *Scale Development: Theory and applications.* Thousand Oaks, CA: Sage Publications.

Henerson, M. E., Morris, L. L., Fitz-Gibbon, C. T., & University of California, Los Angeles. (1987). *How to Measure Attitudes.* Newbury Park, CA: Sage Publications.

Morris, L. L., Fitz-Gibbon, C. T., & Lindheim, E. (1987). *How to Measure Performance and Use Tests.* Newbury Park, CA: Sage Publications.

Reynolds, C. R., Livingston, R. B., & Willson, V. L. (2006). *Measurement and Assessment in Education.* Boston, MA: Pearson/Allyn & Bacon.

part three
Theoretical Perspectives
Design for Learning in Virtual Worlds

seven

Critiquing Virtual Worlds and Virtual-World-based Curricula

Introduction

As you have read, educational virtual worlds in recent years have been created using multiple theory frameworks including (but not limited to) constructivism, cognitive processing theory, behaviorism, and, most often, situated learning. The application of each of these theories in creating virtual worlds helps define the types of activities learners conduct while in the worlds. Understanding these theories and the kinds of learning activities that go along with them provides some guidance when critiquing existing virtual worlds as platforms for learning.

In this chapter, we will describe a framework for critiquing existing virtual worlds that includes aspects of all the theories we covered in Chapter Four, with a particular emphasis on constructivist and situated learning ideas. This framework provides a practical guide to critiquing the quality, impact, and usefulness of existing virtual worlds that you might want to use with your own students or trainees. In addition, the framework offers a basic guide for activities and elements you might want to include when designing your own virtual worlds.

The framework we describe here is based on one first described by David Jonassen, Kyle Peck, and Brent Wilson in their book *Learning with Technology: a constructivist perspective* (1999). As the book's title makes clear, their framework was centered on constructivist philosophy and dealt with more general computer-based instructional and problem-solving environments rather than focusing specifically on virtual worlds. For our discussion here, we have borrowed the concept of an evaluation table and many of the elements from the Jonassen et al. (1999) table for our rubric refocused on multi-theory critique of virtual worlds for learning.

Critiquing Virtual Worlds

When you first set out to design your own virtual world for learning, it can be an incredibly daunting task. The possibilities seem endless. What will your learning goals be? How will you achieve those goals in a virtual world? What activities will you build into your world? How will you know if a student has achieved those goals? We cover all of these points in this book. But, before designing a virtual world from scratch, we believe it is instructive to analyze existing virtual worlds, casting a critical and informed eye on the design of the worlds themselves and the activities embedded in them. Armed with your understanding of the mechanics of virtual worlds through which all activities are realized, along with a sense of the theoretical basis for the activities you can embed in a virtual world, you can critique existing worlds with some confidence, finding examples—both good and not-so-good—that have been created by others. Plus, if you are in a bind and have neither the time nor the money to design and develop your own virtual world, this a great procedure to follow when acquiring the right existing virtual world for your needs.

Without further ado, here is our modified version of the Jonassen, Peck, and Wilson framework applied to the critique of virtual worlds for learning (Table 7.1). First look over the whole framework, and then read on to explore its components in detail. The framework includes a number of focal areas for critiquing virtual worlds, and a rating scale (very poor–very good).

Activities Situated in Context

In the chapter on learning theories, you read about the prominent place of situated learning in the design and building of many virtual worlds for learning. Recall that situated learning is typified by instruction that has students completing activities that look and feel like their real-world counterparts, done in settings that similarly mirror the real world. With this in mind, our virtual-world critique framework includes a focus on the quality of an existing virtual world related to its support for conducting learning activities in context. First, when critiquing a virtual world, you want to examine the extent to which the world has been designed to look and feel like the setting in which the activities being learned would be conducted in the real world.

Imagine, for example, a virtual world designed to teach students how to perform the actions of an emergency paramedic. As a first step to critiquing this imaginary virtual world, you would want to judge the extent to which it supports learning in context (i.e., situated learning). For example, if

Table 7.1 Virtual World Critique Rubric. Adapted from the framework presented in Jonassen, D. H., Peck, K. L., & Wilson, B. G. (1999). *Learning with Technology: a constructivist perspective.* **New Jersey: Prentice Hall.**

Focus	Very Poor	Below Average	Average	Above Average	Very Good
Activities situated in context:					
World look matches real-world setting for practice					
Interaction with real-world objects support					
User manipulation of the virtual world support					
Observation and Inference opportunities availability					
Data recording and management tools availability					
Knowledge Building:					
Intrinsic motivation					
Problem identification					
Problem solution opportunities					
Cooperation:					
Learner–learner interaction support					
Learner–expert interaction support					
Social negotiation support					
Student-centered role assignment					
Authenticity:					
Complexity mimics real world					
Higher order thinking required					
Ill-structured problem identification and solving					
Complex solutions/Multiple answers					
Intentionality:					
Learners expected to contribute to attainment of specific goals					
Learners expected to develop and express goals					
Goal monitoring and reporting tools support					
Activities relate to goals					
Environment features support learning goals					

students are supposed to practice being an emergency paramedic, is the world designed to look like an ambulance, an accident scene, or some other setting that mirrors one in which a paramedic might actually work?

Beyond a visual and auditory similarity to a real-world counterpart, you should assess the extent to which the world includes realistic looking and acting objects appropriate to the setting and the learning tasks. For example, in our hypothetical emergency paramedic virtual world, you would expect to find an array of medical equipment, all functioning in realistic (although probably simplified) ways. The ability for the user to interact with a variety of realistic objects is critical for learning and engagement. Imagine a virtual world in which a learner can't interact with anything. It would be a pretty boring experience—basically a virtual stroll through a 3D slide presentation. Interactive objects provide a mechanism through which the learner can build and demonstrate knowledge about the content and processes that are important to the learning objective(s) designed into the virtual world. For similar reasons, it is sometimes important for an educational virtual world to support manipulation of the world itself. For example, a virtual world might allow a user to design and build houses, plant and grow vegetables, or divert a river's course. This isn't always necessary: the ability to alter the virtual world should exist in support of the learning objective(s), rather than casually being included simply because it is possible from a technical standpoint to do so. In our emergency paramedic world, it could technically be possible to support the ability to construct a new ambulance, but such functionality wouldn't really add to the learning.

Part of the value of conducting learning activities in a context that looks and acts like a real-world counterpart is that such contextualization allows the learner to make observations and related inferences of phenomena they would see in the real world, leading to transferable knowledge about those phenomena. As an example, let's return to our fictitious emergency paramedic world. A world featuring a simulated accident scene, full of accident victims with a variety of symptoms and injuries, provides a nearly endless set of possibilities for students to make observations of the victims, develop inferences about those observations, and then propose courses of actions (CPR, leg setting, medicine, etc.) based on those inferences.

To make the most of opportunities for observation, object interactions, and world manipulation, virtual worlds should provide tools through which learners can record and manipulate data they gather as they interact with the world. One challenge to embedding curricula in a virtual world is that the designed world tends to be complex. The learner needs to makes sense of a large amount of data that may be scattered in the world both in terms of location (spatial distribution) and in time (temporal distribution). Situated curricula in virtual worlds are often designed to represent complex systems, with many interrelated components. In our emergency paramedic example, there could be a huge number of interacting components that learners need to keep track of. In order to make sense of it all as part of the learning process, data recording and analysis tools can be incorporated into the world. Common tools include e-notebooks to record findings, data recorders to store and sort measurements taken, graphs to visualize gathered data, and cameras to snap screenshots of objects seen in the world. More elaborate toolsets may include virtual versions of real-world tools. For example, an emergency paramedic world might include heart monitors, thermometers, blood pressure gloves, etc. Not only do such data tools help support learning, they also provide information that can be used to assess learning.

Knowledge Building

So far we've talked about critiquing educational virtual worlds primarily from a situated learning framework. When designing virtual-world-based curricula, situated learning and constructivism frequently come together to form a cross-theory framework for learning. With this in mind, it's important to appraise existing virtual worlds as platforms for student-centered knowledge building, based on constructivist ideas. Researchers and designers of educational virtual worlds look at the virtual worlds not as spaces for the transmission of information from world to student, but more often as spaces in which students can build knowledge by interacting with the objects inside the virtual world including people, land, the world itself, buildings, and so on. The design elements important for knowledge building in virtual worlds cut across almost every category of Table 7.1. However, for the time being we're going to focus on a specific subset of the critique items that you should look for to see how well a given existing virtual world could support knowledge building for the learner. Several important design elements that support knowledge building include the extent to which the virtual world bolsters a player's intrinsic motivation to conduct knowledge building, the extent to which the world includes "designed dissonance," the ability of the world to support students in identifying problems, and how well the world provides opportunities for the learner to solve those problems.

A basic but critical design element for the success of knowledge building in a virtual world is motivation. An effective educational virtual world must be designed in such a way that it helps spark the intrinsic motivation of the learner to begin building knowledge within that virtual world. Fostering intrinsic motivation in a virtual world is a tricky business. Some designers focus primarily on inclusion of high-quality visual or multimedia elements in order to support motivation. An example of this approach being done well can be seen with The Martian Boneyards in the Blue Mars virtual world (Figure 7.1). This multi-player science inquiry virtual world was developed using a very high-end game engine called CryEngine 2 (see www.bluemars.

FIGURE 7.1 The Martian Boneyards (from Asbell-Clarke et al., 2011)

com). This game engine has been used to create a number of commercial virtual-world-based games including the very popular first-person shooter game Crysis—considered a kind of benchmark for high-quality graphics. Under the Blue Mars umbrella, a group of educational researchers and professional game developers created an educational virtual world that allows students to conduct archeological digs in a virtual boneyard (Asbell-Clarke, Edwards, Larsen, Rowe, Sylvan, & Hewitt, 2011). To help with the sense of situated realism, which in turn can bolster student motivation, this group has been able to take advantage of the power of the game engine.

The high-level graphics approach has worked well in the Martian Boneyards virtual world because it also incorporates good game design. But great visual appeal is in itself not sufficient to maintain motivation for very long if other important elements are missing. A highly realistic, visually appealing virtual world can initially motivate a learner to explore it, but more important than a great look and feel in the virtual world are the game design elements. A deep look at general game design is outside the scope of this book. However, suffice it to say that in critiquing existing virtual worlds you should pay close attention to elements such as storyline, challenge, competition, and so on. When reviewing existing virtual worlds, ask yourself how well the game elements embedded in the virtual world motivate the specific audience for which it has been designed. If you want to pursue general game design more fully, we highly recommend it. We include a list of useful resources at the end of the chapter.

As an example of an educational virtual world that incorporates fun and engaging game elements in support of knowledge building, let's look again at Whyville. As you'll remember from Chapter One, Whyville is a 2D, cartoon-like virtual world initially designed by researchers at UCLA, and now a commercial world (see www.whyville.net). At the time this chapter is being written, Whyville has roughly 6 million users. The majority of these users are girls aged between 11 and 14 years old. From a graphical perspective, Whyville is not cutting-edge. The Whyville virtual world consists of a large series of 2D, cartoon-like locations. The player characters, or avatars, consist of very crude cartoon-like heads and torsos with no lower bodies. Despite this visual simplicity, Whyville supports high levels of intrinsic motivation for its many players. This motivation comes in part from the large community of players who can interact with each other using text-based or voice chat. Intrinsic motivation is also supported in Whyville through the many casual games embedded in the virtual world. Many of these casual games are educational in nature, but they are designed to be so much fun that the user may not "notice the learning." When critiquing existing virtual worlds, or designing your own virtual world, engagement and intrinsic motivation inspired by the gameplay within the world are of critical importance to learning. If the educational virtual world is boring or seems like homework, it is unlikely that much learning will take place.

Another way to support knowledge building in a virtual world is to design the world in such a way that it introduces "dissonance" in the mind of the learner (Jonassen, Peck, & Wilson, 1999). The basic idea is to create a virtual world in which the learners are able to recognize that something is amiss in the world, and then support them in figuring out what that thing is (problem identification and problem solving). You can do this in a virtual world by creating a curriculum or a scenario in which the learner is introduced to some problem upon entry into the world. The learner's goal, quest, or mission is then to interact with the world and all of its elements in order to resolve this dissonance by solving the problem, and building knowledge about the topics and processes related to that problem.

Some virtual worlds directly introduce a problem to the learner rather than making the learner identify it, by simply telling them about the problem impacting the world and asking them to solve it. For example, in many virtual worlds the learner is greeted upon entry into the world by a computer-based character. That character might tell the story of the world's current situation to the learner and/or set the learner on an initial quest that will further introduce the problem. Some virtual worlds include a large number of in-world characters, each of whom introduces a new sub-problem that is part of a larger overall problem inside virtual space. Alternatively, the virtual world can be designed in such a way that the world itself introduces dissonance to the learner through its design. For example, imagine a virtual world with a river running through it. Upon entering the virtual world, the learners might be told only that there is something wrong in the world, and be asked to uncover what it is. By exploring the virtual world, the learners come to understand that there is something wrong with the water in the river. When they look into the river upstream, they see a large number of fish swimming in the water. However, as they walk downstream, they see that there are fewer and fewer fish the farther downstream they go. By the time they reach the mouth of the river, there are no fish to be seen. A scenario such as this allows learners to perceive dissonance in the world on their own. This more subtle way of introducing dissonance enables learners to identify the problem by themselves, an important aspect of constructivist approaches to learning.

Whether by direct introduction or indirect opportunities for discovering problems, learners in virtual worlds should be given the opportunity to identify problems and, through their actions, solve them. The actions taken to solve the problems make up the learning tasks of the curriculum in the virtual world, which lead to knowledge building.

Cooperation

As we discussed in the chapter on learning theories applied to virtual worlds, cooperation between players is often a central feature of socio-constructivist-based and situated curriculum. In critiquing existing virtual worlds for levels of cooperation, you should evaluate the extent to which the virtual world supports interactions between students or between students and experts or mentors. Cooperation in a virtual world can also take the form of the communication between a learner and a computer-based character in the world. In critiquing the cooperation aspect of an existing virtual world or designing in cooperation to your own virtual world-based curriculum, you should pay close attention to the types of cooperation that are supported by the curriculum. For example, does the curriculum foster cooperation that is directly related to the learning goals? Do the tasks and activities that students are asked to perform require cooperation among players? Are there opportunities for mentoring and coaching between players? Does the virtual world or the curriculum embedded in the virtual world include intrinsic motivational elements to encourage cooperation among players? Turning back to our imaginary emergency paramedic virtual world, it is easy to see how built-in tools for collaboration between multiple players would be assets. Computer-based characters could fill an accident scene or emergency room, as accident victims, doctors, nurses, and other paramedics. A multi-player version of the same virtual world could ask players to cooperate in diagnosing and treating accident victims.

In addition to basic cooperation, educational virtual worlds can support multi-player cooperation based on different roles and responsibilities among players completing the curriculum. In critiquing this aspect, you can check whether the curriculum requires that different members of a team of learners take on distinctive roles as they collaborate. If so, are students asked to self-assign roles to play in the curriculum, or are roles assigned by the virtual world in some manner? Is there support in the virtual world for students to negotiate with each other about the roles and rules of participation?

As part of an evaluation of cooperation from a technical perspective, you'll want to examine the availability and quality of any tools in the virtual world that support cooperation and communication between players. For example, basically all multi-player virtual worlds support text chat among players. Text chat tools usually allow players to chat with one, some, or all of their teammates, or to "shout" to all nearby players in the virtual world. Many multi-player virtual worlds also support voice-based chat with similar functionality.

In educational virtual worlds in which the participants will be children, it is important to assess what, if any, parental controls and/or filters exist for chat tools. Chat among players in commercial virtual worlds can be a bit "wilder" than one might want in the classroom or computer lab of an elementary school. Educational virtual worlds and worlds aimed at children might filter the language that is typed, attempting to block foul language. Teacher/parent/administrator controls might be available that can limit the people with whom a given player can chat. The virtual world may also have a self-policing policy in which players earn points for monitoring the behavior of other players in chat, and from completing training courses on chat rules and behavior expectations.

Authenticity

A key strength of learning embedded in a virtual world is the contextual authenticity of that world. In this case, we are not necessarily talking about the level of authenticity of the look and feel of the virtual world. As we described when talking about critiquing the degree to which a virtual world supports learning activities situated in context, it isn't necessary to design virtual worlds that look highly realistic. Instead, an important factor to consider when critiquing an existing virtual world, or when designing your own, is the extent to which it presents learners with authentic problems and offers authentic tools and activities to pursue solutions to those problems. In critiquing the authenticity of problems embedded in virtual worlds, you can look to see the extent to which the complexity of the problems mimics real-world counterparts. For example, do the problems presented in the virtual world you review require the student to engage in higher order thinking? If so, how is this accomplished? It is a real challenge to design a virtual world in which players need to think carefully and respond to problems in a way that demonstrates higher order thinking. In a good educational virtual world it should not be possible for a student to complete a curriculum just by randomly clicking on things. We have described previously that virtual worlds are often used as problem-solving spaces, in which students work to understand the structure and interactions of a complex system from within. Virtual worlds by their nature are good at supporting complex problems with multiple possible answers. There is little point in using a virtual world or creating a virtual world in order to ask students to answer multiple-choice or true–false style questions. In critiquing a virtual world then, you should examine the extent to which the problems embedded in the virtual world are ill-structured and complex; and you will want to see whether the virtual world supports the finding of similarly complex, multi-faceted solutions.

As an example, let's return to our emergency paramedic virtual world. In the real world, the problems that a paramedic must deal with are highly complex. At any given moment, there may be dozens of people in need of attention. Decisions must be made quickly about who to treat first, how to treat them, who to let wait, etc. There are family members to deal with, people who may be intoxicated or drugged, and so on. A high-quality virtual world experience will be designed to allow learners to deal with these kinds of complex and interwoven problems in realistic ways. Conversely, a virtual world with low authenticity might include only a single accident victim with simple injuries and a friendly calm demeanor, provide lots of time to evaluate the injury, and then provide a multiple-choice question in which the player chooses a single perfect treatment.

In addition to critiquing the authenticity of the problems embedded in the world, another question to ask is "how functionally authentic are the virtual tools used to deal with embedded problems?" For example, if students need to measure the composition of water in a virtual river, does the world provide them with tools to do so? If so, how realistically do these tools work? On the low end of functional authenticity, students might click a button on-screen and get a list of components found in a water sample. On the higher end of the authenticity scale, students could have access to a water sampling toolkit. This toolkit could allow them to take samples of water from any location along the river. After taking a given sample, student might see an interactive view of the water under a microscope, and be able to directly organize and count the various types of bacteria swimming in the water. This was the approach taken with the River City world, discussed in previous chapters.

A final aspect of authenticity to consider is the level of complexity in the solution or solutions to the embedded problems in a virtual world. In the real world, there are rarely simple, straightforward answers to complex problems. A virtual world with high levels of authenticity will mirror real-world complexity in the way it supports complex solutions to problems. In our imaginary emergency paramedic virtual world, we have described an authentic problem as one in which the learner needs to juggle multiple accident victims with varying levels of injury, family members, other paramedics, etc. Given this level of complexity of problems, the solutions to the problems should be correspondingly complex. For the emergency paramedic world, for example, the treatment provided each victim, the order of treating victims, and the outcomes of the treatments should not necessarily be "clean." Some accident victims might die. Wrong decisions might be made. The virtual world should allow for this kind of complex authenticity to reflect how things work in the real world.

Intentionality

Educational virtual worlds should be designed to support learner intentionality. It is not enough to simply develop a virtual world and drop students in it in the hope of achieving some learning goal. The design of each virtual world must incorporate curricula, tasks, and interactions that allow learners to clearly and consciously pursue well-articulated goals. Essentially this is a matter of matching worlds and the activities embedded in them to the ultimate goals for learning in ways that require learners to make thoughtful choices as they complete them.

Supporting learner intentionality incorporates the combined aspects of our critique table. For example, our imaginary paramedic world could support learner intentionality by situating learning in a realistic-looking accident scene or emergency room, filled with victims, bystanders, police, etc. The world could require learners to make ongoing choices about victim care based on multiple, interwoven factors. It could provide functionally authentic digital tools that the learners can use to complete tasks. In addition, intentionality in educational virtual worlds can be supported by including tools for use by learners that enable (or require) them to explain or defend their ongoing activities and choices, and to describe how these relate to the learning goals of the virtual world. Such tools could include simple e-notebooks, graphing and drawing tools, information organizers, concept maps, etc. When possible, these tools should also be situated into the storyline of the world, and their use logically consistent with the central activities embedded in the world. For example, in our hypothetical paramedic world, learners might need to explain their choices to a doctor or to a family member of a victim. They might need to record their diagnoses in a report or administer treatment directly. Each of these tasks requires a kind of intentionality of thought: a pause in the action to consider what has been done so far, what those actions and choices mean, and how they were derived.

Conclusion

Analyzing existing virtual worlds is an excellent way to quickly build a strong understanding of the strengths and weaknesses of worlds that have been created by others, and also provides a fantastic way to collect ideas about the kinds of activities and features you might include in your own virtual world. The framework we have covered here offers a solid, multi-theory approach for conducting a thorough critique of existing worlds in terms of their potential to support learning and engagement. Reading about a framework for critiquing virtual worlds is a good start, but the best way to really build expertise is to conduct your own review. Before moving on, spend some time choosing an existing virtual world and critiquing it using the framework presented here, or using your own framework. Later in the book, you will learn about creating a curriculum design document for a virtual world. As you create that document, conduct a simultaneous critique of the world you are planning, paying close attention to how well your world will include elements from the framework.

TEST YOUR UNDERSTANDING

1. The evaluation framework includes a focus on activity in context. What does this mean? How could a learning activity NOT be in context?
2. Think about cooperation among learners in a virtual world for learning. What are the main benefits of cooperation? What are possible drawbacks to a virtual world that includes cooperation as a central component?
3. Is authenticity always a good thing in an educational virtual world? Make a two-column list of the positives and negatives of including highly authentic activities, tools, and settings in a virtual world.

LEARNING ACTIVITIES

1. Pick an existing educational or commercial virtual world. Evaluate it using the rubric presented in Table 7.1.
2. Using Table 7.1, write an outline describing a virtual world and its embedded activities that you could design to address a specific learning goal. Which areas of the rubric would you use in your design? Which would you leave out? Why?

References

Asbell-Clarke, J., Edwards, T., Larsen, J., Rowe, E., Sylvan, E., & Hewitt, J. (2011). *Collaborative Scientific Inquiry in Arcadia: An MMO gaming environment on Blue Mars*. Paper presented at the American Educational Research Association conference, Denver.

Jonassen, D. H., Peck, K. L., & Wilson, B. G. (1999). *Learning with Technology: A constructivist perspective*. Columbus, OH: Merrill Prentice Hall.

Links

The Whyville project offers a great example of an engaging virtual world without using high-end graphics: www.whyville.net

The Blue Mars project, with its Martian Boneyards world, shows a nice example of a high-end graphical world: www.bluemars.com

After writing this chapter, we discovered that a virtual world training game for paramedics had actually been created. You can view a demo at: www.nationalemspreparedness.org

A group at Utah State University has created a virtual world curriculum called H.E.A.T. (Hazard Emergency & Accident Training) that teaches first responders how to cope with fire scenes: http://imrc.usu.edu/heat.php

---

Other Resources

We don't cover general game design here, but as an educator, designer, or researcher interested in the use of virtual worlds for learning, it is a great idea to build a foundation of knowledge in this area. A few good books to look at on game design include:

Schell, J. (2008). *The Art of Game Design: a book of lenses*. Burlington, MA: Elsevier, Inc.

Fullerton, T. (2004). *Game Design Workshop*. San Francisco, CA: CMP Books.

Koster, R. (2004). *A Theory of Fun for Game Design*. Phoenix, AZ: Paraglyph Press.

eight
Designing Curricula for Virtual Worlds

Introduction

Enough with the theories! Enough with the frameworks for critiquing worlds! Enough with all the details about the mechanics! It is time to start designing some curriculum to go into your virtual world. In this chapter, we will walk through a multi-step design process for creating curriculum for use in a virtual world. This process will center on creating a curriculum design document. The curriculum design document has two main sections: Curriculum Overview and Design Details. The Curriculum Overview will provide your audience (your own design/development team or a client) with a vivid picture of the goals, audience, setting, and story of your curriculum. The Design Details section will help specify details of a given curriculum that can then be handed off to a development team to use in the actual development of the virtual world.

As you read through this chapter, you'll likely notice that the goals and processes of designing curricula for virtual worlds isn't all that different from creating face-to-face lessons or training. The main difference is in how you describe what will occur during the curricular unit, and the thought process behind the activities of the curriculum. By now, you have a strong foundation for choosing what kinds of learning/training goals work well in a virtual world, what kinds of curricula can be called upon to achieve those goals, what kinds of activities can be included in those curricula, a list of the available mechanics that you can utilize to represent those activities in virtual space, and a good sense of how to assess whether your audience has learned what you want them to learn while using your virtual world. Given all that, let's start building a curriculum design document.

Virtual-World Curriculum Design Document

When you start designing a virtual-world curriculum, it is useful to spend some time carefully outlining your ideas in a curriculum design document to make sure that your goals are a good fit for a virtual world, and that you have all the major pieces in place to make a successful curricular unit. In our experience, we've seen many teachers, trainers, and designers skip this step and jump directly into development only to find—after working extensively on a developing a virtual world—that their curriculum doesn't really work well in a virtual world. It is much easier to brainstorm, modify, extend, or discard ideas for virtual-world-based curricula via a detailed design document on paper than it is to redevelop the digital components of a virtual world after you've started building.

Putting together a curriculum design document should be a fun and relatively painless process. The main point is to get your ideas on paper and share them with a team of co-creators (subject matter experts, instructional designers, virtual-world programmers, modelers, writers, etc.) and, when you have one, your client. In writing a curriculum design document for an educational virtual world, you can call upon some standard elements that frequently appear in such documents. For our discussion here, we'll draw on some commonsense categories suggested by Alessi and Trollip (2001) in their book on multimedia design. Some of these include: an instructional problem statement, a proposed curricular solution, a justification for why the curriculum will be developed as a virtual world (as opposed to some other platform), a description of the audience and setting, one or more clearly stated learning objectives, an explanation of how achievement of the objectives will be assessed, an outline of the "events" of the curriculum, a flowchart showing the organizational structure of the curriculum, storyboards demonstrating visual snapshots of events to occur in your virtual world, an estimation of the time required to design and develop the curriculum, and an estimate of the costs involved and the people required to turn your curriculum into an actual world.

For our discussion here, we'll include some modified snippets from a curriculum design document written for a virtual world that one of us has worked on as part of a research project called SAVE Science, as well as some freshly crafted material not included in the original design document. We introduced this project way back in Chapter One, but to remind you, SAVE Science places middle school students in a series of virtual-world-based assessment modules. The goal of the project is to have kids complete assessments (tests, basically) of their science knowledge related to areas of content that they study in their classes. The project hopes that by carefully embedding the measures and activities of assessment in virtual worlds, more interesting and useful information about how well kids really understood what they studied in class can be derived than might be determined from more traditional paper-based tests (Nelson, Ketelhut, & Schifter, 2010).

One of the modules created for SAVE Science is called "Weather Trouble." In Weather Trouble, the SAVE Science team designed a module to assess how well kids can remember and apply their knowledge of weather-related concepts such as air pressure, wind, temperature, and humidity (Figure 8.1). The goal of the story of Weather Trouble is to figure out the reasons behind an ongoing drought, and to predict if the drought will be ending soon, and if so why.

Part 1: Design Overview

Instructional/Training Problem

You can start your curriculum document by "setting the scene" for your virtual world. Curricula are designed to address some need or problem. What problem(s) are you hoping to address? To answer this question, you should describe the current state of affairs as it relates to your specific need. The way you describe the instructional problem will depend in part on the intended audience for your design document. Gear your tone, formality, and level of detail for that audience. Here, we're not talking about the people who will use your curriculum as learners, but the people who need to understand your design. What works for a group of colleagues working together to design curriculum for use in classes in their own school might not work for clients from

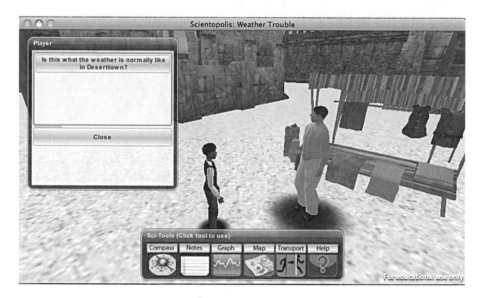

FIGURE 8.1 Weather Trouble

a corporation looking to create training for new employees, which might not work for a government agency trying to decide if they will fund your idea as part of a grant. In all cases, your design document needs to provide a level of detail sufficient for somebody unfamiliar with the project to understand it and to manage its creation.

Regardless of who the audience for your design document is, your instructional problem statement should provide a detailed narrative of the current state of affairs related to your problem, with an explanation of why the current state of affairs should not continue. You might also need to explain how things got to the state they are in now, and why. Again, use your judgment and knowledge of your audience to make choices about how much detail you need to provide and how formal you need to be.

An instructional problem statement for a curricular unit that will be embedded in a virtual world might focus on a clear need for learners to understand and apply knowledge in some content area, often through some specific set of processes. Problem statements for virtual world-based curricula frequently outline existing instructional methods, pointing out their strengths and weaknesses and highlighting the need for some more impactful, authentic approach to teaching the topic.

Weather Trouble Example

In the case of our example Weather Trouble curriculum, the design document was written for an internal team of designers and developers for their own consumption. Consequently, the document didn't need to focus very much on selling the team on the idea of using a virtual-world-based curriculum. Instead, the main goal of the Weather Trouble instructional problem statement was to lay out a "big picture" idea of the problem the team wanted to address, along with some basic ideas of how they might address the problem within a virtual-world-based assessment module. Here's a rough version of the instructional problem statement from Weather Trouble:

> Middle school students in School District X spend 6 weeks studying natural phenomena that contribute to changing patterns of weather. These include temperature, air pressure, precipitation, air masses, humidity, etc. Student understanding of these phenomena is currently measured both by post-instructional unit multiple-choice tests and via district-level summative assessment tests. The existing assessments focus primarily on word definition recognition and basic receptive knowledge,

rather than on mastery and application of concepts and content taught. Further, the data teachers receive from existing assessment approaches provide little insight into student thinking about the content being assessed, making it difficult to pinpoint areas for further study in class and/or improved instructional methods for future students.

Proposed Solution

After laying out the instructional problem, your design document should include a clear, concise statement of how you propose to address the issue you raise. This doesn't need to be a long or detailed explanation (yet). Instead, it serves as the "pay-off" at the end of your instructional problem statement. You will provide the details of what your proposed solution consists of later in the design document.

Weather Trouble Example

To address this problem, we propose to develop a virtual world-based assessment module called "Weather Trouble." In this 45-minute assessment module, students will demonstrate and apply their knowledge of weather-related phenomena gained through completion of related in-class curriculum to uncover the factors influencing an extended dry spell in a fictional medieval city, make predictions about whether the weather will change, and offer evidence for their hypothesis. The assessment module will focus specifically on measuring students' understanding of barometric pressure, humidity, and wind direction in weather patterns.

Justification for the Curriculum

Depending on the audience for your design document, you might need to offer a justification for your solution to the problem you describe. If everyone is already on-board with the idea of doing a virtual-world-based curriculum, and if your team already knows that they need to create curriculum of a specific type around a specific topic, you might be able to skip this part. Otherwise, this section of your curriculum design document offers you a chance to show off your theory and design skills related to the value of virtual worlds for learning ... and a chance to sell the concept of virtual world-based curricula to those folks who might not share your view of their power for learning. In addition, it is a good idea for you and your team to make sure that you understand and can articulate clearly why you want to create a virtual-world-based curriculum, even if you don't need to convince anyone else. Writing this section of your curriculum design document provides an excellent reality check for you and any colleagues working with you. Before diving in to the long hours and sometimes large amounts of money needed to develop a virtual world, you need to be very sure that the curriculum you have in mind really makes sense, and that the solution to the instructional problem you describe can be best achieved in a virtual world versus some other platform.

How do you do that? Make use of the information from the mechanics, theories, world critique, and assessment chapters in this book. Looking at your own instructional problem, analyze why a virtual-world-based curriculum provides a platform that is more useful, meaningful, and powerful for learning than some other form of curriculum. What are the theoretical, practical, financial, and motivational benefits of creating the curriculum you propose? Does the curriculum you plan "score" well on the world critique framework we covered in Chapter Seven? Will your audience learn more deeply in a virtual world? Will they be more engaged in a virtual world? Is a virtual-world-based curriculum more scalable than some other form of curriculum? Why? How about cost? Do you have the money to build a virtual world? Carefully weigh both the pros and cons of designing a virtual world, and present your findings in this section of your curriculum design document.

Weather Trouble Example

For the Weather Trouble module, the team donned its theorist caps and talked about the benefits of situating learning in realistic contexts modeled on the real world:

> By situating assessment of weather-related concepts in a realistic scenario, we believe we can provide a more meaningful approach to letting students demonstrate their understanding of the material studied in class than they would have when tested through more traditional means. Weather Trouble will ask that students not only understand the classroom-taught material, but also demonstrate the ability to apply their knowledge to solve a complex, realistic weather-related problem (understanding the causes behind an on-going drought and predicting upcoming changes in the weather).

Target Audience and Instructional Setting

In your curriculum design document, you should be sure both to carefully describe the intended audience for the curriculum, and fully explicate the setting(s) in which it will be implemented. As you already know, curricular and assessment design decisions vary greatly by audience. For example, a virtual-world curriculum designed for middle school students is likely to be quite different from one aimed at undergraduate students, even if they are covering the same material. Consequently, you should look carefully at who will be using your curriculum. Describe their age range, gender make-up, incoming level of familiarity with the content you plan to teach, language level, and basic technology familiarity. You might also want to find out something about their attitudes toward and experience with computer games, especially virtual-world-based games. While you are at it, it is a very good idea to include any information you have about the teachers, instructors, trainers, or other facilitators who will be leading the implementation of your curriculum. Their experience, attitudes, and motivation toward using a virtual-world-based curriculum can influence how the curriculum is implemented, and most certainly impact your approach to design.

Equally important to consider is the intended instructional setting for your curriculum. In Chapter Eleven, we cover the many elements that need to be considered and handled when actually implementing an educational virtual world. Here, though, we are focused on the overall picture of where and under what circumstances your virtual world will be used. For example, will your world-based curriculum be used in a public school classroom? Will it be done as a voluntary online lesson? Will performance in the virtual world be graded? Will some form of test accompany the lesson, or will performance be automatically evaluated from within the world itself? Whatever the setting, you will want to consider and describe the benefits and potential challenges of implementing your virtual world in that setting.

Weather Trouble Example

For the Weather Trouble module, the team knew the module was going to be implemented in 7th grade classes in a large urban public school district, and in a neighboring suburban school district in the US. The modules would be implemented in tandem with weather-related curriculum taught in class:

> The audience for the Weather Trouble module will consist of 7th grade students in a large urban school district, and 7th grade students in a neighboring suburban district. There will

be roughly equal numbers of male and female students from a variety of ethnic backgrounds. Past surveys have found that nearly all the students in the participating classrooms have had at least some experience playing console games (Wii, Xbox, PlayStation) and/or computer-based video games. There is a sizable group of students whose first language is not English.

The assessment curriculum of Weather Trouble will be designed to match specific science standards of the state in which we implement the module, and aligned with several specific questions from the state-level standardized science assessment [the questions were included in the design document, but left out here]. Implementation of the module will take place after completion of related in-class curriculum on weather and weather systems. Students will complete the Weather Trouble module prior to taking in-class traditional tests on the same material. Participating students will not be graded on their performance in the Sheep Trouble module. Instead, data from their performance in the module will be compared to scores on related questions on their in-class tests, and on state standardized tests. Information on student actions in the virtual world module will be made available to participating teachers.

Learning Objectives

In writing your curriculum design document, you should clearly describe your overall learning goal(s) for the curriculum and indicate how you will determine whether/when a learner using your curriculum has achieved the objective(s). Before you begin the challenging work of creating a virtual world, you need to be certain that you and your team are very clear on what the overall learning objective is for your curriculum. Virtual worlds are not easy to build and creating an effective curriculum inside a virtual world is even more challenging. As we have described, a major motivation for creating a curriculum design document is to make sure that you really *should* be creating a virtual world in the first place. Writing an instructional problem statement and proposed solution help clarify whether you have a strong case for making a virtual world. An analysis of the audience and setting further bolsters your case. But the learning objective is, in a way, the final hurdle to pass. You should be able to clearly explain, in a few sentences, what your objective is and how it will be measured. If you can't do this, don't make a virtual world! Instead, go back to the drawing board and do some more thinking about what your objective really is. It is only after the goal is found to be clear, measurable, and a good fit for a virtual world that you should move forward with your design. In our experience, we have found that it is relatively easy to explicate a good objective. It is often much harder to explain how achievement of that objective will be measured.

Weather Trouble Example

The learning goal statement for Weather Trouble was difficult to construct because the virtual world was not designed to be a learning curriculum, but rather as a kind of situated test in which students could demonstrate how well they had learned the material from their in-class curricular unit on weather. With this in mind, the goal statement reads:

> Students completing the Weather Trouble module will be able to demonstrate the degree to which they have learned the content and processes related to weather as presented in their in-class curriculum on the topic. Demonstration of learning will be measured through analysis of a combination of in-world student behaviors and interactions with embedded data gathering and analysis tools, dialogs with in-world characters, and answers to questions posed within the module.

Virtual World Description

As part of your design document, you should include an overall description of the virtual world "treatment." Basically, this is a short overview of what your virtual world will be, what the curriculum will look like, and how long it will take a user to finish doing whatever you design into it. You can think of this as a "two-minute elevator speech" explaining your virtual world to somebody who has no idea what virtual worlds are. Focus on the look and feel, storyline, and timeframe. Will your virtual world be set in some specific time period, like the Middle Ages? What will your world look like? Will it be a serious-minded, realistic simulation of a real-world place or a fantastical quest set in an imaginary world? Will learners take on real-world roles or take on mythical personas? Will they complete a single large quest or undertake a series of tasks toward some ultimate goal? Will learners spend 30 minutes in your world, or 300 hours? Will learners work through your world by themselves or with other learners?

Again, your description here should not be long, and doesn't need to include deep levels of detail. Those will come later in the document. At this point, you want to paint a big picture view of your world.

Weather Trouble Example

Weather Trouble will be a single learner virtual world set in a mythical town in the Middle Ages. Learners will enter a virtual town that is suffering from a long-term spell of hot, dry weather. Learners, as time travelers from the present day, will be asked by the leader of the town to use their modern scientific knowledge and skills to help uncover the reasons for the long dry spell, to predict whether the weather will change soon, and if so to explain why. Learners will have 30 minutes to conduct their investigation and report back to the town leader. The look and feel of the town will be cartoonish, but fairly realistic. It will be populated by a number of townspeople (computer-based) with whom learners can conduct basic dialogs. Learners will be able to use a toolbox of instruments with which to take measurements of weather-related objects in the world. In addition, the town itself will include a number of embedded instruments and objects learners can interact with to assist with their investigation, such as thermometers, weather vanes, and a compass. Analysis of student use of these instruments, tools, and embedded characters will provide evidence for student learning.

TEST YOUR UNDERSTANDING

1. What is the main purpose of creating a curriculum design document? For whom is the curriculum design document created?
2. Given what you've learned about the mechanics of virtual worlds and the theories that drive their design and use, give an example of a curricular goal that might *not* work well when embedded into a virtual world.

Part 2: Design Details

In Part 2 of your curriculum design document, it is time to focus on the details. While the first part of the document centers on big-picture ideas of instructional problems and solutions, objectives, audience, settings, and offering an overview of the story of the curriculum, Part 2 provides "extreme detail" about the organization, structure, development timeline, and (sometimes) budget/personnel issues related to your curriculum.

For this part of our discussion, we will continue to use the Weather Trouble module as an example, explaining how elements of the document were created. But we won't include actual snippets from the document itself. Including these would add about 50 pages to this chapter, but wouldn't add much to the discussion.

Content Organization (Flowchart)

For the Design Details section of your design document, you should create a flowchart showing the overall organization of your curriculum, as well as details of the quests and tasks within the overall structure of the curriculum. In comparison to organizational flowcharts for procedural and/or presentational curricula, the charts for virtual-world-based curricula can be quite complex. As we have discussed in earlier chapters, the curriculum in virtual worlds often centers on open-ended exploration and discovery. Consequently, the curriculum is frequently non-linear and non-hierarchical. So how can one describe this kind of activity in a flowchart?

One approach is to start with a high-level flowchart that focuses on the overall organizational structure of the curriculum. This style of flowchart shows the structure of the overarching storyline of the virtual world, along with the main structure of any quests that occur as part of the curriculum. Then, in addition to the high-level flowchart, you can create a series of "sub-charts," each outlining the organizational structure of individual quests within the overall virtual-world structure. Continuing in this vein, you keep creating more levels of sub-charts to represent the organization of nested levels of curricular activities in your world until all the curriculum has been included.

More challenging, but equally important, is the creation of flowcharts showing the organizational structure for any GUI elements that will be included in your curriculum. Remember from our discussion of virtual-world mechanics that in-world activities frequently occur in conjunction with GUI tools overlaying the world.

Weather Trouble Example

Weather Trouble centers on a single main quest (to figure out whether an ongoing dry spell will continue and why or why not). Under the structural umbrella of the main quest, there are a number of tasks, or mini-quests, that learners can perform in order to complete the main quest. They can, for example, talk to NPCs in the virtual world to gather local insight on the drought. They can read new and back issues of the town newspaper to look at weather patterns over time. They can view dated paintings of the town showing it in different weather. They can check the temperature and wind direction in town. They can travel to nearby towns to check out weather conditions there. They can record notes in an e-notebook, and so on. To complete the assessment, students can decide at any time to return to the town leader (the NPC who first greets them when they arrive in the world), report their findings, and answer a few questions.

The flowchart for the Weather Trouble world would show all of these elements, providing organizational details for how each will work. More realistically, a member of the design team (most likely the instructional designer/team leader) would create a series of linked flowcharts using a flowchart software program such as Microsoft Visio (see: http://office.microsoft.com/en-us/visio) or SmartDraw (see: www.smartdraw.com). Many excellent open-source tools exist as well, such as Xmind (www.xmind.net). Linked flowcharts allow the design and development teams both to see the overall structure of the curriculum, as well as zoom in on individual tasks and sub-quests to visualize their structure as implemented in a virtual world.

Content Description

Along with a flowchart, your curriculum design document should include a description of the content and story of your virtual world, keyed to the components of your flowchart. Here you can go into more detail about what a learner will experience in the virtual world, from beginning to end. Depending on the complexity of your virtual world, this description can be simple or very complicated. You are working to produce a description of the story of your curriculum that provides enough detail that everyone on the design/development team understands what will occur in the curriculum. It is critical that the team understands, and agrees with, the main points of the virtual world and its curriculum.

There are a number of common elements likely to appear in your description, including an opening, quest descriptions, rules and rewards, and conclusion/wrap-up.

Opening: World Entry and Greeting

How will the learner enter into the virtual world, and what kind of greeting will they receive when they enter? How will your story begin? Will the learner simply appear in the middle of a virtual world, or will she be guided into the world and the story of the world through some form of introduction? It is often a good idea to start your curriculum with a video, an in-game cut-scene, or even a simple text-based story outline that introduces the story of the virtual world to the learner. This helps orient the learner to the world, its goals, and her role in the game. A guided introduction to the world and its story is particularly important for virtual worlds that will be implemented in schools or company settings, since the amount of time set aside for users to complete the curriculum embedded in them is frequently limited compared to the time afforded for completing curriculum in less formal settings.

Weather Trouble Example

In Weather Trouble, learners login through a standard login screen and then choose their character (male or female). Students can modify the appearance of their character, including the color of his/her clothes, skin, and hair; and by selecting a character name from a drop-down box. After choosing and customizing their avatar, learners are introduced to the Weather Trouble story via a short text box that tells the story of the world, and asks for their help (Figure 8.2). The story outline mentions that "Farmer Brown" needs their help. Farmer Brown is an NPC that learners will encounter as soon as they enter the world, and who will give them their main quest.

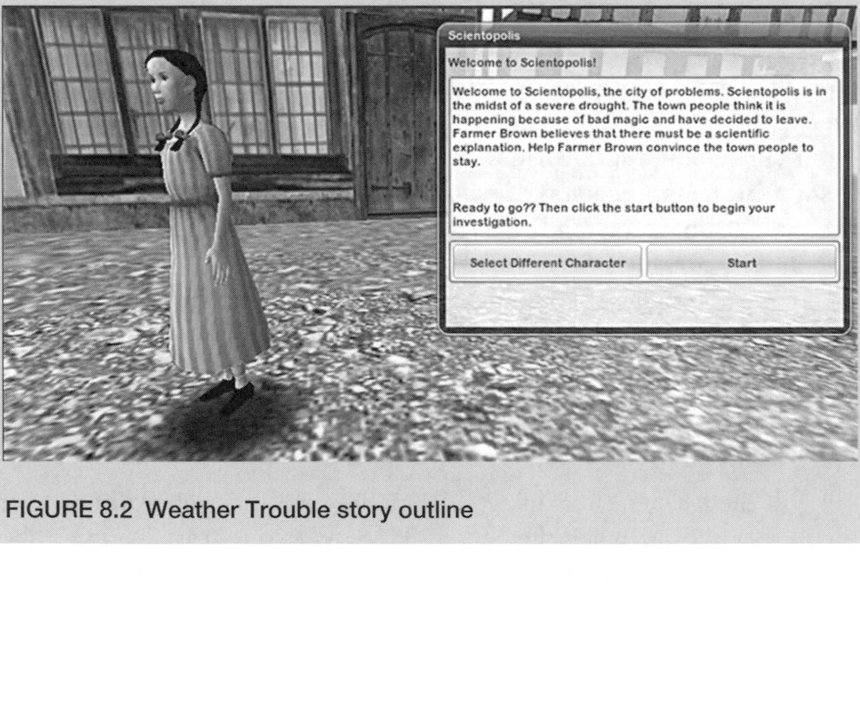

FIGURE 8.2 Weather Trouble story outline

Quest/Task Descriptions

The bulk of your content description is likely to be centered on detailed quest descriptions. If you create a collection of flowcharts to demonstrate the organizational structure of your world, each quest will be represented in its own flowchart. Your description of each quest can follow the structure of the flowchart for that quest, including similar categories as the overall organizational structure: quest opening/introduction, quest task descriptions, quest rules and rewards, and quest conclusions. For each quest, learners are given specific tasks to complete, clear rules and mechanisms for completing the tasks, and explicit feedback when a given quest or task is completed.

Rules and Rewards

In designing and describing tasks that make up a given virtual-world curriculum, it is important to describe the rules for completing each task, and to decide if you will include rewards for completion (or failed attempt) of each task. The rules are simply the goals of the quest along with the structure for how those tasks can (and/or should) be done in the virtual world. In practice, describing the rules for the tasks of your curriculum results in a series of narrative "stories" of the quests. These stories should match the task structure included in any flowcharts you create, and act to provide a readable guide to the activities shown in the flowcharts. Your description of the rules for the tasks of virtual-world quests also provides a textual counterpart to any storyboards or prototypes that you include in your curriculum design document.

In addition to rules governing the tasks of your curriculum, you might choose to include, and thus need to describe, a rewards system. Most commercial virtual-world-based games include rewards for task completion. Rewards are a classic tool in behavioral curriculum: perform a specified behavior correctly and receive positive reinforcement in the form of a reward of some kind. Rewards in traditional instructional software can be as simple as a "Good job!" feedback message and/or some awarded points. In virtual worlds, rewards can be equally simple or can be much, much more complex. A full discussion of the many forms of reward systems in virtual worlds is beyond the scope of our discussion here. But in brief, some typical forms of rewards to consider using in your virtual world might include: points, medals, "money," inventory items, and "fun stuff." Points, money, and medals are straightforward: complete a task and get some points, cash, or a medal. You can define levels of success in completing a given task and then adjust the number of points or medal level (gold, silver, bronze) depending on levels of success achieved in a given task. The rewards can be stand-alone, or can be used as a kind of in-game currency with which learners can buy special objects: weapons, tools, avatar customization items, etc. The points/money/ medals might also be used to "level up" learners: giving them additional powers in the virtual world or simply identifying them as having achieved a certain level of expertise.

Inventory items are also frequently offered as rewards for successful task completion. In educational virtual worlds, these inventory items are often tools that the learner can use to support their efforts in completing subsequent tasks in the curriculum. Finally, rewards for task completion might simply consist of "fun stuff" that learners can use as they explore the world. This might consist of avatar customization elements, special vehicles, or other objects unrelated to the goals of the game but that add to learner engagement. For example, in the educational virtual world Whyville, learners earn virtual money as they complete activities. This money can be used to buy clothes and other adornments that can be applied to their avatars to personalize their appearance.

Storyboards

Along with your content description and flowcharts, your team might want to create a series of storyboards to help demonstrate the look and feel of key elements in your curriculum. These do not need to be incredibly professional works of art. Instead, the goal of creating storyboards should be to allow the team to talk over visual ideas for the curriculum quickly and at low cost. As with your content description, the point of the storyboards is not to pre-visualize every single moment of your planned curriculum, but instead to provide the design/development team with visuals to react to when making early decisions about the curriculum and its design. Celtx (www.celtx. com/index.html) is an open-source storyboarding tool (and so much more, actually) that has taken the media production world by storm. It is quite easy to learn, and you can even make storyboards using any digital camera, no drawing required!

An alternative to storyboards involves drawing out a 2D map of your virtual world, showing the placement of objects, buildings, and characters. A more interactive version of this approach involves creating a 2D map of the world, buildings, and other stationary objects, and then using that map as a kind of stage to playtest curricular ideas. Your team can move characters and objects around on a kind of board game version of your virtual world, acting out the curriculum. This paper version of your world can be used as you move into the development stage as well, to convey ideas directly and interactively to the development team.

With modern virtual-world development tools, it is sometimes possible to mock-up quick scenes in a virtual world, and then include snapshots of those scenes in your design document. This approach is tricky, as your team might be tempted to go beyond basic stick-figure-level visuals and create full-blown 3D models, landscapes, and screen elements in a virtual world-authoring tool.

Weather Trouble Example

Weather Trouble was created based on worlds already built and implemented for previous related assessments. Consequently, as we will discuss in the chapter on developing virtual worlds, the design team was able to take a few short cuts. Rather than doing storyboards on paper, the curriculum team worked closely with the development team to quickly produce a mock-up virtual world, using elements from an existing virtual world. The design and development teams then completed a couple rounds of quick review and revision of ideas for the world look and feel, and for proposed interactions in the main, and only, quest.

Estimated Development Timeline, Personnel, and Budget

By now, you are probably realizing that designing a virtual-world-based curriculum is a major undertaking! Honestly, though, it isn't dramatically more complicated than creating any other curriculum that incorporates similar concepts and tasks. However, when you are working on the curriculum design document for a virtual world, you need to think carefully about how much time and resources will be needed to actually build the curriculum you describe. The fidelity of your virtual world to the curriculum design is tightly connected to the amount of time, person power, and money you have. You may describe a truly outstanding curriculum that is a perfect fit for a virtual world, only to realize that the curriculum you have designed will take a year to develop and require a small army of developers. In the real world of virtual worlds for learning, you usually need to make some kind of compromise on the scale and scope of your curricular ambitions to match the human, time, and financial resources at your disposal.

Consequently, when you are putting together a curriculum design document, you should include a detailed development timeline and budget. Your estimated timeline should be based on several factors including: scope of the curriculum you design; available developers, their skill level, and their available time to work on the project; and resources available in terms of software and hardware, or the money to buy these things.

Weather Trouble Example

Weather Trouble, designed as one of a series of related worlds, did not have its own separate development budget. The design and development team members were primarily university students, on salary as research assistants. The module development timetable was set at 30 days. This is a very fast development schedule. As we have mentioned, though, Weather Trouble was designed and developed as one of a series of related virtual worlds. These worlds shared a common look and feel, common objects, common code, etc. Consequently, the estimated timeline for development could be fairly short. That 30-day window was to produce a first alpha version of the world. At that point, the virtual world was distributed to the team for a round of testing. We'll talk more about this process in the chapter on development.

Conclusion

As you have seen, the curriculum design process for creating a virtual world shares many components with designing any other form of learning curriculum: learning goals, audience and setting information, assessment ideas, etc. For virtual worlds, you also have flowcharts, quest descriptions, storyboards/prototype examples, timelines, and budgets.

In our discussion here, we have included everything but the kitchen sink to provide you with a full picture of elements to consider as you design your own virtual-world curriculum. However, in the real world of design you are probably going to skip some of these elements. For example, you may have no budget to think about. You might forego storyboarding, and instead describe your curriculum purely through text. The key is to make sure that you have thought through as many of the details related to your design as possible to avoid any problems when you get to the development stage.

In this chapter, we have also presented the curriculum design process as separate from the development process, but, in reality, the design and development teams are likely to work in parallel with each other. Doing so helps prevent problems that can occur when a curriculum design idea doesn't match well with the functionalities available in a virtual world. We'll talk about this more in the upcoming virtual-world development chapter.

TEST YOUR UNDERSTANDING

In addition to storyboards, how can you describe/demonstrate the look and feel of your virtual world? What are the strengths and weaknesses of creating storyboards versus other ways of describing and showing the details of your virtual world?

LEARNING ACTIVITIES

Write a tightly scoped, specific learning goal and produce a full design document for a curricular unit to achieve that goal in a virtual world. Base the curriculum design parameters (audience, setting, scope, etc.) on your actual setting.

References

Alessi, S. & Trollip, S. (2001). *Multimedia for Learning: Methods and development*, 3rd Edition. Needham, MA: Allyn & Bacon.

Nelson, B., Ketelhut, D. J., & Schifter, C. (2010). Exploring cognitive load in immersive educational games: The SAVE Science Project. *International Journal for Gaming and Computer Mediated Simulations 2(1)*, 31–39.

Links

Celtx is an open-source storyboarding tool (and so much more, actually) that has taken the media production world by storm: www.celtx.com/index.html

SmartDraw: a good, relatively inexpensive flowchart-making software: www.smartdraw.com

Visio: a good but expensive flowchart-making software package: http://office.microsoft.com/en-us/visio

Xmind is an excellent open-source tool for creating flowcharts: www.xmind.net

---

Other Resources

Applied Research in Virtual Environments for Learning Special Interest Group (ARVEL). This group, associated with the American Educational Research Association, is a very active collection of people who are designing virtual worlds for learning. Their website offers a great collection of tips for designing curriculum, creating worlds, and running implementations. http://arvelsig.ning.com

nine
Designing Measures for Assessment with Virtual Worlds

Introduction

In Chapter Six, we provided a thorough conceptual overview of measurement and assessment in virtual worlds. If you are unfamiliar with these concepts, or just need a quick refresher, please do read that chapter before diving in here. There will be some conceptual overlap in this chapter, but only with the intention to continually bridge between theory and practice—and not enough to forego the necessity of reading the previous chapter. This chapter covers the design pragmatics for evaluation, assessment, and measurement with and within virtual worlds for learning, concluding with a brief section about the adoption and adaptation of existing measurement instruments for use in virtual worlds.

Designing Virtual Worlds for Evaluation

As we've already established, to ensure that learning is occurring in the virtual world in the way you wish, you must evaluate learner outcomes in some way. Remember the evaluation, assessment, and measurement connection we talked about earlier? In this case, as you design or acquire virtual worlds with the specific intent of evaluating one or more learning outcomes, there are several questions you must pose as you begin the design process. What is being evaluated, and why? In order to conduct these evaluations, what must be assessed, and how? In order to make appropriate assessment decisions, what must be measured, and how? In this section, we shall address each of these concerns in order, and the two sections following will further explore assessment and measurement, respectively.

Evaluation

What is being evaluated with or in your virtual world, and why? Based on the title of this book, one can assume that learning is one (or more) of the outcomes being evaluated, and perhaps one or more of the aspects of the virtual world is being evaluated as well. Before making decisions about the assessment techniques and measurement instrumentation necessary for accomplishing the evaluation process, you should ask yourself at least two questions about each different aspect that you intend to evaluate: what (or which) and why? Let's consider these questions for both learning and virtual worlds.

Which aspect(s) of learning is (are) being evaluated and why? Or, to approach this from another perspective, how have you conceptualized "learning?" In the context of your intended evaluation, what are learners going to do or show through their actions in the virtual world, or demonstrate via questions or actions associated with the virtual world to demonstrate that they have learned constructs X, Y, and Z? Or, what must change about the learner to show that learning has occurred? For each of the examples, demonstrations, or changes in learners that you intend to evaluate, you should carefully consider *why* you want to evaluate them. What is it about the examples, demonstrations, and changes you choose that makes them relevant to learning? If you can't find an answer to the "why" question, then it's likely that the aspect in question should not be evaluated in the context of your current intentions for evaluating learning.

In addition to evaluating learning, you might decide to evaluate the virtual world itself. In Chapter Seven, we also described one possible framework for evaluating existing virtual worlds as platforms for learning. If you decide to evaluate a virtual world following this or some other framework, you will want to carefully consider which aspect(s) of virtual worlds is (are) being evaluated and why? For example, are you evaluating the immersive nature of virtual worlds, the technological functionality of virtual worlds, the use of virtual worlds as an alternative to traditional pen-and-paper testing, or perhaps the use of virtual worlds as constructivist open worlds for exploratory problem solving? Are virtual worlds relevant to the aspect(s) of learning that you intend to evaluate? Has this relevance been established, or is part of your intent to evaluate the relevance of virtual worlds for this specific type of learning (i.e., this particular subject domain or demographic of learners)? Whether or not relevance has been established, how is each aspect of virtual worlds (such as those described above) specifically related to each of the aspects of learning that you intend to evaluate?

One good approach to creating an evaluation plan that covers both learning and your virtual world is to create a list of aspects and outcomes that you intend to evaluate, with two columns: one for learning, and one for the virtual world (see Figure 9.1). After you list the aspects and/or outcomes in each column, draw lines between them to cross-reference items from each column, based on relevance and relationships you've established by answering questions posed above. This mapping process will likely help you to get a better picture of what it is that you're *actually* going to need to evaluate based on your original intentions. The connections that emerge across columns will help you to set up an appropriate framework for assessment and measurement that should greatly improve your approach to evaluation in a way that ensures you're actually evaluating both learning and virtual worlds in a way that fully accomplishes your goals.

As you can see in Figure 9.1, there can be quite a bit of overlap across the two sides of your list. Once you're sure you've nailed down what it is you're really evaluating, you've got to facilitate the evaluation process with assessment decisions.

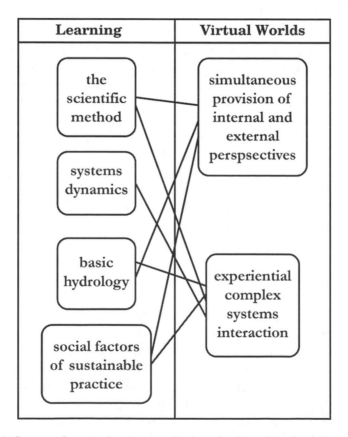

FIGURE 9.1 Cross-referenced outcomes for learning in a virtual world

Assessment (Decisions)

A more thorough exploration of assessment will occur in the next section of the chapter: Designing Assessments for Implementation With or Within Virtual Worlds. However, for the sake of putting assessment decisions[1] into the context of the initial process of designing virtual worlds for evaluation, several quick questions can be addressed, including what, when, where, how, and who is involved in the assessment decision-making process to ensure that the evaluation process is conducted as intended—based on your design.

First, *which* assessment decisions need to be made to ensure the evaluation is conducted as intended? Think again of the connection between evaluation, assessment, and measurement: evaluation outcomes (or goals) lead to construct definitions for assessment (which, in turn, lead to measurement instrumentation). As you consider your evaluation design, you must consider which decisions need to be made about defined constructs to ensure evaluation outcomes are appropriately addressed.

Second, *when* do assessment decisions occur to ensure the evaluation is conducted as intended? The answer(s) to this question depend on the nature of the constructs being assessed to evaluate the chosen outcomes. Should the assessment decisions occur *before*, *during*, or *after* a learner's engagement with a virtual world? Most likely, the timing of decisions will involve a combination of the three. Also, *how often* should the assessment decisions occur (before, during, and/or after a learner's engagement)?

To help answer these "when" questions, let's consider an example of an evaluation design that contains outcomes associated with two different spaces of learning: learning *in* the world vs. learning *because* of the world. To evaluate outcomes of learning that should be occurring in the virtual world (i.e., as the learner actually engages with the virtual world), assessment decisions about constructs associated with these outcomes should probably happen during the learner's engagement with the world—and most likely (depending on the specific nature of the constructs) before and after as well. Further, how often should assessment decisions occur during the learner's engagement with the world for these "in-world" learning outcomes to be appropriately evaluated? At least once, of course, but it might be necessary to make multiple in-world assessment decisions, depending on the constructs being assessed to fulfill the goals of evaluation.

To evaluate outcomes that should occur as a product of the learner's engagement with the virtual world, assessment decisions about constructs associated with these outcomes should probably happen before and after the learner's engagement with the world. Typically, "pre-world" assessment decisions would be made to categorize learners in preparation for engagement with dynamic versions of the virtual world that are modified to support these learners with varied levels of the traits associated with the constructs you're assessing (based on your evaluation plan). Obviously, at least one round of assessment decisions "post-world" is necessary to evaluate each learner's status (and change in traits, etc.) based on his or her experiences interacting within the virtual-world environment. However, for the evaluation of certain constructs—such as those associated with deep learning and transfer (among others)—it would be a good idea to consider additional "post-world" assessments at various intervals following engagement (e.g., weeks and months later) if feasible.

Third, *where* do assessment decisions occur to ensure the evaluation is conducted as intended? This might seem like a strange question to ask, but where assessment decisions need to occur can play an integral role in the process of drafting your evaluation plan. Decisions require tools and evidence, and the location of those decisions can substantially affect the logistics of tool use and evidence delivery (in service of assessment decisions). Let's briefly explore these locational logistics for assessment decisions that might be made before, during, and after a learner's engagement with a virtual world.

Where should assessment decisions occur before a learner's engagement with a virtual world? Logistically, what works best for the tools and spaces you have at your disposal for your approach to evaluation? Who is making the assessment decisions, and where are the decisions happening? Is it a different location from that of the learner? How do these logistical issues apply differently or similarly to assessment decisions that might be made during or after a learner's engagement with a virtual world?

Fourth, *how* must assessment decisions actually happen to ensure the evaluation is conducted as intended? Or, to put it another way, what is the mechanism for the decision-making process? How does the decision maker form and communicate his or her decisions? How is this process different if the decision maker is a computer software application? Once the pragmatics of the decision-making process are settled, as an evaluation planner you must also decide which decisions must be made by the assessor to properly conduct the intended evaluation. Or to take a different perspective, which assessment decisions are relevant to the intended evaluation, and which are not?

Finally, *who* needs to be involved in assessment decisions to ensure the evaluation is conducted as intended? Who is making the final authoritative decision(s) about the evidence collected for an individual learner under evaluation? Are multiple parties involved in the decision-making process? If so, is there a hierarchy amongst the decision makers? Are humans and computers both involved in the decision-making process, or is it one or the other? Are those being evaluated also contributing in the decision-making process through one or more self-assessment procedures?

As you can see, there is the potential for quite a bit of overlap when considering the where, when, and how of assessment decisions in service of evaluation with (or of) virtual worlds. Also, the combination of *who* is making the assessment decisions and about *what* they are making assessment decisions substantially influences the where, when, and how of assessment decisions as you formulate your design for the development or acquisition of virtual worlds for evaluation of learning. Not only do the who and what of assessment decisions heavily influence the other logistical aspects of assessment, they also directly affect the choices you as an evaluation designer must make about measurement instrumentation.

Measurement

As with the previous subsection on assessment, to put measurement instrumentation into the context of the initial process of designing virtual worlds for evaluation, the same what, when, where, how, and who questions can be addressed concerning the relationship between measurement and evaluation to ensure that the evaluation is conducted as intended—based on your design. Many of the questions can be explored using the example of a simple ruler used to measure length (Figure 9.2).

First, *what* must be measured to ensure evaluation is conducted as intended? Based on your evaluation design, what are the constructs you've defined for the requisite assessment decisions? Based on your definitions, what actually

FIGURE 9.2 A folding ruler

needs to be measured? Remember, learning cannot be directly measured. Consider learning to be a complicated type of growth. If you measure a person's growth in terms of change in height or girth, you would most likely measure the length or width of the person to begin assessing the person's growth in these dimensions.

Second, *when* must measurements occur to ensure evaluation is conducted as intended—before, during, and/or after the learner's engagement with the virtual world? Remember, assessment decisions require reliable evidence, which comes from measurement instruments (such as the ruler). Since the evidence must be delivered to the assessor before he or she (or it) makes the decision(s), when must these instruments be implemented in order to facilitate appropriately timed assessment decisions? For example, if a carpenter needs to cut boards a specific length, should she measure the boards before or after cutting?

Third, *where* must measurements occur to ensure evaluation is conducted as intended? Measurements can be conducted within or outside the boundaries of the virtual world. As you formulate your evaluation design, you must take into account the locational logistics of measurement so as to best facilitate the collection of evidence in a manner that is reliable for the types of assessment decisions that must be made. Considering the ruler example: to measure the length of an object, you must hold the ruler flush with the object. If you hold the ruler at some distance from the object, the length data (evidence) you collect isn't as reliable. When measuring to collect evidence about changes in a learner within and because of a virtual world, you must consider strategic placement of the necessary measurement instrumentation to best collect the necessary evidence: in the virtual world, outside the virtual world, or most likely some combination of the two. Of course, make sure you justify your strategy through alignment with assessment decisions in service of evaluation goals.

Fourth, *how* should measurements happen to ensure evaluation is conducted as intended? Or, in other words, how does the instrumentation function, and how does this functionality affect the assessment process in service of your evaluation design? Considering the ruler example: how should you hold the ruler to make sure you can still read the numbers when you measure an object? Do you also need to hold the object in a certain position to ensure that accurate, precise measurement can occur (for the collection of reliable evidence)? You must consider the specific mechanics of chosen measurement instrumentation and how these mechanics will affect the learning and assessment processes taking place.

Finally, *who* does the measuring to ensure evaluation is conducted as intended? Someone (or a computer) must conduct the measurement operations necessary for evidence collection. In other words, who holds the ruler? Is the assessor also the measurer, or are two separate entities involved? Is this always the case, or does the protocol (and its inherent roles) change depending on the context of assessment in service of your chosen evaluation design? If more than one entity is involved, how does the communication process work between the assessor(s) and the measurer(s)? Are the measurer(s) and assessor(s) human or machine?

As noted in the previous section, there is quite a bit of overlap when addressing these questions about measurement in service of evaluation planning. Similarly, the influence amongst factors of measurement is substantial. Additionally, the influence between measurement and assessment must not be ignored. While we've briefly addressed assessment and measurement in service of evaluation, there are additional considerations to be made when crafting your evaluation design.

Additional Evaluation Considerations

While the possibilities for additional considerations to be made with your evaluation plan are limitless, here we can focus on a single issue as an example of what else should be considered as you formulate your evaluation design. In addition to the evaluation of learning, you might decide to evaluate the relationship between the learner and the virtual world. In this case, the relationship in question can be seen as the "user experience"—or UX—that the learner has while engaging with the world.

Of course, the UX can be a significant factor in a learner's engagement with in-world content. It is important to know if the virtual world provides an inherently poor UX for users (learners), as a poor experience typically leads to less user engagement, which can inhibit any learning that is intended to occur while a learner should be engaging with in-world content. However, simultaneous UX testing and evaluation of learning within and because of virtual worlds—with both procedures conducted at a level of acceptable quality—is extremely difficult to achieve. Specifically, asking a user (learner) to evaluate UX aspects of the virtual world while they are in it breaks the immersive state that is desired for authentic assessment of learning as they engage with the in-world content. So, as you make decisions in the process of developing or acquiring a virtual world to meet the needs of your evaluation plan, do not plan on evaluating the UX of the world at the same time that you will be conducting the procedures necessary to carry out your evaluation of learning outcomes. This is not to say that UX evaluation should be overlooked—especially if you are developing a new virtual world to meet the needs of your evaluation plan.

There are potentially many other issues you will take into consideration as you craft your evaluation plan. As with any other design process, it can be helpful to show your design plan to other people—both designers and those with other types of expertise—to receive feedback from multiple perspectives. It's best to leave no stone unturned, as you never know what you might find under that last stone—perhaps some factor that will make or break your overall evaluation process.

Designing Assessments for Implementation With or Within Virtual Worlds

Remember: assessments are decisions about interpretations of evidence. When it comes to designing virtual worlds for the purposes of assessment, there are basically two ways in which these worlds can be used for assessment: decisions can occur separate from the virtual world experience, or in conjunction with (or in other words, within) the learner's virtual world experience. Additionally, these assessments can be conducted, and decisions can be made about them, by either human beings or machines (Table 9.1).

In any case, there are several key elements of the assessment decision process—whether they occur with or within virtual worlds, made by humans or machines—that we will describe in detail here: evidence and interpretation, the meaning of interpretations and their resulting decisions, and putting the decisions to use. Each of these key elements will be illustrated using the same example: a virtual-world-based driving simulation.

Evidence and Interpretation

Of course, as a decision-making process, assessment involves some form of interpretation of data collected as evidence about an individual learner. In our driving simulation example, a learner, James, must pass several tests built into the simulation to receive a certificate that allows him to engage in a real driving examination. One such test involves James' ability to parallel

Table 9.1 Variations in Decisions and Decision Makers

	Separate from World	Within World
Human	A teacher chooses and assigns a different virtual activity for each student in her classroom based on current test scores of each student.	A human-controlled mentor character decides which tasks to assign an apprentice character in a current quest based on the immediate prior performance of the apprentice.
Machine	At a science center kiosk, a learner enters extant data (such as demographics and grade level) into a digital form, and the computer program uses these data to unlock certain aspects of the ensuing virtual environment at appropriate levels of difficulty.	A computer program unlocks increasingly difficult levels of a 3D puzzle simulation as a learner progresses in his or her ability to solve these puzzles.

park three different sized vehicles—a compact car, a station wagon, and an oversized SUV—in a regulation-sized street parking space (Figure 9.3). For each vehicle, he must park between two other vehicles on a city street without breaking any traffic laws, without hitting either of the two other vehicles or the curb, using a minimal number of forward and backward movements—all within a specified amount of time.

How is the interpretation of evidence of James' simulated parking performance going to happen, and how must the evidence be prepared in order for the interpretations to take place? Who will make the decisions for interpretation of James' parking performance? Will it be humans, machines, or some combination of the two? Machines could easily make decisions about whether or not James collided his vehicle with the other parked vehicles, made too many moves, or took too much time. Each of these are discrete quantitative values that involve binary "yes/no" decisions. Computers thrive on binary decision-making. Humans might make decisions about the overall quality of James' combined performance across all three vehicles. Did he do better with the smaller vehicle or the bigger vehicle, and why? Humans can handle higher-order interpretive decisions better than computers (for now, anyway). Perhaps that is a good way to delineate between the potential responsibilities of humans and machines as you design assessments for your virtual world: the who, the what, the when, and the where questions are based on more discrete variables that can be interpreted by machines, whereas the how and the why questions are more complex, and humans are still a better fit for these interpretations.

FIGURE 9.3 Parallel parking in Washington, DC (with a little help from a friend!)

When will the interpretive decisions be made? How soon after measurements are implemented and data are collected must decisions occur? Does the relative temporal proximity of measurement to decision-making require that these decisions occur within the timeframe that the learner engages with the virtual world? In the case of James' parallel parking performances, are there any time-sensitive assessment decisions that must be made between each of his three attempts with different vehicles? Consider also the learner's time before and after engaging with the virtual world—such as pre-tests and post-tests. Assuming that James must past a preliminary examination before gaining access to the driving simulation, then interpretive decisions about evidence collected from his pre-test must be made quite soon after he completes the exam, especially if the general expectation is that learners complete a pre-test, the driving simulation, and a post-test all in one continuous session. Many designers solve this temporal issue by making preliminary decisions about acceptable percentages of correct answers which represent a level of quality acceptable for a learner's continuation to the next phase. However, this may or may not be the case, depending on your specific situation, so be prepared to spend some time during your design process accounting for this issue.

Finally, what will it take to turn data into decisions? In other words, how much work is necessary to prepare the evidence collected about James' parallel parking performances so that the evidence is in a form appropriate for use by the interpretive decision maker(s)? If machines are making decisions, the raw quantitative values representing physical attributes of James' performance might suffice, so long as the virtual world is programmed in a way that understands these numbers in such a format. If humans are making decisions, a bit more semantic information (or metadata) might be useful in the decision-making process. So, in the process of designing the transition from measured data to meaningful evidence, you should consider the following for your assessments: What is the evidence necessary for the assessment decisions, and how must that evidence be prepared and delivered? To whom must this evidence be delivered, and when?

Decisions and Meaning

Interpretations of evidence—and the resulting assessment decisions—pertaining to a learner's performance have substantial meaning. The outcomes of certain decisions carry much more weight than others, of course, but every single assessment decision made about a learner—whether that decision is made by a human being or a machine—has some level of impact on the learner's current experience, and, likely, his or her future. As you design your assessments for learning in virtual worlds, keep in mind what impact these assessment decisions have upon the learner. Assessments must not inhibit the learning process.

How important is the evaluation for which the learner is being assessed? What does it mean if a learner passes the assessment? Will he or she be certified to operate machinery that is potentially dangerous for themselves or others? If James doesn't pass the driving simulation, will he still be able to legally drive a vehicle? If he doesn't pass the parallel parking test, will he still be able to pass the rest of the simulation assessments, and if so, does failing the parallel parking test prevent him from receiving a driver's license? Depending on your own enthusiasm for motorist safety, these questions may seem more or less important. Consider, however, a virtual world that features emergency response scenarios for paramedic trainees, or a virtual world that teaches harbor navigation to oil tanker captains. In each case, different stakes—or levels of accountability—for the assessment decisions are involved, both human and ecological. You certainly wouldn't want a paramedic who failed the emergency response training to be first on the scene after James (who subsequently failed the driving simulation) manages to knock you off your bicycle as he swerves haphazardly into a parking spot, careening through the clearly marked bike lane.

Finally, does the fact that a machine (instead of a human) is making a particular interpretive assessment decision change the meaning of that decision? If so, how much of a difference does it make? Well, that's for you to decide, but the ramifications of the extent of this difference in meaning should be heavily considered as you design your assessments for your intended evaluations.

Beyond Decisions

Regardless of the meaning of the interpretive decision(s) made about collected evidence—and regardless of who (or what) makes the decision(s)—the last issue to be considered when designing assessments for implementation with or within virtual worlds is to decide if a given assessment decision leads to a change in the virtual world itself and, if so, when should that change occur. In other words, once an assessment decision has been made, should changes to the virtual world be implemented to present an appropriately timed response to the learner, and if so how quickly? Of course, it is possible that no changes to the virtual world will be necessary—especially in the case of assessments occurring after the learner has concluded his or her engagement with the virtual world scenario.

In any case, the heart of the issue in question is something called the learning-assessment-guidance loop, or the LAG loop (Figure 9.4). Ideally, assessments should be designed so that interpretive decisions can serve as an efficient and effective bridge that facilitates the connection between learning processes and appropriate support systems (guidance). In Figure 9.4, the spiral represents the path of a single learner through a single virtual world in one contiguous session.

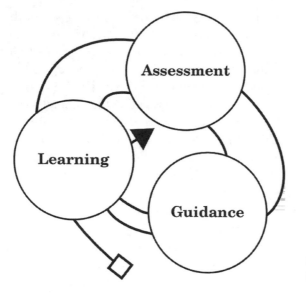

FIGURE 9.4 A hypothetical
LAG loop for a single learner

Depending upon the intended evaluation procedure, the way the LAG loop is implemented for assessment with or within virtual worlds can vary quite drastically from one scenario to the next. For example, it might be the case that no post-assessment guidance is intended to be implemented for the learner as he or she engages with a particular virtual-world scenario. Table 9.2 presents different scenarios for implementing the LAG loop with and within virtual worlds. Each of the scenarios shown in the table displays one of potentially many iterative cycles of learner engagement and assessment.

As you may see in Table 9.2, when designing virtual worlds for learning, there are two main questions to ask about the LAG loop: (1) where is the loop, and (2) how tight is the loop? For example, in Scenario 1.1, the learner is assessed before and after engagement in the virtual world, but not during his or her engagement—and no guidance is delivered within the virtual world. In this case, the LAG loop doesn't exist, so the answer to both questions is "not applicable." Scenario 1.2 includes a second engagement for the

Table 9.2 A Selection of LAG Scenarios

LAG Loop Scenarios	
1. Assessment *with* Virtual Worlds	**2. Assessment *within* Virtual Worlds**
Scenario 1.1: A → {L} → A	Scenario 2.1: A → {LAG} → A?
Scenario 1.2: A → {L} → A → {G?}	Scenario 2.2: A → {LA} → A? → {G}

A = Assessment; G = Guidance; L = Learning
{} = Duration of a learner's singular contiguous engagement within a virtual world

learner with the virtual world, in which some form of guidance is provided post-assessment. In this case, the LAG loop fits loosely (how tight?) across multiple visits (where?) to the world(s). Scenario 2.1 contains a tighter LAG loop that occurs within a singular engagement of the virtual world by the learner. Scenario 2.2 contains a looser LAG loop that occurs over one or more sessions of learner engagement (depending on whether or not the intermediate "out of world" assessments are conducted).

Can you think of ways that each of the four scenarios displayed in Table 9.2 might apply to James' virtual driving scenario? Further, can you think of realistic educational scenarios that match each of the scenarios displayed? Obviously there are many combinations of engagement and assessment missing from Table 9.2. Can you think of any specific examples that aren't represented? This brief exercise should reify the concept that—as we've mentioned in other chapters—different contexts require different approaches to the engagement assessment cycle. For example, in Scenario 1.2, it is entirely possible that the post-assessment guidance takes the form of a paper workbook (or digital document) assembled dynamically for the individual learner—or perhaps the guidance comes in the form of in-world discussions led by the teacher. Even in the 21st century, the most advanced technologies are not always the best solution for every problem. Keep this in mind as you design your assessments. And, of course, remember to keep in mind that you must have good measurement tools to make good assessment decisions.

Designing Measures for Use in Virtual Worlds

There is a plethora of literature available for appropriate design of traditional measurement instruments (i.e., paper-based tests), so the focus of this section of the chapter is strictly upon designing measures for collecting evidence during the time that a learner engages with the virtual-world scenario—in-world measurement. Three major issues are addressed: which data should be collected as evidence, how much data is too much data, and, finally, efficient and effective collection of evidence through in-world measurement.

In order to make the assessment decisions necessary for adhering to the intended evaluation plan, which data (if any) must be collected as the learner engages with the virtual world? First, revisit the constructs defined in your assessment plan. Is the nature of one or more of these constructs such that evidence about changes in these constructs must be gathered synchronous to the learner's engagement with the learning scenario presented in the virtual world? If so, then in-world measurement instrumentation should be considered, and an in-world data collection plan should be folded into the design process before commencing development of the virtual-world application. To structure this data collection plan, consider again the constructs identified as necessitating in-world measurement. Specifically, which evidence is needed about a learner to assess in-world changes in his or her traits directly associated with these identified constructs?

Of course, *how* to collect the necessary data as evidence should also be considered. Unfortunately, the vast range of computer programming approaches to collect specific types of in-world performance evidence is beyond the scope of this book. Even so, the issue of whether or not the evidence you'd like to collect actually can be collected should be addressed as early as possible in the design process. For example, consider again the driving simulation world: you're counting on the ability to collect evidence about a learner's high-speed pursuit driving ability using a measurement instrument built into the fabric of the virtual-world experience—one that relies heavily on the recording of real-time simulated physics of the vehicle. The end of the development cycle arrives and you find out that it's technically impossible to build the tools necessary for such in-world evidence collection—or perhaps the time and money allocated for the project development have been exhausted—and you've failed to include a backup plan for assessing these constructs. Depending on the stakes of the assessment of these particular constructs, this lack of ability to collect evidence about controlled high-speed pursuit driving could be a disaster!

Beyond whether or not data *can* be collected in-world during a learner's engagement with it, the more important question is whether or not it *should* be collected. Just because a given kind of evidence can be collected doesn't mean it should be. As you create your data collection plan, ethics of data collection should always trump technological advancement; always consider the morality of when, where, and how the data (and which data) will be collected.

Next, how much data must be collected as the learner engages with the virtual world? Of course, at the least, your data collection plan should include the minimum amount of data necessary to make good interpretive decisions about the identified constructs. Beyond this minimum, a good rule of thumb is to collect as much data as you can. However, *how much is too much*? In this age of information overload, remember that, most likely, human beings will be processing much of the data. Consider the intended tightness of the LAG loop: how much time does the assessor have to deal with the evidentiary data? Use this time limitation as a primary guideline for deciding how much data to collect during the learner's engagement with the world. Of course, software solutions abound for parsing data into condensed forms that could be much more useful as evidence to the human assessors making the interpretive decisions—the details of which are again beyond the scope of this book. A second guideline to follow when deciding about in-world data collection is the maintenance of student engagement for the duration of the in-world scenario. Does any aspect of data collection (e.g., frequency, amount) have the potential to create a noticeable disturbance (i.e., a lag in world rendering) that will cause a reduction in learner engagement with the virtual world? If so, then your data collection plan should be scaled down to prevent such potential disturbances.

Despite the warnings about collecting too much data, another perspective to consider is the efficiency of data collection and the fact that, in many cases, there most likely will be only one chance to collect valuable evidence of a learner's in-world performance. In fact, once a particular event has occurred in a virtual world, the same event can never happen again in exactly the same context. This is similar in concept to the adage that one can never step into the same river twice. As such, as you create your data collection plan consider another adage: "Make hay while the sun shines." In other words, collect as much evidence as possible while learners are engaging with the virtual-world scenario—as much as possible within the two aforementioned guidelines, of course. If it turns out that there is room in your data collection plan for the collection of this extra evidence, be sure to include in your plan a structure for organizing data into that which will be used immediately for interpretive assessment decisions and that which will be saved for later use.

As you craft your data collection plan during the design process, reality will set in, and it may be the case that there isn't enough time to create new measurement instrumentation to collect the evidence called for by your learning evaluation plan. If this is the case, the ideal (although painful) scenario would be to postpone full-blown public deployment of the virtual-world application until new measures can be properly designed and developed. Depending on the stakes of the evaluation plan, it might be acceptable to implement existing measurement instrumentation—such as lower stakes evaluation. For high-stakes evaluation such as end-of-grade testing in US public schools, it would be best to design and develop new measurement instrumentation that is thoroughly validated with the intended population of learners.

Implementing Existing Measures for Assessment in Virtual Worlds

Depending on the assessments you need to conduct based on the constructs identified and defined during the development of your evaluation plan, there is most likely an existing measurement instrument out there that will seem to fit your needs. Using available research literature, you can identify existing instruments that reliably measure traits associated with constructs X, Y, and Z, adopt them and adapt them for your specific purposes. Unfortunately, you've likely got a bunch of square measurement pegs that fit nicely into slightly larger round holes. Most often, adopted existing measures won't actually be a reliable, valid option for use with the population of learners to be assessed in your virtual world, for a variety of reasons.

First, unless it's your lucky day—and you find peer-reviewed literature to support your claim—the reliability of your chosen instrument(s) likely has not been verified for your targeted population of learners. As a hypothetical example, just because an instrument has been shown to be statistically reliable for measuring change in 5th graders in California doesn't mean it's reliable for 5th graders everywhere. Many variables must be controlled to ensure appropriate reliability, of course, and so fairly early in the assessment planning process you must make decisions about how closely these reliability statistics match your needs—and whether the ascertained level of closeness in the match is good enough (or not).

Similarly, it's likely that the traits measured by the chosen instrument(s) are not directly aligned with the traits you've identified for each of the constructs you need to assess. So, in addition to a likely mismatch in reliability, you've got a likely mismatch in several types of validity. Again, early on in the design process, figure out how close you need the match to be (for each type of validity) and make decisions about whether these matches are good enough.

Speaking of different types of validity, one major issue that is almost guaranteed to exist when choosing measures for assessing constructs associated with learning in virtual worlds is the fact that most existing measures have likely never been used in conjunction with a virtual-world platform before— especially measures integrated into the fabric of the learner's virtual experience. For example, if you need to integrate a science quiz into the interactive experience of water sampling at a virtual creek, most likely the wording is going to need to be changed on each of the test items to allow for seamless delivery of the test items in a way that does not break the immersive experience for the learner. A change as seemingly simple as test item wording can actually have quite a drastic effect on reliability, so imagine the potential effect of all the other changes you'll make to test items as you integrate instruments into the virtual-world scenario. When it comes to the virtual, we're still establishing the frontier of reliability and validity in measurement and assessment. Always keep this issue in mind as you conduct your designs.

If you want to ensure a high standard of reliability and validity in your approach to measurement and assessment for evaluating learning in your virtual world(s), what follows is a useful procedure. Depending on the learner traits you've identified from constructs you've defined, one or more new instruments can be developed (or heavily modified from existing instruments) according to the specific traits (demographics, prior knowledge, etc.) of the population to be measured for assessment. Each of these new instruments should be piloted, verified, and validated with an acceptably sized sample of the population you intend to measure—and these pilot studies should take place within the virtual-world environment in which the actual learning experiences will occur.

Again, reality sets in. Your funding for designing, developing, and implementing your virtual world runs short—if you had any funding at all. You're the only person on the project, wearing 12 different hats. So, realistically, do the best you can! At a minimum, take the time to test the instrument(s) you wish to use within a virtual-world setting before you use data collected with the instrument as evidence. However, if you don't have strong reliability statistics and validity justification for these instruments, than you cannot (and should not) make any substantial claims about learning (or any trait changes) in your chosen population.

Conclusion

Once again, we've covered a lot in this chapter, including the pragmatics of evaluation, assessment, and measurement with and within virtual worlds. This might seem strange, but hopefully you've got more questions now than you had before reading this chapter. Much like good research, proper design practice—especially when it comes to evaluation, assessment, and measurement—often involves asking lots of good questions that lead to better questions. The most important thing to take away from this chapter is that, while there will be common threads between each approach to assessment and measurement for the evaluation of learning in virtual worlds, every specific scenario will have enough unique variables that you as designer—whether you're wearing one hat or 12—must continuously ask better questions.

Note

1 You might be wondering why we've used the term assessment *decision*, not assessment. Yes, it may be confusing, but let's clarify: often, the term assessment is mistakenly used to refer to what is really a measurement instrument—a test. Yes, the process of assessment does require some form of measurement, but the crux of what makes assessment different from measurement is the fact that a decision of some type is necessary for assessment to occur.

TEST YOUR UNDERSTANDING

1. What is the difference between measurement and assessment in virtual worlds?
2. Describe specific differences between assessment with and within virtual worlds.

LEARNING ACTIVITIES

1. Create an evaluation (of learning) plan for an existing virtual world, or for one you plan to create.
2. Perhaps you already have a few instruments in mind for implementation with the virtual world that you are designing or acquiring. Think about the viability of these instruments for transformation into the context of a virtual world.
3. Think about one or more of the constructs you've identified and defined as part of your evaluation plan. If you haven't got an evaluation plan yet, then just think of one or more constructs for the sake of the challenge. Write up a critical reflection of the design pragmatics for measurement of traits associated with these constructs—specifically oriented to a learner's performance within a virtual world built for the learning domain you've chosen.

Other Resources

The Journal of Technology, Learning, and Assessment (JTLA) http://ejournals.bc.edu/ojs/index.php/jtla—from the website: "The *Journal of Technology, Learning and Assessment* (JTLA) is a peer-reviewed, scholarly on-line journal addressing the intersection of computer-based technology, learning, and assessment."

This open access journal is a veritable treasure trove of intellectual discussion of the pragmatic application of advanced technologies for situated assessment practice. All articles are freely available for download as PDFs.

part four

Beyond Design

Development and Implementation of Virtual Worlds

ten
Developing Virtual Worlds for Learning

Introduction

The primary focus of this book is the *design* of virtual worlds for learning. There are already plenty of books out there that talk about the technical aspects of developing computer games and virtual worlds. Frankly, those details are beyond the scope of this book. But it would be silly to bring you on this trip through theory, mechanics, design, assessment, and all the rest without talking about how virtual worlds actually get built. Plus, both of your authors *love* to build virtual worlds, and to talk about building them. So, this chapter will provide an overview of the development steps that should be considered as part of the process of designing virtual worlds for learning. Additionally, we'll cover issues of project management, specifically from the perspective of ensuring a smooth transition from design phase to development phase.

In Chapter Eight, we walked through the process of creating a comprehensive curriculum design document. You'll remember we talked about the incredible benefits of creating such a document before starting on the development of your virtual world. Some of these are: making sure you have clear, measurable learning goals; making sure you know how learners can achieve those goals through use of a virtual world; providing a reality check to see if the learning goals and activities best suited to reach those goals are good matches for a virtual-world-based curriculum; and creating a timetable and budget estimate to see if embedding your curriculum into a virtual world, even if it is a good fit, is worth the time, effort, and cost of development.

These are all great reasons to create a detailed design document, but they are only "part 1" of the benefits. An equally important reason to write a curriculum design document is to provide a blueprint for the creation of the virtual world, its objects, and its activities. In order to ensure a smooth transition from design to development, your design document should be as clear and detailed as possible. A good way to think about it is that the document you produce should be able to stand alone as a complete record of design. You should be able to hand the design document off to a team of developers and have them create exactly what you want without further communication … although of course you should never do that! Regular communication between the design and development teams is imperative to achieving good results.

Experience has taught us that achieving an appropriate level of detail in the design document is vital to avoiding costly problems with development. Developers cannot read the minds of the curriculum designers—if something isn't in the design document, it won't appear in the virtual world. Likewise, developers should strive to "stick to the script": their job is to realize the vision of the curriculum design document in virtual space. This doesn't mean that developers shouldn't bring their own ideas and expertise to the table. They know best how to make a curricular vision a reality in a virtual world. But they should not stray too far from the design document to pursue personal flights of development fancy.

When you first start creating virtual worlds, it may be that you alone are the designer and developer (and subject matter expert, graphical artist, writer, coder, etc.). When going solo, it's easy to stick to the script, or to adjust it however you want. But as you move into serious design of virtual worlds, you'll likely need to bring in other people to help produce your worlds. As the team grows, the need for a clear process for development grows too. Everyone on the design and development teams should understand and adhere to a clear set of rules throughout the development process to make sure things go smoothly.

Development Process

For this chapter, we'll continue to refer to the Weather Trouble module from the SAVE Science virtual world as an example (not a perfect model, but a real-world example, complete with problems and issues). Our discussion of the development process in this chapter will assume that you are working in an educational setting, rather than as part of a professional development team or commercial game development company. The development process we describe is one that is contextualized to the unique culture of amateur educational development (i.e., development taking place in schools, universities, and informal settings). Large commercial organizations would likely follow a more formal ADDIE (Analysis, Design, Develop, Implement, Evaluate) approach than what we describe here.

Throughout the chapter, we will situate our development discussion in the Unity game engine (Figure 10.1). Unity is a powerful development environment for creating virtual worlds and other kinds of games, simulations, and training platforms. There are multiple flavors of Unity, including basic and pro, and versions that let you publish your virtual world to iPhones, iPads, Android devices, and gaming consoles (Xbox, PlayStation3, Wii, etc.). The basic version of Unity is free, and is plenty powerful enough to create educational virtual worlds that can be published on Windows and Mac computers or run within most modern web browsers. You can download the free version of Unity at http://unity3d.com. If you discover that you need some special feature that isn't part of the free version (although this is unlikely), you can purchase yearly licenses for the professional version of Unity at a steep academic discount by contacting sales support through the Unity website or through third-party online retailers such as the Academic Superstore (see: www.academicsuperstore.com). If you are not in an academic setting, you will have to pay the full price, which is considerably higher.

Although we will talk about Unity within the framework of our discussion of virtual-worlds development, we will not give a tutorial on Unity itself. For that, you can find a large number of excellent online lessons and tutorials. Many of

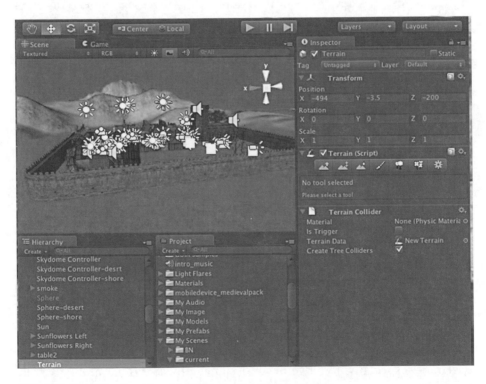

FIGURE 10.1 Weather Trouble in Unity development tool

these lessons are free, although the best tend to require a monthly tuition fee. We will list some good online Unity resources at the end of the chapter.

Also, Unity is only one of several good virtual-world development systems. We think Unity offers the best combination of power, flexibility, and cost. However, it has a fairly steep learning curve and requires some programming skills to take full advantage of its functionality. Two other systems, Second Life (http://secondlife.com) and Activeworlds (http://activeworlds.com) are easier to use for teams without strong technical training, but are both less flexible and powerful than Unity. Also, neither system allows for virtual-world development across multiple platforms.

The Development Team

Before you start building your virtual world, you'll want to make sure that you have an adequate development team in place. Depending on your circumstances, the size of your team may run from one (that's you) to a dozen or more people. Again, we are assuming in this chapter that you are not developing your virtual world as part of a huge team at a large commercial software company, but are instead working in an educational or training setting. A bare-bones development team, once you move beyond solo development, consists of an instructional designer/game designer, programmers, and 3D modelers/graphic artists. If you have the money, you should also include a sound artist, voice-over artists, and story writers. Although not directly a member of the development team, you'll need a subject matter expert on hand as part of the curriculum design process.

Instructional Designer/Game Designer

This person manages the development process by interacting with both the development team and the curriculum design team. Ideally, she will have some training in instructional design and/or experience with creating computer-based learning materials. Even better would be training and/or experience in designing and developing educational games. This person does not need to be an expert programmer, artist, or curriculum designer, but should possess enough knowledge of all aspects of the project to understand and be able to translate between other team members, and enough management experience and/or talent to keep the development process moving along as smoothly and quickly as possible. Ideally, you should actually have two people working together, one instructional designer and one game designer. At a minimum, you should consult with a game designer—especially if you've never designed any sort of game-like virtual world before.

Programmer/Virtual-World Builders

These people write the code that runs all the interactions and events in the virtual world, as well as code to control the GUI elements associated with your world. Note that we use the plural here. If possible, your development team needs more than one programmer. Also, your programmers should be real programmers: people with training in programming languages, math, and logic. Virtual-world creation tools such as Unity make it relatively easy to create basic interactions via pre-written chunks of code. However, for all but the most simple virtual-world interactions, you need programmers who can write custom code. This might seem obvious, but in virtual-world development set in educational settings it is not uncommon to see projects begun without anyone on the team having programming skills or experience.

The programmers often also assemble the virtual worlds, using multimedia elements such as 3D models, avatars, 2D graphics, sounds, and music created or purchased by other members of the team. Building or assembly of the worlds using the Unity development system is similar to arranging furniture and set pieces on a stage for a play. Unity allows for simple drag and drop placement of 3D objects in virtual space. Once the objects have been positioned in the virtual world, code is attached to the objects to make them interactive.

3D Modelers/Graphic Artists

Every virtual-world development team needs at least one 3D modeler/graphic artist. Ideally, of course, you want more than one. These skill sets (3D modeling and graphic artistry) are not always found in the same person. For educators hoping to create virtual worlds, this aspect of development can be the most challenging. Simply put, good 3D modelers and graphic artists can be very expensive, and the typical educational virtual-world project is not flush with cash. So, what do you do? Virtual-world developers working in educational settings (especially universities) have a great resource not readily available even to large-scale commercial developers: students. For virtual-world projects being built in an educational setting, you can draw upon the skills (and relatively low wages) of student artists. Collaboration with students is a win-win situation. The students get the chance to build their portfolios while still in school, gain valuable experience producing content for use with a real audience, and earn some money. The designers and developers gain the ability to create virtual-world-based curriculum on a limited budget with a small development team.

But what do you do if you aren't in a setting where you have access to students who can help create 3D models and graphic elements? One option is to make use of digital libraries of pre-made objects. Many such libraries exist, and a good number of them offer free objects. For example, Google 3D Warehouse (http://sketchup.google.com/3dwarehouse) has a very large collection of free user-created 3D objects. Other digital libraries such as TurboSquid include a mix of free and for-purchase 3D objects (http://turbosquid.com). Independent artists also create 3D objects and graphical elements aimed at users of specific development tools. For example, included in the Unity development tool there is an asset store containing 3D models, graphical elements, programming code, and other useful materials for creating games and virtual worlds. At the end of the chapter, we will provide links to a number of these content libraries.

There are weaknesses to relying on libraries of existing material, mostly that the quality of free content is not always high, there is a limited amount of free material available, and use of existing content limits your ability to design your virtual world to your own specifications. Another challenge is to find enough material with a unified look and feel to create a virtual-world-based curriculum. On the other hand, use of this free material allows you to quickly create and deploy virtual worlds for learning.

Another possibility is to seek out freelance artists and modelers to create the items you need. If you cast a wide net and know where to look, you can often find very skillful "starving artists" who can work quickly and cheaply. With Unity, for example, there is an online community forum where artists can advertise their availability and show their portfolios. In the same forum, virtual-world designers can post help wanted advertisements (see: http://forum.unity3d.com/forums/31-Commercial-Work).

Weather Trouble Example

In developing the Weather Trouble module as part of a funded research grant at a university, the development team had resources typical to such settings: a small team of dedicated student workers and researchers, and some grant money for development. The virtual-world development team included two programmers/world developers, one graphic artist, and an instructional designer. The instructional designer also helped with the programming tasks as needed. All members of the development team were part-timers, working on the Weather Trouble world around classes, conferences, and other jobs. All but one member of the development team was a student. While all development team members had had training in their area of development, only the graphic artist and instructional designer had done professional work in their specific areas. The development team also paid an independent artist living overseas to create a few custom 3D models for the project.

The world development team worked with a strong curriculum design team from another university. This group consisted of several PhD students with expertise in science education, a supervising science education professor with experience designing curriculum specifically for virtual worlds, and a professor with expertise in teacher professional development and implementation of technology-based learning environments in schools.

A Basic Development Process

Once you have your team in place, you can begin to build by converting the design document into a fully realized virtual world. The development process is never, in our experience, a clean linear sequence of steps from curriculum design to fully developed world. Instead, the virtual world is created via a "rapid development" iterative cycle of development, testing, review, and revision. This iterative cycle is just that: some development will take place, problems and challenges will be discovered, revisions to the curriculum and virtual world will be made, follow-up versions will be built and tested, more revisions will be made, and so on.

Below is a basic series of steps that you can follow as part of your own iterative virtual-world development process. These steps are not necessarily universal, but they offer a commonsense approach to development of virtual worlds that we have found useful in our work.

Table Read

Like actors on a television show, it is a good idea to start the development process with a table read of the script. The script in this case is the curriculum design document described in Chapter Eight. The development and curriculum design teams read through the design document together and then discuss the big picture of the virtual-world development. All the team members should complete a pre-read of the document before coming to the table read, paying careful attention to the elements of the document that pertain to their role on the team. The goal of the table read is to make sure the development and curriculum design teams share a common understanding of what the virtual world will look like, what its storyline will be, what the main quests and tasks will be, how learning will be assessed, and who will be in charge of each aspect of development. It goes (almost) without saying that this shared understanding needs to mesh with the overall vision and details of the curriculum design document.

Virtual-world design and develop teams are often not housed in a single location. In fact, it may be more common that members are distributed across distance, and that most interactions take place electronically. In such cases, the table read is even more important than it is for in-house development teams. Misunderstandings and miscommunication that can be relatively easy to clear up when development of a virtual world is taking place in a single location can flare up into very large problems when team members are working solo in different locations.

Weather Trouble Example

When creating the Weather Trouble virtual world, the development and curriculum design teams were based at two universities on opposite sides of the United States and, apart from rare face-to-face meetings, operated almost entirely at distance. Consequently, the table read took place via teleconference. Development team members read through the design document created by the curriculum team beforehand, and then the whole team met electronically to go line by line through the document. Members of the development team asked questions, raised technical issues with aspects of the curriculum, and sought clarification on several aspects of the curriculum design. Curriculum team members explained difficult or complex elements of the curriculum design in greater detail than what was in the design document when necessary. The proposed development timeline included in the design document was discussed and (as is usually the case) modified. One member from both teams took notes recording all issues raised, revisions to be made, and next steps. These notes were then compared, combined, and sent to all team members as a shared "contract" of work to be done for creating the virtual world.

Resources Listing

After the development team has a thorough, shared understanding of the design requirements of the virtual world, team members should assemble lists of the multimedia and programming resources that will be needed for development. For example, the graphics designer and 3D modeler should read through the design document and compile a comprehensive list of the graphical elements and 3D objects needed for the world. The programmers should look through all the events/tasks/interactions that will take place in the curriculum and create a list of the programming scripts and functionalities that will be needed. The instructional designer looks at those same events with a different set of goals: she creates a list of the design approaches that need to be included to best support learning in the virtual world. For example, the instructional designer might decide to include use of visual signaling in the world. As we described in Chapter Four, visual signaling is an approach used to direct a learner's attention to interactive objects in the virtual world and/or in the GUI that are important to goals of the curriculum. Ideally, this list of design approaches and accompanying functionalities, objects, and materials will be added to the design document before reaching the development stage, but this doesn't always happen.

Resources Gathering

Once a master list of required resources is created, members of the development team start gathering existing resources to use in the new virtual world. When you first begin developing virtual worlds, you will probably not have many ready-made resources on hand. But as you complete development projects you will begin to develop a digital library of resources that can be reused on future projects. As your team reviews the design document, they can quickly identify and gather up existing resources that can be used and/or modified for use in the latest project.

If you haven't yet developed a personal digital library with resources that fit for the existing project, you can turn to one of the online repositories of materials we described earlier to hunt for graphics, objects, and code snippets that will work for your project. This approach is often faster, easier, and cheaper than developing your own materials, although as we have pointed out, there are drawbacks to the online library approach in terms of getting the look and feel that you want and that is consistent with the vision of the curriculum design document.

Weather Trouble Example

With the Weather Trouble virtual world, about 90 percent of the resources needed for the project had already been developed, purchased, or scavenged from digital libraries for prior projects. Weather Trouble was the third in a series of related curricular units all set in the same, vaguely medieval, cartoonish virtual world. Consequently, a wealth of 3D objects could be reused or repurposed from earlier worlds. These included buildings, "set piece" objects (chairs, tables, etc.), roads, farm animals, NPCs, and landscape elements (rocks, trees, water, etc.). Similarly, many of the 2D graphical elements developed for earlier projects could be reused. These included most of the GUI elements (buttons, GUI panels, etc.) and textures for the 3D objects. On the programming side, nearly all the code used in Weather Trouble consisted of edited versions of Unity source code developed for earlier worlds (Figure 10.2).

For elements that hadn't already been created, the development team looked first to online digital libraries for items that could be purchased or downloaded for free. They bought many items including medieval buildings, stone walls, and fences. They also found free (and royalty-free) graphics and associated code for an animated virtual sky with clouds moving across it.

FIGURE 10.2 Weather Trouble world with bought, built, and found objects

Resources Creation

When you don't have the resources you need, and/or you are unable to locate acceptable resources from an existing free or for-purchase online library, it is time to create new resources. Speaking broadly, the challenges to creating your own resources come down to: people, money, and time. As we have described, it is not easy to find and hire skilled artists, modelers, or programmers. Skilled professionals in these areas are often expensive and usually already working on other projects. Less experienced, but still skilled resource creators might be easier to find and cheaper to hire (university students, for example), but will likely need more time to develop the resources and require more oversight. You'll need to balance these competing challenges to get your materials created.

Another challenge is to maintain a consistent look and feel throughout your virtual world. The most typical scenario for educational virtual-world development is that you will use a mix of existing, purchased, and freshly developed resources for your project. To both match good design practice and to stay true to the curriculum design team's vision, you need to have a clear, consistent look to your virtual world. When developing new resources to go into a virtual world, the artists and modelers need to work to carefully match both existing resources and newly created ones to the overall look and feel of the world.

Weather Trouble Example

Although the development team was able to reuse a large number of existing resources in Unity for the Weather Trouble world, the curriculum design document included a number of elements that needed to be developed from scratch. Some of these were: new NPCs, a number of new 3D objects related to the specific content of the curriculum (weathervanes, thermometers, flags, etc.), and new GUI elements including a compass and teleporter (to jump from one area of the world to another without having to walk).

Geography Creation and 3D Object Placement

As you gather and create the resources for your virtual world, you can begin to build the geography of the world. By geography, we mean the large-scale indoor or outdoor spaces of the world. For example, if your virtual world is set in a small town, you can build the geography of the town, including hills, valleys, plains, trees, bodies of water, etc. If your virtual world will be all indoors, you can construct the structures in which the curriculum will take place. You create the world's indoor or outdoor geography to provide a stage that you will then fill with 3D objects and characters. As soon as the geography has been built, the 3D objects can be placed in the virtual world. It is often the case that the geography is ready before all the 3D objects have been developed. In this case, to save time and maximize efficiency, placeholder objects can be arranged in the virtual world. These placeholder objects provide the programmers and GUI developers with temporary target objects with which to test their code.

Weather Trouble Example

Weather Trouble takes place in a world that looks something like a town and countryside in the Middle Ages. Specifically, the curriculum has students exploring a small town, a desert outpost, and a shorefront. The development team created a single terrain object in Unity that was large enough to contain all three locations. Unity has a built-in tool that allows for simple creation of landscapes. Using this tool, the development team set up the overall geography of the world quickly and then placed all the buildings needed on each of the "stage sets" of the world (Figure 10.3). Once the main sets were ready, all other 3D objects were brought in and set into their appropriate places, ready for code to be attached for interactions and related GUI elements.

FIGURE 10.3 Weather Trouble landscape and objects

GUI Creation

As we have discussed in previous chapters, virtual-world-based curricula usually make extensive use of 2D GUI elements. GUIs are used to provide information about objects that appear in the world, as a conversation system for talking to NPCs in the world, as inventory systems, toolkits, etc. When developing a virtual world, the GUI system, including programming and graphical elements, can be created in parallel with the world itself. That way, as 3D objects are being placed in the world, any GUI elements associated with them can immediately be added and tested.

Weather Trouble Example

The Weather Trouble world made extensive use of an elaborate GUI system for NPC dialogs, object interactions, note-taking, and embedded quizzes. The programmers and graphic artist worked in tandem to create the GUI system using a graphical design program (Adobe Photoshop) and Unity as the other elements of the virtual world were under development (Figure 10.4).

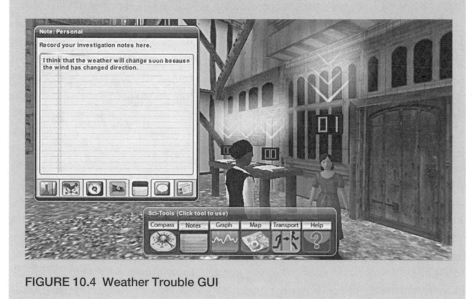

FIGURE 10.4 Weather Trouble GUI

Programming

Although we've listed programming after geography creation and object placement, you shouldn't wait to write code until these things happen. Programming should be going on in parallel with these other development activities. Ideally, as soon as the sets of the virtual world are in place, the programmers should be able to start testing, revising, and tweaking their code. With programming of in-world interactions, it is particularly important to keep communication channels open between the development and curriculum design teams. Interactions are quite difficult to explain and to visualize in the curriculum design document. The table read should help to clarify how interactions should work. But there is nothing like trying them out as soon as possible in the virtual world itself. Using placeholder objects and GUI elements, programmers can quickly put together basic versions of interactions in the world. Together with the curriculum designers and instructional designer, these interactions can be tested and modified as necessary. Frequent testing and revisions in the early stages of development can prevent major headaches later on.

Weather Trouble Example

On Weather Trouble, the instructional designer doubled as an assistant programmer and created the geography of the world with its three distinct areas (desert outpost, seaport, and downtown). He also placed the buildings, walls, and some of the objects. The lead programmer placed the rest of the objects, developed all the interactions, and implemented the GUI system. As we have described, most of the code for the project consisted of existing scripts, modified for use in the Weather Trouble world.

Alpha Version Testing

As soon as your team has a basic version of the world developed, it is important to begin conducting alpha testing of the world among team members. The purpose of alpha testing varies depending on the role of the team member doing the testing. For example, the curriculum designers should pay careful attention to how their design looks in the "real" virtual world. Graphic artists and modelers focus especially on the look and feel of their artwork in virtual space. But perhaps the most valuable task during alpha testing is to have everyone on both the design and development teams try to break the world. They do this by performing all possible interactions built into the world looking for functional or programmatic errors, misspellings in the text, and logic errors. In trying to break the world, team members should also do unexpected things, like try to escape from the world (more than once we have found invisible holes in the landscape of our built worlds that allowed learners to drop through the ground and fall endlessly through virtual space!).

Weather Trouble Example

With Weather Trouble, the curriculum design and development teams participated in a single round of alpha testing of a version of the world that was about 90 percent finished. The testing resulted in a short list of necessary revisions, mostly related to the dialogs between learner avatars and NPCs in the world. Some of the curricular design elements also needed to be changed from their original concepts. For example, the curriculum design document had learners checking the temperature of different places in the virtual world by using a thermometer they carried with them. Carrying a thermometer around "felt weird" when alpha tested in the world, and the team realized that it made more sense to place working virtual thermometers on buildings around the town.

Revisions

Alpha testing will inevitably reveal a collection of programming bugs, spelling and grammatical errors, graphical and 3D model glitches, etc. These kinds of problems are usually relatively easy to fix in subsequent revisions. More challenging, but also common, are problems with the design of the curriculum that are revealed only when the design document is converted into a world. Ideas that made sense on paper and through the table read are sometimes found to be less useful, meaningful, or logical when actually experienced in the virtual world. It is critical to identify these kinds of issues as early as possible in the development process. The later your team catches them, the more expensive they become in terms of time, money, and personnel resources.

Pilot Testing and More Revisions

After conducting alpha testing and making revisions to your virtual world (at least one round of this, but more are better), your team should arrange to conduct one or more rounds of pilot testing of the virtual world with a sample population drawn from its target audience. Your goals for pilot testing are similar to those in the alpha testing round: testing for programming, graphical, and textual, and multimedia bugs. Importantly, pilot testing also allows your team to gather data on how well your virtual world and the curriculum built into it actually supports the goals of the curricular design, and to learn whether it engages users in the ways that you hoped. The target audience is nearly guaranteed to interact with the virtual world in ways you did not anticipate. Pilot testing lets you see how well your vision matches with the real-world behaviors of the target audience.

> ### Weather Trouble Example
>
> With Weather Trouble, the team piloted the virtual world with several classes of middle school students at a single school. They ran a full implementation of the curriculum, complete with pre- and post-surveys for students and teachers, classroom observations, and data analysis. Everything went smoothly except that it was discovered that the school where the pilot study was conducted had computers that were below the minimum technical requirements to run the virtual world well.

Sign Off on a "Milestone" Version

After one or more rounds of pilot testing, it is time to sign off on a milestone version of the virtual world. This milestone version will be the default version of the world that you run for a set period of time with the target audience. As you use this version of the virtual world with your audience, you should continue to gather data on how well the world and its curriculum work to support the goals of the curriculum design. These data can be used later as the basis for yet another round of revisions to the virtual world toward a later milestone version for some future set of implementations. Importantly, once the team has signed off on a milestone version, it should be "set in stone" for a clearly specified period of time. That means that any new features or other changes to the virtual world will have to wait until a specified period of time has passed. Following this rule prevents a never-ending cycle of on-going changes to the virtual world, helping to avoid serious implementation problems.

Conclusion

Development of virtual worlds is challenging, difficult, time-consuming … and incredible fun. Seeing the design choices you have made, the theories you have considered, and the curriculum you have designed come to life in your own virtual world is a fantastic experience. In this chapter, we have presented a very basic overview of the development process for creating virtual worlds. We covered just the bare facts. It would take a full book to really dig deep into all the important aspects of the development process from an educational perspective (Hey! There's a good idea … dear editors!). But this overview will get you started. We hope that you enjoy the experience of seeing your design become a virtual world as much as we do.

TEST YOUR UNDERSTANDING

1. What is the minimum number of people needed on a development team?
2. What's the role of the instructional designer on the development team?
3. What are the main reasons to conduct alpha testing? Pilot testing? What are the differences between the two?

LEARNING ACTIVITIES

1. Assemble (on paper) your own virtual world development team using the people and resources available to you in your own setting. Do you have all the people you need? If not, how can you fill in the gaps?
2. Write out a version of the development steps situated to your own setting. Are there any particular challenges to development? If so, how can you address the challenges? In what ways would you alter the development steps to best match your own situation?
3. Compare and contrast the development tools Unity, Second Life, and Activeworlds (see the links below). Which one seems the best fit for your virtual-worlds development project?

Links

The Unity development engine has become the flagship environment for creating games and virtual worlds, for both commercial and educational purposes. http://unity3d.com

Second Life is a popular environment for creating multi-user virtual worlds. It is relatively easy to develop basic virtual worlds at a relatively low cost. http://secondlife.com

Activeworlds.com offers similar multi-user building tools to Second Life. The graphics quality is lower in Activeworlds, but the level of control over development, deployment, and security for educational worlds is better than in Second Life. It is also cheaper to use than Second Life: http://activeworlds.com

The Academic Superstore sells annual licenses for Unity at a steep discount over the professional licenses: www.academicsuperstore. com

Other Resources

If you decide to use Unity for your development work, there are a number of very good web sources for tutorials, community support, and multimedia resources. A few include:

Unity community: a bulletin board for Unity users to share information, tutorials, and resources: http://forum.unity3d.com

Unity Answers: a user to user Q&A site for getting things done in Unity: http://answers.unity3d.com/index.html

Design3: a great collection of Unity tutorials. Requires a monthly subscription: www.design3.com/unity

Buzz3d: a strong collection of Unity tutorials. Some free, some not: http://www.3dbuzz.com

Goldstone, W. (2009). *Unity Game Development Essentials*: http://amzn.com/184719818X

Creighton, R. (2010) *Unity3D Game Development By Example*: http://amzn.com/1849690545

eleven
Implementation and Evaluation of Virtual Worlds in Multiple Contexts

Introduction

You might ask yourself why a book about designing virtual worlds for learning contains a chapter covering implementation and evaluation. Typically, the design process is considered done well before a virtual world is implemented with its intended audience of users. Further, in most cases, usually the process of evaluating the success of an implementation is an afterthought—if any evaluation occurs at all. However, we propose here that the process of designing any virtual world for learning should include a thorough consideration of the implementation and evaluation procedures—due to the distinct possibility that each or both of these procedures could, in fact, heavily influence the design of the virtual world.

As such, this chapter covers these two procedures from the perspective of how they should be considered during the design process. What is implementation and when does it actually start? How does the implementation process differ across various contexts of learning, such as formal education, informal learning, and educational research? What separates evaluation from implementation, and why is evaluation so important for design and development? Specific to virtual worlds, what are the primary differences between formative and summative evaluation?

Implementation

What exactly *is* implementation? For our purposes here, the following definition works pretty well: implementation is the phase of software application

187

design and development in which the software application is released to the public for use as it is intended—as it was *designed*. Speaking of design and development, how is implementation different from design and development? Design is the process of planning a solution for an identified problem, development is the process of building the planned solution, and implementation is trying out the solution to see if it really solves the problem. So, hopefully you've got a problem to solve!

By now you might have guessed that the implementation process doesn't start until after both the design and development phases have been completed. Typically, this is true. However, in the grand scheme of things, the process of design is never really finished, and implementation is merely another phase of design. Technically, though, the implementation phase of an application begins when a stable version of that application is released to the public. The transition between development and implementation usually involves a series of testing phases (alpha and beta) as shown in Figure 11.1.

As we mentioned in the chapter on virtual-world development, alpha testing has more of a technical orientation, typically conducted by the development team and trained professionals with the intent of finding programmatic flaws in the application. Upon completion of alpha testing, developers use feedback from the alpha testers to make final programmatic fixes to the application before releasing the beta version for beta testing. If you are new to the process of designing and developing virtual worlds, alpha testing might seem like a necessary evil that hinders the development timeline. However, alpha testing provides assurance that your virtual world, when released to the target audience, functions as intended. You wouldn't want to lose a learner's engagement due to malfunctioning software. If you are acquiring a virtual world as opposed to designing and developing your own, you should inquire with the developers of each of the worlds you are considering to find out the details of the alpha-testing process to which these candidate worlds have been subjected.

Beta testing is considered to be a more qualitative procedure, typically conducted by a relatively small group of users sampled from the intended target audience of the application. Upon completion of beta testing, devel-

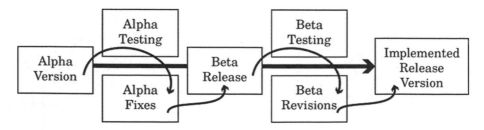

FIGURE 11.1 Transition from development to implementation

opers work with designers to resolve any final issues of user experience that have been identified by beta testers before approving the "final" version of the software application that is ready for public consumption. Here we put final in quotes due to the fact that, as we've mentioned before, design is never truly finished, and the post-beta version of any software application is—and yet isn't—final. The next version of the same software application will likely go through beta testing (and potentially alpha testing, depending on circumstances). For example, consider the popular Firefox web browser developed by Mozilla (www.mozilla.org). Each major version release (1.0, 2.0, 3.0, etc.) is typically beta tested before finally being released to the general public.

A Variety of Contexts

Obviously, as you finish design and development, alphas, and betas—or upon making the acquisition decision—the wait is over and implementation must begin, and exactly *how* this implementation process occurs depends entirely upon the context of learning for which the virtual world is implemented. Table 11.1 provides an overview of the implementation process—including categories of approval, support, and functionality across three main contexts: formal education, informal learning environments (such as museums or after-school programs), and laboratory research.

Formal Educational Environments

Implementation of virtual worlds for learning in formal educational environments typically involves one or both of two procedures: (1) integration of the virtual-world experience into regular classroom activities, or (2) special trips to a central computer lab. You will likely need approval—from district- and/or school-level administrators—well before implementation in any formal environment. Of course, this need for approval will vary from one place

Table 11.1. Overview of Differences in Implementation across Contexts

Context	Approval	Support	Functionality
Formal education	District/school	Teachers Tech. staff	Stable release Updates permissible
Informal learning	Program organization	Administrators Tech. staff	Stable release Updates expected
Laboratory research	Funding source(s) University, college, department, etc. Human subjects review	Collaborators Tech. staff	Distinct variations for investigating specific constructs Research assistants No changes during individual implementations

to the next. To boost your chances of getting the necessary administrative approval when implementing in the United States, it helps to align most if not all of the outcomes, goals, and/or objectives for learning within the virtual world with articulated grade-level education standards for the state(s) in which you plan to implement. Proper standards alignment for formal use can be more difficult to justify when adopting off-the-shelf commercial games for in-class use. If you are planning to implement your virtual world nationwide, you should familiarize yourself with the Common Core State Standards Initiative (www.corestandards.org), which has been adopted by an overwhelming majority of the 50 states in the US. Currently the standards address only language, arts, and mathematics.

Who is involved in the implementation of virtual worlds in formal environments? As previously mentioned, administrators at various levels must give approval, and administrators at the school level will likely need to give continuous decision-level support as the implementation continues. Teachers at each school must "buy in" to the implementation process through an understanding of the virtual world (e.g., purposes and goals, standards alignment, additional student benefits, etc.) that is good enough to justify continued support through the additional work that might be required by the teacher to conduct the implementation (i.e., assessment and reporting). Often it helps to create teacher materials to serve as a pragmatic guide or support system for the specific procedures involved in the implementation process. Of course, the creation of these materials should first be considered during the design phase of the virtual world.

Depending on the particular staffing organization within the district, system, and school where your virtual world will be implemented, one or more technical support specialists might be available to provide continued support of the implementation process. If this is the case, it's a good idea to work directly with these individuals before implementation begins, discussing specific technological issues the school, system, or district might have in place—such as integrated network security features that may or may not inhibit certain aspects of back-end communication performed during the implementation of your virtual world. The more preliminary interaction you have with available technology support staff, the more likely you are to cover all the potential problems that could arise during implementation to cause an unnecessary disruption in the learner's experience. The last thing you want to have happen is a disruption of learning thanks to technical difficulties.

Finally, the most important participants in the implementation of virtual worlds in a formal environment are the students. These people are the primary reason that the technology even exists, and they should be considered the main beneficiary of the facilitation provided by the technology. If they are not engaged with the learning scenarios that are delivered by your virtual world, you do not want this lack of engagement to occur because of technological issues in implementation, nor from poor design. Again, this is why proper alpha and beta testing are such important parts of the design and development process. Imagine the potential differences inherent in two different virtual worlds—X and Y—designed for 5th grade students. World X is properly alpha tested using professional alpha testers that understand interaction perspectives typically held by 5th grade children, and properly beta tested with an appropriate sample of 5th grade children. World Y is neither alpha tested nor beta tested. Both are intended to be used in conjunction with 5th grade science, including in-class experimentation and out of class field studies covering the entire school year. Which of the two virtual worlds is more likely to suffer mechanical failure? Which of the two is more likely to hold students' engagement? Of course, there is no way to know for certain without more evidence, but based on the hypothetical situation presented here, it is likely that world X would stand a better chance of avoiding mechanical failure *and* maintaining learner engagement.

Informal Learning Environments

Contrary to formal environments, implementation of virtual worlds for learning in informal environments does not follow any patterns of typicality. Technically, any virtual world used in any context of learning, such as a person of any age interacting individually (under their own volition) with a virtual world in the privacy of their home. In many cases, the actual learning that occurs is entirely incidental—learning that occurs without intent.

However, some of the more common structured informal environments in which virtual worlds are often implemented are after-school programs, interactive exhibit spaces in museums and science centers, and in-home personal use of applications. Still, with more and more sophisticated virtual worlds existing entirely on the web or available to download at no cost to the user, it is entirely likely that any single virtual world would be implemented in all three of these environments—perhaps in a multitude of environments over time by the same user.

Consider Celestia (www.shatters.net/celestia), a free open-source, cross-platform, 3D space simulation intended for galaxy exploration (Figure 11.2). A mother and daughter could discover and enjoy Celestia during a weekend visit to their local science center, and this excited girl might then engage with Celestia the following week at the library where she goes after school until her mother comes to pick her up. The mother and daughter could then download Celestia to the home computer to share her progress with her mother after dinner one evening that week.

Who is involved in the implementation of virtual worlds in informal environments? Obviously, this can vary greatly depending on the informal environment. For in-home use, probably just the user (and perhaps a parent)

FIGURE 11.2 Screenshot of Jupiter as seen in the Celestia virtual worlds application

is supporting the implementation of the virtual world. In after-school pro-grams, museums, and science centers, it is likely that some form of admin-istrative buy-in will be necessary, and it is possible that technical staff will be available for mechanical support—with both of these factors depending on the size and structure of the given organization or program. In any case, the most important thing to consider when designing or acquiring a virtual world for implementation in informal settings is the enormous variety of technical savvy inherent in the people supporting these settings. As such, it would be a very good idea to integrate some form of thorough support system—to allow any implementation supporter channels for troubleshoot-ing the virtual world. These support systems exist in many forms, such as downloadable documentation (installation guides and user manuals), wikis (similar content to documentation with additional user contributions), or web-based forums where communities of users can discuss any number of issues regarding mechanics of the virtual world. For example, Celestia users are highly active on the associated support forums (see, for example, www.shatters.net/forum). As a side note, you've probably considered such support systems to be just as handy for the implementation of virtual worlds in formal educational environments.

In the case of choosing an existing virtual world—as opposed to designing and developing your own—the existence of a solid support system for the virtual world should be considered during the decision-making process. When designing and developing a new virtual world, whether or not to construct a complex web-based support system—as opposed to more simple documentation that can be packaged with the virtual world itself—is a decision that should be based on the scale of implementation. The higher the number and variety of formal environments in which implementation will occur, the more likely a complex web-based support system will be necessary.

One last issue to consider for the implementation of virtual worlds in informal environments is the fact that, even in the most structured informal environments, you can never count on the persistence of use and engagement that is more likely in formal educational environments. Consider a virtual world that has 16 learning scenarios, with the intention that a learner complete one scenario each week for 16 weeks. Such an implementation schedule is more feasible in a formal environment where students are more likely to at least be present in school to attend the classes or labs where the scenarios occur.

Laboratory Research Environments

Whether you are designing and developing or acquiring a virtual world for implementation in experimental studies that take place in a controlled laboratory setting, the primary issue to consider is the necessity for a clean break between development (or modification of an acquired virtual world) and the beginning of implementation. Most likely, if you are conducting studies in such a setting, patterns of change in learning outcomes from people engaging with one or more controlled variations or versions of the virtual world will be analyzed in hopes of finding significant correlations to support hypotheses established for relationships between independent and dependent variables associated with one or more constructs of learning. If this is your intended approach to research, then you should absolutely avoid modifying the virtual world during data collection for any given study—in order to avoid the unintended introduction of one or more unwanted variations in the sampled data. If anything changes about the user experience with the virtual world due to changes made to the world mid-implementation, you might not be able to use the data collected to make valid comparisons between participants, and the given experiment will fail.

When considering the timeline for implementation of virtual worlds for experimental research, it is imperative to account for the additional time needed for any necessary funding approval, human subjects review, and participant recruitment. This is especially the case when designing and developing your own virtual world. Typically, acquiring the amount of funding that is necessary to support large-scale implementation—even in a laboratory setting—requires evidence of successful pilot implementation with the virtual world. Additionally, in most cases, the final working version of the virtual world to be implemented must be completed (and potentially demonstrated) before approval can be obtained from a human subjects review board.

Assuming all goes well and implementation moves forward as planned, who is involved in the implementation of virtual worlds in university-based laboratory settings? In most cases the principal investigator (PI) (i.e., the head of the research project) is the primary decision maker—or perhaps one or more co-PIs if the laboratory setting is spread across multiple locations with a co-PI leading each location. Depending on the hierarchy of the laboratory staff, one or more postdoctoral researchers or senior research assistants will likely take care of the pragmatics of implementation (e.g., logistics, participant administration, etc.). Technical support staff might be available to assist with mechanical function of the virtual world, but more often than not this responsibility also belongs to the postdoctoral researchers or research assistants. Often, it is the case that design, development, and implementation of a particular virtual world are done in-house—or even by a single individual. Even so, it is important to consider the potential for scaling up the implementation of any virtual world during the initial design and development process.

TEST YOUR UNDERSTANDING

1. We've covered three major types of implementation environments for virtual worlds. Can you think of issues specific to formal, informal, or laboratory implementation scenarios that we've missed?
2. Can you think of additional implementation issues applicable to all three types of scenarios? How is your own scenario for implementation different from, and similar to, these three?
3. Consider the differences inherent in implementing a virtual world for on-the-job training—in commercial scenarios and industrial scenarios. Who might typically be involved in each type of scenario, and when, where, and how might implementation actually occur? What about various fields of medicine? What about military training?
4. Can you think of other contexts or scenarios different from these that might require attention to unique aspects of the implementation process? In any case, no matter what the specific details are for the context or scenario of implementation for any virtual world, every single virtual world implemented for the purpose of learning should be properly evaluated.

Evaluation

What is the overall purpose of evaluation? When designing virtual worlds for learning, evaluation takes two forms. The first form concerns the design and development of the virtual world, for which evaluation is an inquiry process about the quality of the software application and the associated user experience. The second form concerns student learning—an approach to evaluation that we've already covered in two other chapters. While a separate, dedicated evaluation of the product (virtual world) may or may not seem as important as the evaluation of students' learning as a result of exposure to the virtual world, care should still be taken to ensure proper procedure is followed: when conducting any sort of evaluation, you must make valid assessment decisions using evidence collected with reliable measurement instrumentation.

This section of the chapter will focus specifically upon proper evaluation of the virtual world and associated user experience, specifically in terms of two primary types of evaluation: formative and summative. Briefly, *formative* evaluation is generally conducted for the purpose of improving an application via continued iterations of design and development. Formative evaluation typically involves designers, users, administrators, and any other key stakeholders directly affected by the implementation of the software application. Contrary to formative evaluation, *summative* evaluation is generally conducted for the purpose of helping an organization to make a final adoption (or rejection) decision for a given software application. Summative evaluation typically involves administrators, a select subset of users, and other affected stakeholders. Ideally, an independent program evaluator should be involved whether the process is formative or summative. Realistically, for your virtual-world project, this evaluation procedure will likely be conducted by you or another member of your team. In any case, a thorough evaluation should not be avoided. Good formative evaluation procedure leads to better virtual-world design (and better user experiences), and good summative evaluation leads to better long-term implementation of your virtual world within the deciding organization.

Ample resources are available in print and on the internet for a thorough understanding of both formative and summative evaluation in a variety of contexts. Here, we focus on procedural elements of formative and summative evaluation that should be considered specifically with the implementation of virtual worlds for learning. As a foundation to the procedural elements for these two types of evaluation, we look to Fournier's (1995) general logic of evaluation, which contains four basic steps:

1. Establish criteria of merit.
2. Construct standards.
3. Measure performance and compare with standards.
4. Synthesize and integrate data into a judgment of merit or worth.

Simply put, the establishment of criteria of merit involves making decisions about the dimensions of evaluation. The construction of standards involves deciding how well the evaluand—the thing being evaluated—should perform in each of these dimensions. Measuring performance for comparison is the process of gathering evidence about the evaluand for the purpose of rating the evaluand's performance based on these established standards. Finally, the process of data synthesis, integration, and judgment of merit involves making assessment decisions about each evaluand based on the comparisons made in the third step.

As we progress through the pragmatics of formative and summative evaluation of virtual-worlds implementation, we'll use Celestia as a recurring example—as it may be implemented across three types of previously identified environments: formal, informal, and laboratory research. In fact, you might want to download the free Celestia application to use as a tangible example as we explore the two evaluation processes (see: www.shatters.net/celestia/download.html). We'll start with formative evaluation.

Formative Evaluation of a Virtual-World Implementation

To dissect the process of formative evaluation, we'll proceed through each of the four logical steps of evaluation—criteria, standards, measurement, and synthesis—with specific focus on the pragmatics involved in each step. We'll follow up the four steps with a brief discussion of the different participants typically involved in formative evaluation. The section concludes with a discussion of why the process of formative evaluation should be considered during the design and development of any virtual world.

Criteria

In formative evaluation, there are at least two different sets of criteria that must be considered: the direct user experience (or UX) and the overall process of implementing the virtual world. Typically, evaluation of UX covers the following criteria: utility, usability, stimulation, value, and aesthetics.

The criterion of utility is concerned with whether the virtual world's functions are both useful and fit for the purpose of the implementation. As you can see, in formative evaluation, there is some overlap between UX and the implementation process. In Celestia, one of the main goals is to enable the user to freely explore the known universe by flying to specific locations. Are the system functions (i.e., the exploration flight controls) useful and fit for this purpose?

Usability is concerned with whether or not the tasks required of the user can be easily and efficiently accomplished within the standard system functionality of the virtual world. Do you find the task of universe exploration easy to accomplish in Celestia? Would you say that it is also an efficient process?

Stimulation is concerned with whether or not the user perceives his or her interaction with the virtual world to be inspirational (or motivational, in academic terms). When you interact with Celestia, are you inspired to find out more about this solar system or the rest of the known universe? Why or why not?

Value is concerned with whether or not the user perceives the virtual world itself to be important, according to his or her own needs. In other words, does the user consider time spent using the virtual world valuable or wasteful? Within the parameters of science education (or informal science learning), how important is Celestia? Does this perception change with a narrower (e.g., learning about astrophysics) or wider (e.g., everyday life) perspective of use?

The criterion of aesthetics is concerned with whether or not the user perceives the virtual world to be visually attractive and experientially engaging at the sensational level. This might be a hard criterion to wrap your head around, and a good reference for better understanding of this quality of UX—especially for game-like virtual worlds—is Swink's (2009) book on "game feel." Swink writes that game feel consists of three interacting parts: real-time control, simulated space, and polish. Essentially, better game feel comes down to how well realistic details of user-world interactions—designed to mimic real-world interactions—can be simulated in real time to the user. As you fly through Celestia, how does it feel?

The second set of criteria for formative evaluation involves the actual process of implementing the virtual world in a particular context. Russ-Eft and Preskill (2001) have a great set of questions to serve as a foundation for formative evaluation of any implementation process. Are there barriers to implementation? If so, what are the specifics? For example, do the computers intended for use in the implementation process meet the minimum standard hardware requirements for successfully installing and operating the Celestia software application? Beyond the minimum requirements, does Celestia run smoothly on the computer?

What are the effective strategies for implementation, with or without barriers? If challenges for installing and operating Celestia are present in the implementation environment, how are they overcome effectively? Do middle school students need to work in groups at single-computer workstations in the computer lab and take turns "driving" the Celestia exploration? Are certain arrangements of the computer kiosk on a museum floor better for encouraging longer periods of use of Celestia than others?

Are any staff involved in the implementation process appropriately prepared? For example, should teachers spend time exploring the universe through Celestia themselves before students do? Would a teacher guide for successful operation of Celestia be a beneficial addition to the implementation process? In your particular implementation environment, how much technical support is necessary from the support staff? For example, what happens if the Celestia application crashes in the middle of an exploration experience?

Once the implementation is under way, which parts of the process are working well, and which are not? This question is a catch-all of sorts. Of course, each implementation scenario will have pragmatics relevant to its own character, so it is important to form additional criteria for evaluation that are specific to the character of your implementation. For example, what additional criteria must be added to a formative evaluation of implementing Celestia in a special education environment? Additional focus on accessibility certainly comes to mind right away.

Speaking of pragmatics, we've hinted above at different contexts such as formal and informal environments. Of course, the criteria must reflect the pragmatics of the context for implementation, whether it's informal, formal, laboratory research, commercial, industrial, or government. How might the context affect the criteria of UX? Should simulation and aesthetics matter as much in formal education as they do in informal learning environments? Concerning the implementation process, how might the context affect criteria for barriers, effective strategies, and, especially, staff preparation? Imagine the differences in criteria for implementing Celestia in the science classroom, an informal environment such as a science center or museum, and in a laboratory for research on innovative assessment techniques for learning with virtual worlds. In any case, always remember that the process of establishing criteria for evaluation is your chance to define the dimensions of evaluation. Once you've defined the dimensions, then you can move on to establishing standards for these criteria.

Standards

Upon establishing criteria for evaluation, you must then define and describe parameters for standards of quality for each of the criteria. In other words, for each criterion, what are the boundaries of quality? As you set these low and high boundaries, remember that constructing the standards involves deciding how well the evaluand should perform in each of these dimensions. Remember that, in this case, you are not evaluating the performance of the learner (in terms of learning outcomes, at least). During formative evaluation, your two evaluands are the virtual world (in terms of UX) and the process of implementation.

For UX, we've established criteria for utility, usability, stimulation, value, and aesthetics. What are the qualitative dimensions for each of these criteria, and how should the virtual world perform to meet the minimum, moderate, and maximum levels of quality for each criterion? For example, let's think about the criterion stimulation, which, if you have forgotten, is essentially whether or not the user perceives his or her interaction with the application to be inspirational. If you were to create standards for this criterion for the UX of Celestia, what would the qualitative dimensions be? What, specifically, would be the difference between minimum, moderate, and maximum levels of perceived inspiration for each user that encounters Celestia?

Standards for criteria of the implementation process will likely depend much more heavily on the environmental context of implementation, since the process of implementation can be much more directly affected by these contextual factors than the user's experience with the software application. Remember, the basic criteria we've established for evaluating the implementation process are barriers, strategies, staff preparation, and the catch-all "what's working, what's not?" criterion. As an example, let's consider the implementation of Celestia in an informal environment—casual in-home use by a parent–child combination of users. How would you define dimensions for barriers in such an implementation? What makes a barrier a barrier? Are some barriers worse than others? If yes, how so—or to put it another way, *how much worse*? Some barriers to implementation in the home environment could be deal-breakers (i.e., the user gives up attempting to successfully implement the virtual world) and some could be easily overcome. Ranges of "barrier severity" (for lack of a better term) should be defined for each potential barrier that could occur in the implementation process, and these ranges of insurmountability can serve as a definition of the boundaries of this criterion.

Considering this example with Celestia in the casual informal environment, think about how the pragmatics of other implementation environments—such as formal classroom settings, laboratory research, commercial, industrial, or military training might change the way that standards are formed for the criteria of evaluation for both the user experience and the implementation process. What about your own virtual world? How is it similar to Celestia, and how is it different, and what effect might these differences have on your own approach to standards for evaluation? And, of course, as you form the standards, you should always keep in mind how you are going to measure the evaluand based on these standards. It's possible that the chosen approach to measurement can actually have an effect on how the standards are formed for each criterion of the evaluation.

Measurement and Comparison

Remember, this phase of evaluation is focused upon gathering standards-based evidence about an evaluand (through performance measurement) for the purpose of rating the evaluand's performance and comparing these ratings to standards—or the ratings of other evaluands with similar performances. Even though earlier chapters focused on evaluation, assessment, and measurement of constructs associated with *learning*, those chapters can also serve as a foundation for the process of gathering evidence for comparison of evaluands in regards to the criteria and associated standards for user experience and the implementation process. For that matter, these chapters can serve the same purpose for synthesis and judgment, too—but we'll get to that phase soon enough.

You've established your criteria and your standards, and you need to strategize about measurement of the evaluand for the purposes of comparison. For UX, typically the self-report and "think aloud" approaches are most commonly used, but it's up to you to decide if these approaches to measurement and assessment are reliable and valid enough for your own purposes. Do you need direct measurement of your evaluands through clickstream data logging (i.e., recording data recorded automatically by the virtual world when students interact with it) and perhaps even biofeedback such as pulse monitoring or posture shift measurement? To put it another way, can your virtual-world users assess themselves accurately enough to provide the reliable evidence that you need for making valid assessments in your formative evaluation? If not, how will you go about implementing appropriate direct measurement techniques?

The same line of logic applies to measurement of the implementation process. Can student interviews provide the evidence you need? Do external observers need to log timed notes about the strengths, weaknesses, and other nuances of the implementation process? Consider another example implementation of Celestia—this time in a 5th grade classroom. The teacher has two computer workstations in the back of the classroom that can be used for "free learning" experiences, including open exploration of the universe using Celestia. Will children this age be able to accurately self-report on constructs associated with user experience and the implementation process? You'll need to consider such psychological phenomena as social desirability (among others) and the fact that, from a UX perspective, children are being asked to compare free time playing with a computer game against sitting at a desk and paying attention to a lecture or presentation. Obviously, many of the pragmatics of this process will vary according to your own specific contextual needs. Again, if you re-read the earlier chapters on measurement and assessment with an eye toward evaluation of UX and the implementation process—using the criteria and standards we've already discussed—you should be able to piece together a rather comprehensive measurement plan that fits your specific needs. Now, on to synthesis and judgment.

Synthesis and Judgment

Remember, the final logical step of evaluation—data synthesis, integration, and judgment of merit—involves making assessment decisions about the evaluand using the comparisons of measured evidence gathered as a result of the previous logical step. As you create your formative evaluation plan for both the UX and the implementation process of your virtual world, you must carefully consider all the pragmatics of assessment: the who, what, when, where, and how.

Exactly how and when synthesis and judgment of evidence will occur is especially important for formative evaluation, since much of what comes from the assessment decisions will be directly and (hopefully) rather immediately used in iterative design and development of the virtual world. Therefore, streamlining the logistics of this fourth step in the logical flow of evaluation can be paramount for the continued improvement of any implementation of any virtual world. Can you think of specific examples based on previously described contexts of use for Celestia? What about the specifics of your own context for your own virtual world? What might be some major differences in the approach to synthesis and judgment for formative evaluation in a military training context versus a corporate environment?

Participants

Who is involved in the formative evaluation of the implementation of any virtual world? While there will be variations in participants based on the context of implementation, typically four parties should be involved: designers, administrators, implementation participants, and at least one independent evaluator. The designers should maintain at least a passive role in the formative evaluation process, as they will be taking the results of the evaluation and improving the virtual world—in collaboration with the developers, of course. As a side note, assuming that you are the designer (or a member of the design team), it is imperative that the designer maintains an appropriate distance from the heart of the evaluation process, as the evaluand (the virtual world) is "your baby," so to speak, and you will likely be one of the biggest sources of bias in the formative evaluation process, despite your best intentions.

At least one administrator of the organization or institution supporting the implementation (such as a school principal, museum director, or corporate training supervisor) should be involved to assist with gathering of evidence relevant to the organization itself and to serve as an inside collaborator to assist with any internal barriers to evidence collection—such as scheduling time to interview teachers implementing the virtual world in their classrooms. Implementation participants included in the formative evaluation process are those stakeholders that are most directly engaged with the implementation, such as virtual-world users, instructors, technological support staff, and perhaps even parents, if users are minors.

Finally, the formative evaluation process should be conducted by an independent evaluator whenever possible. Not only is the formative evaluation process a major administrative job in and of itself, but maintaining an unbiased approach to evaluation is much more likely if an independent evaluator is involved. As you might have already realized, due to the effort typically required for procedural administration of the formative evaluation process—as well as the fact that an unbiased third party unfamiliar with the virtual world will need to work efficiently and effectively—formative evaluation should be considered during the design phase of the virtual world.

Design Considerations

The primary reason that formative evaluation should be considered during the design and development of any virtual world is efficient and effective data measurement for the administration of the evaluation process. Depending on the measurement and assessment methodologies intended for the evaluation process, the potential for data *mismanagement* can be high. As embedded measurement techniques become more sophisticated, the amount of real-time data that can be collected for criteria related to both UX and the factors of the implementation process continues to increase. As a designer of a virtual world with an eye on improvement through iterative cycles of design, the last thing you want is for your friendly evaluators to be "swimming in data" when they're synthesizing and judging the merit of the evaluand based on the established criteria.

Consider the following example in which a modified version of Celestia (remember, it's open source!) is implemented in a local science center. The modifications include special add-on scripts (www.celestiamotherlode.net/catalog/scripts.php) developed specifically for the science center to highlight issues of space exploration relevant to the regional population served by the science center. To evaluate the implementation process of this modified version of Celestia with teenaged visitors to the science center, you intend to compare self-reported responses to questions in a brief exit interview (conducted by museum docents) with real-time clickstream data captured as the users interacted with the application at a kiosk station in the museum.

For more efficient comparison of the self-reported responses with the user data, it might be better to streamline the process of collecting these responses in a digital format that is stored directly on a server in the same location and format as the clickstream data collected during the user's interactive experience. This removes at least two human-powered steps from the data management process—the manual collection and entry of interview responses into a database—which removes that many opportunities for human error, as well as the need for staffing volunteers at the kiosk during opening hours. There are always pros and cons, of course. One drawback to removing volunteer interview procedures from the evaluation process is the potential for more users to walk away from the kiosk without filling out the survey questions.

For this issue, compromise could be found if museum volunteers conducted the exit interviews using a tablet computer that synchronized wirelessly with the kiosks, thereby unobtrusively linking visitors' responses (keyed in by volunteers) with the kiosk experience they've just had with Celestia. Of course, designing and developing such a system must be done in concert with the design and development of the scripts used to modify Celestia, as there will likely be interaction between the two applications to ensure synchronization of responses and clickstream data.

As you can see, one seemingly simple example can become quite complicated—all the more reason to continuously consider formative evaluation during the design and development of your virtual world. Think of your own context of implementation and the nuances of the evaluation process that would be more efficiently and effectively conducted if considered early on in the design process. One final thought: the more efficient and effective the evaluation process is, the more unobtrusive it seems to the participants, which typically means they are more likely to fully participate in the evaluation process.

With that, we've covered all four logical steps of formative evaluation. Let's move on to summative evaluation.

Summative Evaluation of a Virtual-World Implementation

Similar to the previous section on formative evaluation, as we dive into the process of summative evaluation, we'll proceed through each of the four logical steps of evaluation—criteria, standards, measurement, and synthesis—with specific focus on the pragmatics involved in each step. We'll follow up the four steps with a brief discussion of the different participants typically involved in summative evaluation. The section concludes with a discussion of why the process of summative evaluation should be considered during the design and development of any virtual world.

Criteria

It is possible that the criteria of UX will be included in the summative evaluation of a virtual world, but if so, not with the intention of improved design of the application. Remember, the intended outcome of the summative evaluation process is a final adoption/rejection decision of the evaluand. As such, it might seem that UX—which is primarily intended for design improve-ment—would never be appropriate for summative evaluation. However, if the administrative decision makers are concerned with UX factors as part of the adoption/rejection decision-making process, then the criteria of UX should certainly be included in the dimensions of the summative evalua-tion. For specifics on these criteria, please refer to the previous section of the chapter addressing formative evaluation.

As for summative evaluation of the implementation process itself, Russ-Eft and Preskill (2001) emphasize that there are actually four different types of summative evaluation that can be conducted: monitoring, outcome, impact, and performance. A monitoring evaluation is concerned with the ethics of implementation, such as whether or not the implementation of the virtual world violates the rights of the users in any way. For example, if the appli-cation collects personal identity data about each user (as part of the sign-in process) in a non-secure fashion, there is an obvious problem with the potential for identity theft. Or, if required corporate training is conducted on workers' unpaid time, this may or may not be an ethical concern, depending on the context.

An outcome evaluation is concerned with learning. In any educational set-ting—formal, informal, or training—obviously the factor of whether or not any learning occurred with the users of the application is of vital importance to whether or not the application is adopted for continued implementation. Of course, the stakes of the criteria for learning can change substantially from one context to the next (e.g., paramedic training versus informal casual learning). An outcome evaluation might be subsumed by an impact evalua-tion, which is a much more holistic approach to understanding the full effect of any implementation on participants. Impacts an implementation has on participants beyond learning can include affective factors (such as emotional perspectives) as well as secondary or peripheral benefits a person is exposed to through engagement with the application. Often, the impact evaluation centers around an estimated comparison between actual learning gains of participants in the implementation with ways those same gains may or may not be possible in learning environments that do not involve the implementa-tion of the evaluand. For example, can students experience similar learning outcomes and emotional experiences when reading an illustrated text about the solar system—or interacting with a two-dimensional multimedia applica-tion—as they do when interacting with Celestia?

Finally, a performance evaluation is concerned primarily with thorough documentation of results of the evaluand, which in this case is the implemen-tation process. Typically, there are three aspects of the evaluand that make up the documentation: process, outputs, and outcomes. Process is, as you might have guessed, the various activities that occur between the user and the vir-tual world during the implementation. Outputs are the products and services delivered to the user as part of the implementation process. Outcomes are the specific results experienced by the user during and after interacting with the products and services delivered during the implementation process. Can you think of examples of process, outputs, and outcomes that could be documented as part of the performance evaluation of an implementation of Celestia in the previously described casual in-home use by a parent–child pair of users? In any case, the documentation process inherent in performance evaluation should have at least a rudimentary presence in any summative evaluation procedure. Furthermore, regardless of the context, a summative evaluation should typically consist of some combination of all four types of evaluation described above. From one context to the next, more emphasis may be placed on monitoring and impact evaluations or outcome and performance evaluations—all depending on the unique needs of the adoption/rejection decision makers.

Across all types of summative evaluation, Russ-Eft and Preskill (2001) note that several questions drive criteria selection as dimensions of the evaluation are formed. What are the goals and outcomes of the implementation? Continuing with the example of in-home casual use of Celestia, what might be the goals and outcomes of the parent–child combo of users as they engage with Celestia? A cost-benefit analysis works its way into most summative evaluations: is the implementation of Celestia worth its associated costs? Remember—costs to consider are more than just financial. For example, the Celestia software application is free to download, but the time and effort taken to install (and possibly troubleshoot) the application are a separate type of cost. If the computer on which the parent–child combo wishes to run Celestia doesn't meet the minimum requirements of the application, upgrading the computer will require additional time and effort, as well as financial costs. Of course, an investigation into benefits must accompany the questions of cost. What are the benefits a user receives for participating in the implementation—emotionally, intellectually, financially, etc.? Are there secondary benefits made available to the user as a result of participating in the implementation? What might be the benefits obtained by the parent–child pair implementing Celestia at home? One obvious benefit is the convenience of being able to engage with Celestia in the comfort of their own home.

Another common type of questions refers to extensibility of the implementation—is the process reproducible in other locations? Can acceptably similar experiences be had by Celestia users in different geographical regions, speaking different languages, with different cultural backgrounds? What about users from different socioeconomic backgrounds, or users with drastically different levels of technological savvy? Each factor of extensibility of the implementation of the application will be more or less important depending on the contexts of any summative evaluation, of course.

Two types of questions usually only apply in more professional or commercial implementation processes. First, is the virtual world a viable product? While an investigation of the product viability of any application might seem as though the application itself is the evaluand, in fact the implementation process is still the evaluand, but certain outcomes of the implementation process—such as extensibility—can be used as criteria to make judgments about the viability of the virtual world as a product. Second, does implementation lead to improved productivity in the given profession or work environment? Of course, an argument can be made that productivity would be a desirable outcome of any implementation of a virtual world in a formal classroom environment, but this question typically refers to the traditional type of productivity associated with commerce and industry.

To review our progress so far, we've covered the four types of evaluation procedures that typically occur in a summative evaluation, and we've explored the typical types of questions that can be asked to help form the criteria to serve as the dimensions of a summative evaluation. Now it's on to the formation of standards for these criteria.

Standards

Remember, based on the logical steps of evaluation, the construction of standards involves deciding how well the evaluand should perform in each of the dimensions established with the criteria selected for the evaluation. Let's go through how this standards construction process might happen for each of the four types of summative evaluation. As we did with formative evaluation, let's explore the qualitative dimensions for at least one criterion associated with each type of summative evaluation. How should the implementation of the virtual world occur to meet the minimum, moderate, and maximum levels of quality for each criterion?

For an example of constructing standards of ethics for a monitoring evaluation, let's again consider the issue of data security. What are the minimum and maximum levels of quality for data security? In any case, the minimum level of maintaining the security of users' personal data should still be somewhat high, but there might be times when lower standards of security are acceptable. For example, the strength and consistency of data security might need to be higher for implementations of Celestia that occur in public shared kiosks than those that occur in the privacy of one's home.

For an outcome evaluation of learning, what might be the minimum and maximum levels of quality used to construct the standards for the established learning criteria? For example, how much should a user know about the solar system after engaging with Celestia for a given period of time? Or, from the perspective of learning gains, how much should a user's knowledge of the solar system improve as a result of engaging with Celestia for the same period of time? It's likely that the standards for learning gains would be much lower for a user in an informal science center setting where the amount of time spent with Celestia may be minimal, as opposed to our beloved parent–child pair that has ample time to explore Celestia over the course of many sessions.

An impact evaluation is one case where UX criteria can be useful in a summative evaluation. Consider the affective factor of emotional experience, which is similar in many ways to the UX criterion of stimulation. How much emotional stimulation should a user experience while engaging with your virtual world? Even though it is a UX criterion, remember that this is summative evaluation, so no redesign is intended. As such, it may be that the standards for stimulation are set much lower, especially if stimulation is less of a requisite factor for a user to continue engagement with the application—such as any case where the user is required to use Celestia whether he or she likes it or not (perhaps in a formal educational environment). Obviously, this is far from the ideal implementation scenario, but it is a definite reality.

Finally, for a performance evaluation, what might be the minimum and maximum levels of quality used to construct standards for the processes, outputs, and outcomes associated with the evaluand? For example, consider one process that might occur during the in-home use of Celestia: downloading and installing the add-on script (and associated material files) that allows the user to experience the "Cassini-Huygens Mission GT (Enhanced)." At a minimum, how easy should it be for a 6th grade student to go through this process on his or her home computer? What about the parent? Should the standards be different based on the age of the user?

Again, the importance of these four types of evaluation will vary with the context of the adoption/rejection decision being made. As such, the standards established across the four types of evaluation might be prioritized based on the particulars of the given context. Consider, for example, an implementation of a modified version of Celestia in a laboratory research environment at a university. How might ethics, learning, affect, and performance documentation be prioritized? Ideally, the standards for the ethics of the implementation process should maintain a high priority. Depending on the nature of the research studies being conducted, standards of learning or affect may take priority over one another. While procedural documentation is often critical in research studies to maintain certain types of validity, standards for processes, outputs, and outcomes might take a lower priority than standards for ethics, learning, or affect. Whatever the prioritization may be for the context of the adoption/rejection decision to be made as a result of the summative evaluation, as you form the standards, you should always keep in mind how you are going to measure the evaluand based on these standards—just as we discussed in the previous section on formative evaluation.

Measurement and Comparison

How might your measurement strategy to gather standards-based evidence for comparison—leading to synthesis and judgment—differ in a summative evaluation versus a formative evaluation? What sort of evidence should you measure to assess the ethics of an implementation in the process of conducting a monitoring evaluation? How will you measure this evidence? Using the Celestia example, which aspects of data security should be measured, and how? When, and how often? Where is the evidence stored, and what does it look like?

Think about an impact evaluation that is primarily focused on the secondary or peripheral benefits received by participants in an implementation of a virtual world. What if the effects of these peripheral benefits don't fully manifest until long after the adoption/rejection decision needs to be made? Do you collect evidence as best you can, or do you remove these criteria from the evaluation? That will depend on your own particular situation, of course! These are the types of questions that should come up during the crafting of the measurement plan for a summative evaluation of a virtual world.

Finally, for performance evaluation, let's revisit the process of downloading and installing an add-on script to extend Celestia in the casual in-home implementation. What sort of evidence would you need to collect to measure the quality of this process, and how would you collect it? Can you think of outputs and outcomes resulting from this process that might serve as evidence? How would you measure the outputs and outcomes? How should the evidence be stored to facilitate the documentation of processes, outputs, and outcomes in a way that leads to efficient synthesis and judgment? In the end, with summative evaluation, the primary goal of measurement is efficient and effective delivery of reliable evidence to ease the process of synthesis and judgment for the evaluator, so that he or she can quickly deliver a high-quality recommendation report to the adoption/rejection decision makers.

Synthesis and Judgment

As you are forming your measurement strategy, you've got to prepare for the assessment decisions that must be made by synthesizing and integrating collected evidence for the judgment of merit (assessment decisions) about the evaluand—based on the standards defined for established criteria. The key factor of this logical step when conducting summative evaluation is the fact that these assessment decisions are intended to lead directly toward the creation of a report that will be handed off to administrators for a final adoption/rejection decision. As such, you should work to set up a system for data synthesis and assessment that streamlines the process of evaluation report creation.

For example, consider once more the classroom implementation of Celestia. Instead of a single 5th grade classroom, this implementation is being piloted across all seven middle schools in a school district. Put yourself in the shoes of a consultant who is hired by the school system to conduct the summative evaluation and draft the final report for the superintendent of the school system. Collecting and synthesizing standards-based evidence measured from several different classrooms of seven different schools sounds like a data management nightmare. With proper logistical planning, it doesn't have to be so bad. Diving into the details of such a plan for any type of evaluation process is beyond the scope of this book, but the fact that a management plan needs to be in place should be quite apparent. For further reading on the matter, chapter 14 in Russ-Eft and Preskill (2001) is a great place to start.

Participants

In contrast to formative evaluation, summative evaluation of a virtual world usually does not involve the designers of the evaluand under consideration, since no redesign will stem from the results of a summative evaluation. As such, typically three parties should be involved in summative evaluation: administrators, implementation participants, and at least one independent evaluator.

Similar to formative evaluation, deciding which administrators and participants will be involved in the summative evaluation process really depends on the criteria, the measurement plan, and the synthesis and judging process that occurs for the particular context of implementation. In any case, it cannot be stressed enough that involving an independent third-party evaluator is of utmost importance—especially in the case where the administrator decides to reject the evaluand and discontinue implementation of the virtual world. It's never easy to take rejection, and if you the designer are also the evaluator, the sting of rejection might be amplified by the confusion of whether or not the evaluation was conducted in an appropriately objective manner. In other words, you might not know if it was a poor evaluation, bias, or a poor design that caused the rejection. If you ensure that the evaluator is independent of the designers and implementers, you can hopefully eliminate bias and poor evaluation from the equation. If a poor evaluation still occurs, well, don't hire the same evaluator again.

Design Considerations

As with formative evaluation, the process of summative evaluation should also be considered during the design and development of your virtual world. The data management concerns mentioned in the "Design Considerations" portion of the previous section on formative evaluation apply here as well. Beyond these considerations, one additional aspect of summative evaluation should be considered when designing your application: the streamlined formation of evaluation reports. Think about all the potential contexts of implementation that your virtual world might have, and think about all the different participants and administrators that could be involved in different summative evaluations of your virtual world. How should they be linked into the process of summative reporting?

One final caveat: remember that while these participants and administrators aren't focused on specifically improving the design of your virtual world, they might still want to provide useful information on the improvement of the design. Because of this, you should consider implementing some sort of provision in your virtual world (or the associated website) that allows any user to provide feedback—the more direct the better. Make sure the design feedback doesn't impede the overall experience and the resulting summative evaluation. It is also entirely possible that the provision of a direct feedback channel for design issues for your virtual world could actually score positive points in a summative evaluation for certain contexts of implementation. So, it can't hurt to include the option.

As you can see, there are quite a few similarities and differences between formative and summative procedures for evaluating a virtual world. In either case, the main point to remember is this: the more time you spend planning for both types of evaluation during the design process, the better off you will be.

Conclusion

While the finer details of implementation and evaluation are mostly beyond the scope of this book, we felt it was necessary to cover enough of each topic to appropriately focus the design process for virtual worlds intended to be used for learning. So, to review, we started with a basic overview of the implementation process, including what it is and when it starts. Then, for the sake of comparison, we explored three specific contexts for implementation: formal educational environments, informal learning environments, and laboratory research environments. Then, we moved on to evaluation, starting with a general overview including brief definitions of formative and summative evaluation. We then explored both types of evaluation using Fournier's (1995) logical steps of evaluation (criteria, standards, measurement, and synthesis/judgment) for both UX and the implementation process.

TEST YOUR UNDERSTANDING

1. What separates evaluation from implementation, and why is evaluation so important for design and development?
2. Specific to virtual worlds, what are the primary differences in formative and summative evaluation?

LEARNING ACTIVITIES

1. Your target audience is at-home users of Celestia, within the learning domain of introductory astronomy. Define goals and objectives for an implementation of Celestia, as well as criteria and standards for a formative evaluation of this implementation—including UX for children and adults.

2. As an added challenge, move forward with the creation of a measurement and assessment plan for the at-home implementation of Celestia—a plan that allows for efficient and effective collection of standards-based evidence for the creation of a thorough evaluation report to be sent back to the designers of Celestia.

3. Consider your own target audiences for your own intended virtual world. Based on the learning domain(s) associated with your design, define goals and objectives for an implementation of your virtual world with at least one of the intended target audiences. Create a measurement and assessment plan for summative evaluation, and make notes of any techniques to infuse effective evaluation strategies into the design of your application.

References

Fournier, D. M. (1995). Establishing evaluative conclusions: A distinction between general and working logic. *New Directions for Evaluation, 68*, 15–32.

Russ-Eft, D. & Preskill, H. (2001). *Evaluation in Organizations: A systematic approach to enhancing learning, performance, and change.* New York: Basic Books.

Swink, S. (2009). *Game Feel: A game designer's guide to virtual sensation.* Boston, MA: Morgan Kaufman Publishers.

Links

Mozilla Foundation: www.mozilla.org—From the website: "The Mozilla community produces a lot of great software and acts as an incubator for innovative ideas as a way to advance our mission of building a better Internet."

Common Core Standards: www.corestandards.org—From the website: "The Common Core State Standards Initiative is a state-led effort coordinated by the National Governors Association Center for Best Practices (NGA Center) and the Council of Chief State School Officers

(CCSSO). The standards were developed in collaboration with teachers, school administrators, and experts, to provide a clear and consistent framework to prepare our children for college and the workforce."

Celestia Space Simulation: www.shatters.net/celestia—From the website: "The free space simulation that lets you explore our universe in three dimensions. Celestia runs on Windows, Linux, and Mac OS X. Unlike most planetarium software, Celestia doesn't confine you to the surface of the Earth. You can travel throughout the solar system, to any of over 100,000 stars, or even beyond the galaxy."

The Celestia User Forum: www.shatters.net/forum
Where to Download Celestia: www.shatters.net/celestia/download
Add-ons for Celestia (The Motherlode): www.celestiamotherlode.net

Other Resources

User Experience (UX) has many different definitions—an aspect of UX that contributes to confusion of the matter. However, many good resources are available to find out as much as you want to know about the subject, such as:

- UX Magazine: http://uxmag.com
- UX Myths: http://uxmyths.com
- UX Booth: http://uxbooth.com
- UX Matters: http://uxmatters.com
- *Game Feel*: www.game-feel.com
- ACM Special Interest Group on Human–Computer Interaction: www.sigchi.org

The process of evaluation is rather complex, but luckily there are many organizations and peer-reviewed publications that can help you on your way (in addition to the Russ-Eft and Preskill text mentioned above), such as:

- The American Evaluation Association—http://www.eval.org
- Evaluation at the Research Methods Knowledge Base: www.socialresearchmethods.net/kb/intreval.htm
- *Evaluation* (a peer-reviewed journal): http://evi.sagepub.com

Index